A Struggle for Holy Ground

A Struggle for Holy Ground

Reconciliation and the Rites of Parish Closure

Michael Weldon, O.F.M.

LITURGICAL PRESS
Collegeville, Minnesota

www.litpress.org

1   2   3   4   5   6   7   8   9

Library of Congress Cataloging-in-Publication Data

Weldon, Michael (C. Michael)
    A struggle for holy ground : reconciliation and the rites of parish closure / Michael Weldon.
        p.   cm.
    Includes bibliographical references and index.
    ISBN 0-8146-2155-4 (pbk. : alk. paper)
    1. Catholic Church—United States. 2. Parishes—United States. 3. Church closures—United States. 4. Pastoral theology—Catholic Church. I. Title.

BX1407.P3W45   2004
264'.02099—dc22

                                                        2004004585

Contents

Foreword

Michael Weldon has done a signal service to the Church in writing about church closings and consolidations. This is not the work of a detached observer. Father Weldon was pastor of a parish in San Francisco which experienced the paroxysm and rage involved in closing and consolidation.

To his personal, pastoral experience, he has added the depth and perspective which come from study and research and from some distance from the actual experience.

This work is notable for its scholarly care and its use of sources. Works of this kind can be dry and exacting to read. The pleasant surprise is that this study is not only well written and easy to read but imaginative and informative as well.

From now on no diocese should attempt closings or consolidations without carefully reading and studying this book. There is no problem-free way of closing parishes or consolidating them no matter how obvious the reasons for doing so. People will always be profoundly hurt and angry even when every effort is made to avoid or reduce these feelings. But Father Weldon shows a way to approach the closing and consolidation which has potential to greatly reduce these powerful negative reactions and make the whole experience life giving. Among the many merits of this book are the appendices which give various rituals for grieving and going through the process of closing, letting go, and beginning a new life.

I strongly recommend this book and the wisdom, insight, and practical suggestions which make it so valuable.

Archbishop John R. Quinn
Retired Archbishop of San Fancisco

Reconciliation, Liturgy, and New Life

God . . . has reconciled us . . . through Christ and given us the ministry of reconciliation, namely, God was reconciling the world to himself in Christ. (2 Cor 5:18-19)

The hallmark of Christian spirituality that distinguishes it from other religious traditions is its insistence on reconciliation. Because of God's love poured out for us in Jesus Christ who suffered, died, and rose again, Christians individually and as a group are called to be ministers of reconciliation in a world often alienated from God and divided one from the other by myriad causes—language, culture, financial status, social caste, and sexual orientation. The wonderful contribution of Fr. Michael Weldon is that he offers a constructive perspective on how to be an agent of reconciliation in one of the most tension-charged and divisive contexts in which ministers can find themselves: the closing and consolidation of parishes.

Because of demographic and economic change, dioceses throughout the country continue to be confronted with the death of parishes—especially in large cities that have hosted ethnic enclaves for generations. Surprisingly for Roman Catholics, one of the most neglected aspects of ministering to people grieving over the impending loss of their parish is the ritual aspect. While we say that liturgy is a defining part of our life, even go so far as to claim the Eucharist as the source and summit of the Church's life, relatively little systematic attention has been paid to the role that our ritual and sacramental tradition can play in ministering to people whose lives are sometimes shattered by the loss of ecclesial identity that a parish has traditionally provided.

This book fills the gap. Michael Weldon is a sensitive observer who has "walked the walk" of a minister who has been in the midst of this painful and stress-filled context. Reflecting on his own pastoral experience in San

Francisco and through interviews and research in Chicago, he articulates an approach to parish closing and consolidation that can serve as a model for pastoral agents in the same circumstances in other areas of the country. Drawing on the liturgical traditions of the Church, he offers a rich array of ritual models for helping a parish grieve the loss of its church building and embrace a new communal identity in the process of consolidation. No bishop, pastor, or pastoral council involved in closing and consolidating parishes should miss this invaluable resource that offers crucial insights into transforming a situation of grief, anger, and loss into an opportunity for hope, reconciliation, and new life.

Very Reverend Mark R. Francis, C.S.V.
Superior General
Clerics of St. Viator, Rome
Pontifical Liturgical Institute of Saint Anselmo

Acknowledgments

This book is located on the experience of two remarkable Christian communities, St. Anthony of Padua/Immaculate Conception in San Francisco, and Saint Benedict the African East and West in Chicago. It has been my pleasure and privilege to know both communities of people and journey with them a bit. After the struggle with the consolidation of the parishes in San Francisco, I was humbled by the providence of meeting the people of the Catholic community of Chicago's Englewood. Listening to their stories brought so much healing to mine. It is my conviction as we enter this new era of U.S. Catholicism, that the most effective agents of reconciliation will be those who have weathered the restructuring of their neighborhood parishes, forgiven, and together created a new vision of local Church. I tip my hat to these courageous people and call them to join me in making their stories known.

I am grateful to the Franciscans of St. Barbara Province for the opportunity to take this pastoral experience and shake the life out of it. It is my hope that any insights I may have discovered on this issue will be of service to the reconfiguration of our centuries-old ministry on the West Coast. I thank God for the privilege of living with the Capuchin friars of St. Clare Friary, Chicago. Their sense of Franciscan friendship and hospitality rekindled some of the same within me. I am extremely grateful to my readers and classmates at the Catholic Theological Union. I owe a debt of gratitude to Professors Mark Francis, C.S.V.—my mentor and friend, Robert Schreiter, C.PP.S., and Dianne Bergant, C.S.A., for coaching me through this study. Mrs. Indiana Blandón and Dinah Shaw lent a professional, yet heart centered objectivity to the interview process. The experience, strength and hope of the staffs and parish leadership who made available their insights for this study continue to inspire me—especially Dominican Sr. Johnellen Turner. Mrs. Patty Hughes, Rev. Dave Baldwin and Rev. Arturo Perez lovingly read and critiqued my sometime hasty opinions. This work honors a "gang of four" friends: Revs. Luis Vera, O.S.A., Patrick McGuire, and Richard Young, who listened, cajoled, laughed and sometimes wept with me through the chapters of this text. Finally, I would like also to acknowledge the community at the Franciscan Renewal Center in Scottsdale, Arizona—most especially Cheryl Thomsen, my editor in arms, who wrestled a year of revisions from "dissertation-ese" to a more readable form.

Introduction

Catholics Redesigning Themselves

> There was a feeling of sadness. Though my church was to be the re-
> maining one, I felt sad for those in the merged church for it seemed
> that they were losing their church; their identity; their autonomy;
> their existence. I wanted to do what I could, by joining others in the
> merging process, to ease the pain and to make those from the other
> church feel welcome and a part of our—theirs and my [own]—parish.[1]

A lot dies when a parish is closed. I tried to slow it a little—or soften
it at least—for folks in a church in San Francisco where I served as pastor.
I feared that the whole weight of that loss would drive people away as we
attempted to redraw the boundaries between what the above parish council
member called ours, theirs, and mine. "Consolidating resources will make
us a better church," I told them. Some believed me. I believed myself.
The paschal mystery, the great Christian story, lies across the horizon of
all "church life." Any blended family or blended community has to first
die before it can be reborn or resurrected. Like many other former urban
Catholic enclaves, we still had schools and social services to run. And we
lost many anyway.

Regret is a hard word. "Would've, could've, should've" brings smiles to
the lips of even the most cynical. But we live in an era of great ecclesial
transition, what some social scientists have called the greatest religious
reorganization in U.S. history. Even an Internet search at the time our
bishop announced the consolidation turned up next to nothing in the way

[1] Carmen [pseudonym], interview by author. San Francisco, Calif., November 10,
2002.

of resources. There was little precedent in American Catholicism for closing local churches. And in the midst of it all, I came to regret some of the pastoral calls I had to make.

There is no indication that Catholic Christianity is dying out in this country. The latest statistics in fact show growth with infant and adult baptisms every year. Still, the skylines of our cities are marked with the spires of an age of Catholic church life now gone, shattered by history and social movements beyond all of our control. And maybe the best we can do is grieve it well.

In the first few years after leaving my assignment after the San Francisco consolidation, I revisited and often revised the rituals and communication processes we had used. During the penitential rite of my final Eucharist as pastor of the combined parish in San Francisco, I knelt and asked both communities I had served for forgiveness of any hurts and injustices for which I was responsible during those years. It was deeply moving and left a tender sense of closure to my professional and personal relationships of that time. But several years later, I realized that I still had some intense emotional energy wrapped around my storytelling about those days. My sense of "church" has changed and grown. It will always reflect the people and staff, the conflicts and dreams of that era of feisty San Francisco Catholicism. But forgiveness was not complete. The memories, for many of us, were still raw or (at best) tender. I had asked forgiveness of the assembled community but had not offered mine to those who assaulted my leadership and reputation during that conflicted time. Letters of protest that remain in one's diocesan personnel file reminded me how long healing takes.

In 1995, the Archdiocese of San Francisco completed a pastoral planning process and made the decision to close or consolidate ten parishes in urban San Francisco County. As a pastor there, I ended up implementing the process I had seriously questioned and even sought to undermine. A small, formerly Italian national parish in the Bernal Heights neighborhood was eventually merged into the territorial parish where I served. With that decision, a tidal wave of rage and resistance began with constituents that lasted for the next few years. The volume and depth of that emotional backlash from parishioners and former parishioners toward the parish leadership overwhelmed even the services of professional conciliation. Attempts to bring together the two parishes and school communities over the next several years were met with a stubborn active and passive resistance. This book emerged from the struggle to understand that experience.

Faith crises lead some religious professionals to question their vocations, others to go to school. I did both. A sabbatical, including postgraduate studies at Chicago's Catholic Theological Union, was a privileged opportunity to wrestle with my dilemma with some of the best practical theologians in the U.S. Church. With an eye toward new strategies of pastoral care, I conducted interviews with people who had walked through parish consolidations in the last decade from two distinct locales. A method of "participant observation" saved me from the rigors of statistics and a strictly quantitative analysis. It is based on conversation and presumes an environment of mutuality, employing open-ended questions to elicit feelings and impressions from the participants of the events described.

The issues raised by these interviews cannot be shaped to conclusions in the common understanding of the term. Rather they will suggest new venues of pastoral care for communities experiencing the upheaval of parish restructuring. St. Benedict the African in the South Side of Chicago was formed from eight parishes in the late eighties and St. Anthony and Immaculate Conception were merged into a single parish in San Francisco in the late nineties. These consolidations provided the foundation for the case studies and interviews. The cultural landscapes of the two settings were quite distinct. One reflected a primarily northern-urban and African American setting, and the second a multicultural West Coast setting of Hispanic, Filipino, Italian, and a smattering of several other cultural groups. Parochial schools were involved in both settings. Although separated by geography, culture, socioeconomic levels, and time, they each offer some common insights into the challenges posed by consolidation and the options for future pastoral care in these settings.

Parishioners were invited to participate in town hall meetings, round-table discussions, surveys, and onsite visitations and discernment processes composed of clergy, religious, professional staff and laity. Some found them empowering. Others found themselves at variance with the final decisions of these processes and their bishops, and further estranged from the local church. Some communities had wrestled with the issues of declining numbers and resources and had themselves initiated creative programs and collaborative structures to address them. Others were surprised at massive restructuring plans initiated by their bishops and chancery staffs to address burgeoning diocesan-wide fiscal and personnel crises. The future impact of these pastoral-planning experiences (whether initiated from the top down or at the level of the local church) on the shape and vitality of the future American Catholic Church will be profound.

Common issues emerged from the interviews in both settings, including the desire for non-manipulative processes of rite and decision making, adequate time to grieve, accountable listening by those entrusted with decision-making authority, and finally, extended follow-up or pastoral aftercare. Human beings negotiate the perimeters of relationship with ritual. Initiating relationship, saying good-bye and renegotiating these boundaries of human affiliation are often culturally prescribed dances. Among its many functions to social scientists, ritual is both prescriptive and descriptive of human experience. The rituals, therefore, used by these communities to walk through the closure of a parish offer a window with which to look into their experience and access the factors that shaped it.

There are no officially approved Roman Catholic rituals for closure or consolidation of a parish. The Church, whose fundamental identity includes the mission of reconciliation, grapples with itself in times of internal conflict, particularly when the decision of its leadership is perceived as the source of trauma. This has often been the case around church restructuring. By critically attending to experience, tradition, and culture in this context, the mission of reconciliation can perhaps be discovered in a more profound way.[2] Rather than expecting the Church to somehow be above the conflict effecting other institutions, the effective negotiation of internal conflict could leave the Church in a position to mentor other human institutions undergoing significant change.

Throughout the U.S., in many cases—not all by any means—the processes around church restructuring have been laden with conflict. In Gospel imperatives, the Church as an assembly of Jesus's disciples sees itself as a force of reconciliation in the world. But when the Church itself is perceived as the source of the social breach or even trauma, its sense of itself as a reconciling agent becomes muddled. The traditional source of reconciliation becomes one of the parties in need of reconciliation itself. Interviews with people who participated in local consolidations or parish closures often reflected elements of emotional or social trauma—the tearing apart of internal worlds as a result or in the wake of this experience. Somatic distress, preoccupation with the loss, hostility reactions and loss of familiar patterns of conduct are symptoms often associated to traumatic

---

[2] This method of practical theology first carefully attends to relevant information in each of these three sources then actively engages this information by bringing each of the perspectives into assertive dialogue. See James D. and Evelyn Eaton Whitehead, *Method in Ministry: Theological Reflection and Christian Ministry* (Kansas City: Sheed & Ward, 1995) 5–8.

loss. What made this experience traumatic for some and not for others was an ongoing question.

There seems to be a thin line in the Catholic imagination between Church as people and church as buildings. Creative ritual and pastoral care can serve related issues from forgiveness, public apology, "good grief,"[3] cleansing of memory, lament-protest, revision of narrative, exorcism of cycles of rage and recrimination, to celebration, thanksgiving, leave-taking and memorial. A practical theology asks where the world's wounds need to be bound up and directs preferential care there. This movement is an opportunity to dance with alternative responses to the consolidation-closure issue, and it selects how to apply the Christian tradition in alternative or more effective ways. It is an invitation, according to Don Browning, to new or renewed pastoral practice toward social and individual transformation.[4]

Inherent to reconciliation is the reframing of conflict: to address, integrate, and embrace the—sometimes painful—past and a necessary shared future as a means of dealing with the present.[5] The patterns of forgiveness and reconciliation can be an important resource and a lens into the conflict generated around the restructuring of local church. As parishes across the U.S. are closed, altered, and consolidated—and new configurations created—people are being asked to cross (often old) territorial boundaries. Local communities are asked to significantly broaden and extend their experience of church. People at the grass roots are being challenged to change patterns of thought and behavior. Racial, class and socioeconomic boundaries are being called to significant adjustment.[6] Transformation of

---

[3] This term was originally coined by Granger E. Westberg, *Good Grief* (Minneapolis: Fortress, 1971). Successful grieving leads a mourner to gradually make attachments and investments in other persons and things once again. Ultimately it is a process in which a belief system, although significantly challenged by loss, is restored. See also Kenneth R. Mitchell and Herbert Anderson, *All Our Losses, All Our Griefs: Resources for Pastoral Care* (Philadelphia: Westminster, 1983) 96–97.

[4] Don S. Browning, "Toward a Fundamental and Strategic Practical Theology," in *Shifting Boundaries: Contextual Approaches to the Structure of Theological Education*, ed. Barbara G. Wheeler and Edward Farley (Louisville: Westminster/John Knox, 1991) 295–328.

[5] John Paul Lederach, *Building Peace: Sustainable Reconciliation in Divided Societies* (Washington, D.C: Endowment of the United States Institute for Peace, 1997) 30–36.

[6] Patricia Forster, O.S.F., "The Chicago Story and Boundaries to Parish Restructuring," in *Diocesan Efforts in Parish Reorganization: A Report* (Clearwater, Fla.: Conference of Pastoral Planning and Council Development, 1995) 83–84.

the geographical boundaries around a group of people (like a parish) does not happen simply because a higher up writes an official document declaring it so. It takes place when people begin to sense common ground, a shared humanity, and some consensus about the future goals.

Forgiveness is one of the key moments to reconciliation in the conflicts around changes to dedicated space. A conviction is growing from the works of one of my mentors, forgiveness makes social change possible.[7] It implies a way of "reframing" social and individual relationships after some traumatic breach. It is linked to remembering the stories of people's lives and the revision of those narratives against the great narrative mystery of the passion, death, and resurrection of Christ. Culture often dictates the norms by which interpersonal and social breeches of relationship are reconciled. The words and gestures employed for public apology and those that invoke the absolution are culturally prescribed. One cannot understand human forgiveness without grappling with culture and its ritual expressions.

Ritual in its broadest perspective is deeply embedded in the network of ordinary human social relations, not something external to them. It includes all the aspects of human biosocial behavior that are patterned, repetitive and conventualized. Hence, interpersonal forgiveness is usually performed in ritualized action. Ritual is a way to establish order, affirm meaning, bond community, grapple with ambivalence and encounter mystery. It is a safe locus for encountering the Ultimate and Transcendent.

In this context, ritual emerges as a potent vehicle for transformation and social change. It cannot act of itself to heal trauma around the losses of a local church, but together with pastoral care, its energies can be directed to social and/or individual change. Liturgical theologian Edward Foley defines pastoral care in a way that helps one see its relationship to processes of reconciliation. He calls it "the Church's response to the personal, relational and spiritual needs of persons in the context and through the agency of the local community."[8] Human beings across nearly every culture employ patterns of ritual to bear on any rift of social relationships. Ritual and pastoral care dance together at the service of reconciliation in innerchurch conflict. They serve the process of accompanying people through the obstacles that would impede or prevent them from entering into a

---

[7] Robert Schreiter, C.PP.S., *The Ministry of Reconciliation: Spirituality and Strategies* (Maryknoll, N.Y.: Orbis Books, 1998) 66.

[8] Edward Foley, Capuchin, "Pastoral Care as Liturgical Common Ground" *New Theology Review* 13, no. 3 (August 2000) 31.

reconstituted (reconfigured) community of a newly formed parish, or of completing the transition to another worshipping community. It is restoration of communion.

Changing Catholic ethnic demographics in the United States, diminishing finances, deteriorating facilities, and personnel shortages have necessitated the restructuring and closures of religious institutions built during the great Euro-American immigrant period extending from the mid-nineteenth through the mid-twentieth centuries. These institutional closures and reconfigurations have impacted both the religious communities and the neighborhoods around them in powerful ways. Parish staffs, members of affected local communities, and diocesan leadership will continue to face the reality of parochial restructurings through the next decade. Each stratum of people affected by these parochial changes requires a specific form of pastoral care. If they are to work through issues like grief and powerlessness evoked by the loss of a local church institution and reaffiliate in another form, the proper rites must be observed. Ritual performs a different function for those in diocesan leadership, the pastor or local administrator implementing the closure of a parish, and the people in the pews.

With the great expansion of lay ministry since the Second Vatican Council, the numerical decline of ordained personnel and vowed religious, some shapes of parish, significantly different from the past, are evolving. The closure and consolidation of parish churches has become a symbol of this great change. Catholics, redesigning themselves on the local level, are writing a new chapter to American religious history. It is an opportunity to experience some of the foundational narratives of a unique expression of Catholic culture, to embrace the resulting conflict with the values that emerge from those stories, to grieve the tremendous losses of autonomy and identity, and to engage the widest consultation of voices in the formation of new configurations of U.S. church. My conviction: new faces of Catholicism are being birthed from the midst of the crisis, as well as some new faces of reconciliation.

Chapter 1

The Best We Could Do with Church?
Demographics, Finances, and Culture

Announcements of closures and consolidations by chancery offices were testimony that the Catholic culture of the immigrant period of U.S. church was dead or dying. Many people in Chicago identify themselves by the parish they lived in. We had to be willing to look at that. Holding up a building or a piece of architecture or a school . . . was that the best we could do as church? To close a church had an impact on the whole culture of the neighborhood. But we had to be willing to do that. The Catholic culture was already dead. We were just saying the truth. We couldn't afford to pay for that any more. The people with the money had moved out of the neighborhoods already. We had big buildings in need of great care and repair. Is that the best we could do with church? We had to help people have a bigger sense of church.[1]

The immense vitality of the Catholic Church in the United States has depended largely on the strength of its parish life. Indeed, the parish was the heart of American Catholicism,[2] a fundamental institution around which Catholics gathered during the time period of the Euro-American immigrant church. The above quote from one of the pastors involved in

---

[1] Fr. Donald [pseudonym], interview by author, Chicago, Ill., February 19, 2000.
[2] Allan Figueroa Deck, S.J., *The Second Wave: Hispanic Ministry and the Evangelization of Cultures* (New York: Paulist Press, 1989) 58.

1

the early stages of the consolidation in Chicago's Englewood district spoke a beautiful yet harsh truth. An era of incredible vitality was coming to an end. In fact a culture was fading away, a reality provoking the most profound grief for those whose religious identity and history was anchored to it. Among the new communities who moved into these neighborhoods, especially from African American and Hispanic heritages, "the Church" had an opportunity to create something new or surrender to slow death those very places that just a century before were teeming with Catholic life.

An Extensive Effort at Religious Reorganization

At the beginning of the twenty-first century, American Catholicism presents a figure of substantial paradox around sacred spaces. Despite an increasing Catholic population, clergy numbers are decreasing. Concurrent with this, and the economic factors around changing Catholic demographics, closings and consolidations of local parishes are becoming a somewhat commonplace occurrence. Scores of parishes have been suppressed in large cities like Detroit, Pittsburgh, Chicago, and San Francisco, as well as in rural townships like Holbrook, Iowa and Steelton, Pennsylvania. Nearly every major metropolitan area of the U.S. and Canada has been affected.

Diocesan pastoral planning committees, as well as religious and secular media, attribute the increase of parochial consolidation, particularly in the last three decades, to a complexity of issues. A Canadian newsmagazine attributed the recent closures in Alberta to the "turbulence of the liberalizing tendencies of the Second Vatican Council with its vernacular services, more attention to social justice than reverence, and great dialogue with Protestants."[3] The closing of churches has a way of bringing out a host of fears, grief, and unfinished narratives from the last generation of immigrant Catholics. Archbishop John R. Quinn in his letter closing twelve formerly ethnic churches in San Francisco articulated the pastoral task with the closure of parochial institutions:

> The closing of a parish church is a difficult and traumatic event for a faith community. There will be special needs which will arise from these communities. I call upon the parishes of our city to assist these faith communities in this period of transition by supporting them in

[3] Carla Yu, "Big Box Catholicism," *Alberta Report/Newsmagazine*, December 7, 1998, 41.

their grief and by welcoming them into the new parishes they will attend.[4]

Pastoral care for those affected by the closure of a parish needs to address trauma, grief, transition, and welcome.

With Catholics in large numbers relocating to the suburbs, the large urban churches, remnants of the past immigrant era, found themselves competing for worshipers and resources. Changing population demographics showed new immigrant groups moving into areas previously occupied by other ethnic communities, profoundly altering the Catholic institutions remaining there. This landscape has been further shaped by changes in Catholic liturgical and devotional life in general since the Second Vatican Council. Language and devotional customs of the newer ethnic communities, including the African American and the various Hispanic and Asian populations, continue to impact the urban church profoundly.

The decline in the numbers of vowed religious (sisters, brothers, and some clergy) and ordained diocesan ministers, as well as the legitimization of lay ministry in the Church, gives a new face to leadership. Parish life has seen an explosion of professional lay ministries assuming roles previously restricted. Six basic staffing models have emerged throughout the country as dioceses responded to these changes: (1) multi-parish pastors, (2) multi-parish teams, (3) parish clusters, (4) nonordained parish directors, (5) a parishioner emerging as pastoral leader,[5] and (6) change of status to oratory or shrine.

Perhaps the area that weaves through all of the above parochial models is finances. Funding parishes, schools, and other Catholic institutions has changed tremendously as the pools of volunteer labor and ministries have shifted. As a result of post-Vatican II models of ministry and the crises of personnel and finances, "renewal" and "replacement" have emerged in discussions concerning aging buildings, ecclesial structures of decision making, and traditions of stewardship. The immigrant church built a tremendous education and social service system by inspiring the generosity of people themselves with very limited resources. The fiscal crisis revealed the need for a sense of stewardship built on another experience of church.

---

[4] Archbishop John R. Quinn (a letter read at the weekend Masses of the archdiocese, November 19, 1993). The original transcript is in the archives of the Archdiocese of San Francisco, Menlo Park, Calif.

[5] National Pastoral Life Center, "Alternative Staffing of Parishes," *Center Papers* (1987) 3.

The calling forth of people to share their gifts of time, talent, and financial resources in the service of their parish and greater Catholic community required a new ecclesial vision beyond the traditional boundaries of parish. This transformation often began with the schools.

The 1983 Code of Canon Law *(Corpus Juris Canonici)* gave bishops "sweeping authority to merge or suppress parishes" (CJC 515), that they did not have before the Second Vatican Council.[6] This change combined with a series of diocesan fiscal emergencies in various parts of the country opened even the most timid bishops to wield that authority. Canonist James A. Coriden notes that canon law often made it easier to close a parish than to change its name or its use.[7]

Among these various restructuring options has been the movement toward parochial closure and consolidation. The statistics from the 2000 *Official Catholic Directory* listed 19,627 Catholic parishes in the United States. In 1990, they listed 19,860—a reduction nationally of only 133 in one decade.[8] Yet since the late sixties, nearly one hundred parishes have closed in the Archdiocese of Chicago alone. The U.S. Catholic population continues to increase from 248,312,134 in 1990 to 273,961,528 in 2000, an increase partially due to another migration of new ethnic groups from the Hispanic nations to the south. The total number of priests (religious and diocesan) continues its decline from 53,111 in 1990 to 46,603 in 2000. The number of active diocesan clergy will nearly equal the number of parishes in the country by 2005. An anticipated influx of 1,515 priests from abroad will lessen but not significantly alter the continuing clergy shortage in the United States.[9]

National statistics as of the year 2000 seemed to indicate that parishes being closed or merged nationally are generally equivalent to those new parishes being established. These figures however will be further challenged as the number of clergy continues to decline through the next decade. Richard A. Schoenherr and Lawrence Young's 1993 study *Full Pews and Empty Altars* charted a 19 percent decline in priests between the years 1966–84. The most moderate of their projections estimated an over all 40 percent decline in American priests from the years 1966–2005. These

[6] James A. Coriden, Thomas J. Green, and Donald E. Heintschel, eds. *The Code of Canon Law: A Text and Commentary* (New York: Paulist Press, 1985) 415.

[7] See CJC 1218 and 1222. See James A. Coriden," Getting Down to Cases: Parish Closings," *New Theology Review* 9, no. 3 (1996) 103–6.

[8] *Official Catholic Directory* (New York: P. J. Kennedy & Sons, 2000) 2133.

[9] Joseph Claude Harris, "The Shrinking Supply of Priests" *America* 183, no. 14 (November 4, 2000) 16–17.

initial projections, although dismissed as conjecture by many analysts at the time, most notably Cardinal Mahony of Los Angeles, are proving surprisingly accurate to within 1 percent.[10] David Yamane, who edited Schoenherr's final book after his death in 1996, noted that if extended a further decade, there will be approximately a 46 percent decline in U.S. priests by 2015. The parish to priest ratio gets larger with each passing decade.

The announcement in September of 1988 by Detroit's Cardinal Szoka to close one third of the urban parishes of his archdiocese was a marker event for this major transition of the American Church. Catholics were startled by the news, and there were howls of protest by pastors, religious, and laity mobilizing to save their churches. In the fifties and sixties, the dedications of new Catholic churches and schools were almost "an annual Catholic rite of spring."[11] The Detroit experience dramatized what had been taking place quietly in nearly every major metropolitan center of the country for nearly thirty years. Against the ensuing crisis, a group of social scientists from Wayne State University concluded that they were witnessing one of the most extensive efforts at religious reorganization in American history. Interviews conducted over the next year by their College of Urban, Labor and Metropolitan Affairs confirmed the extent of this decision's impact on the cultural and religious landscape of the city of Detroit.[12] The conviction that the closings would have lasting and negative impacts on the immediate neighborhoods and the larger urban makeup of the city could easily be applied to San Francisco, Chicago, and other large urban centers of the United States. Reactions were sometimes loud and immediate.

Concurrent with the reduction of mainline Protestant denominations and the frequent sale of their church buildings to new religious sponsors, the religious fabric or "cultural presence of religion" in the inner city changed according to the Detroit study:

[10] Richard A. Schoenherr and Laurence Young, *Full Pews, Empty Altars: Demographics of the Priest Shortage in the United States Catholic Dioceses* (Madison: University of Wisconsin Press, 1993) 28–30. For projections and further implications of these statistics see also Richard A. Schoenherr, *Goodbye Father: The Celibate Male Priesthood and the Future of the Catholic Church,* ed. David Yamane (Oxford: Oxford University Press, 2002) xiv.

[11] Jay P. Dolan, R. Scott Appleby, Patricia Byrne, and Debra Campbell, *Transforming Parish Ministry* (New York: Crossroad, 1989) vii.

[12] Thomas J. Duggan "Massive Church Closings and Changing Urban Religion: the Current Detroit Experience" (an abstract prepared for the annual meeting of the Society for the Scientific Study of Religion, Virginia Beach, Va., November 1990).

Perhaps the obvious transition was from a dominance of hierarchically organized religion to congregationally based religion, from centrally and clerically controlled religion, to locally and substantially laity controlled religion. Often accompanying this transition was the movement from religion integrated into and endorsing contemporary secular institutions to religion, which served as a haven from the injustices and inequalities perceived in the secular realm.[13]

The religious groups replacing the mainline Protestant and Catholic groups often reflected a different sense of investment in the neighborhoods around them. They tended to be transitional churches that followed their constituencies out of the area with any economic advancement. This is a different kind of church environment than previous generations had seen. Catholic parishes were canonically based with geographical boundaries and usually owned by the larger church body, the diocese. As bishops across the country have implemented processes for planning and development in these neighborhoods, the structures used were those of community organizing. Conference table discussions which included representatives of the people, structures of mutual communication, and consensus building were new to Roman Catholicism.

"Catholicism is not democratic," participants and leadership frequently lamented. The oft-repeated mantra reflected a clash of the ecclesial structures between church (as a subset of the larger Church) as a hierarchical communion and the participative processes used in diocesan "strategic planning."[14] Fears of regression to lay trusteeism, that still unhealed nineteenth-century leadership controversy, seemed to linger behind the conversations. Often elements of what was labeled as "congregationalism" clashed with the more traditional hierarchical, "the buck stops here" leadership structures of many U.S. dioceses. The archbishop of San Francisco repeatedly reminded participants and clergy in his planning processes that the decisions were his alone as local ordinary. The individual bishop's role as "corporation sole" found itself in tension with the perceived tasks and processes of the conference table. When bishops intervened to remind local processes that their task was only "consultative," participants spoke of feeling powerless and demoralized. Strategic planning often experienced itself as living between two definitions of

---

[13] Ibid.

[14] Suzanne Clark and Robert Duggan, "Strategic Planning: What It Did for One Parish," *Church* 12, no. 2 (Summer 1996) 26–31.

Church, pre- and post-Vatican II.[15] The rites of the conference table and those of the eucharistic table seemed to be at odds with one another.

Parishes had performed a unique social role—a stabilizing function, according to the Wayne State study—in many of the neighborhoods where they have been located. This role frequently extended significantly beyond their own membership. One of the pastors involved in Chicago's Englewood consolidation called them "grounding institutions." Their loss impacted an entire community beyond its own membership:

> When these institutions leave a neighborhood, the whole neighborhood community is deeply impacted. People find security and identity in them. Community services locate near them. Community gatherings happen there. Worship and meaning evolves around those institutions. This was the greatest loss to Englewood as the parishes closed.[16]

The ethical dimension of this displacement of institutions is a significant issue for future Catholic leadership. What is left behind as Catholic institutions withdraw? What ongoing responsibility does the broader Church have to the neighborhoods where their populations were formerly located? As leadership of the South Chicago Englewood area began renegotiating their cluster relationship in the mid-eighties, they realized that the largest neighborhood service provider was still the Catholic Church. This included the parish and parochial schools, Catholic Charities and Catholic healthcare. Philadelphia psychologist Patricia Kelly makes the point that the Catholic Church is not first and foremost a social service agency or a school. It is, rather, a faith-based community:

> The basis on which we are operating, the parish, exists to manifest the kingdom . . . to realize the reign of God, nothing more—not to maintain a school, not to be a social center. The key to growth in this notion is leadership with vision. The process needs to be faith based not social service based.[17]

The reasons given for the closure of schools and parishes across the urban centers of the United States were quite consistent. Large church

---

[15] Patricia Forster, O.S.F., "The Chicago Story—and Boundaries to Parish Restructuring," in *Diocesan Efforts in Parish Reorganization: A Report* (Clearwater, Fla.: Conference of Pastoral Planning and Council Development, 1995) 83.

[16] Fr. Nick W. [pseudonym], interview by author, Chicago, Ill., February 12, 2001.

[17] Patricia Kelly, phone interview by author, Chicago, Ill., October 16, 2000.

facilities without enough members to keep them operating was the simplest explanation offered by Church officials. The most repeated response in Chicago's Englewood area for the closure of their eight churches was finances. "We couldn't pay the bills." In a 1988 homily, the pastor of St. Martin's in South Chicago held up a copy of a utility bill for heating his facility for one of the winter months. This bill was larger than the weekend collections. The people began to realize they could not continue. By the time of the Englewood consolidations, all of the parishes and schools of the cluster were on significant archdiocesan subsidies. This crisis in regard to church subsidies was echoed in chanceries across the country.

The Archdiocese of San Francisco was forced to come to grips with this reality following the 1989 earthquake. City building codes were changed for un-reinforced masonry buildings and the estimated cost of sixty million dollars to bring to code older church buildings far exceeded archdiocesan savings.[18] Programs of pastoral service, such as worship and ethnic ministry offices, were scrapped because of already depleted endowments for the care of urban grammar and secondary schools.[19] In the last decade of the twentieth century, these calls for financial relief indicated a far deeper crisis facing the U.S. Catholic Church in the large urban centers: a migration of its population to the suburbs.[20]

A reverse trend, that sociologists came to call gentrification, began to occur by the end of the decade. The more upwardly mobile were tired of the long daily commutes to work and began moving back into the areas abandoned by the previous migration. These migrations back into the city have not been overwhelmingly Catholic—leaving the parish problem virtually unchanged. The churches and schools originally built for the former ethnic populations were aging facilities often in need of major renovation and often significantly larger than needed.

The figures of the 1990 census indicated that nearly all of the major cities of the Midwest and Northeast continued to lose population to the suburbs. As households with money left the cities for the safer environ-

[18] "A Journey of Hope toward the Third Millennium: The Pastoral Plan of the Pilgrim Church of San Francisco" (first-phase recommendations of the Archdiocesan Planning Commission, November 19, 1993) 37–38.

[19] Archbishop John R. Quinn, "A Shepherd's Call" (a homily on the occasion of the initiation of the archdiocesan planning process, December 15, 1995) as quoted in "A Journey of Hope Toward the Third Millennium: The Pastoral Plan of the Pilgrim Church of San Francisco," 55.

[20] Andrew Greeley, *The Church in the Suburbs* (New York: Sheed & Ward, 1959) 31, 58.

ment of the suburbs, this urban core deteriorated and became more dangerous. The churches became poorer and less capable of providing basic services that might retain a population. It became a downward spiral. In a 1994 speech, "The Church in the City," delivered to the National Pastoral Life Center's Urban Ministry Conference, Bishop Anthony Pilla summarized the situation:

> As population has shifted, so has the tax base of cities. As people of greater means have moved from central cities to suburbs, our cities and our city parishes remain home to growing concentrations of people of reduced income, fewer educational opportunities, and with little or no access to employment in the suburbs where jobs have moved as well.[21]

The slipping tax base impacted the "somewhat isolated worlds" of national and ethnic territorial parishes that remained behind in the old neighborhoods in several ways. Many were built for the cultural and language needs of ethnic populations that had moved into the mainstream of U.S. society. In short, the congregational base had moved away from the neighborhoods. In Chicago one woman spoke dramatically of the realization that the home parish she was fighting to preserve was built by another culture for their unique needs and lifestyle.

> When we looked at the history of it, it put a different slant on it. "They left them because of us." She said during the time of the strongest emotions, her husband came home from a meeting and said to her that these churches were built for another people and another time. They were built in the style of the mother churches in their home countries of Ireland and Germany. We didn't inherit these churches, they were abandoned![22]

In San Francisco's "mission district," the ethnic Italian base of a small national parish likewise had moved away. It however continued to support the church from the suburbs, utilizing the facilities for special events like sacraments and funerals. The population of its grammar school was primarily commuter, some of whom were descendents of the original Italian founders. As the archdiocesan planning process began to look at the possible closure of the Italian national parish of Immaculate Conception in

---

[21] As quoted in Joseph Claude Harris, "The Shrinking Church in Big Cities," *Church* 10, no. 3 (Fall 1994) 29.

[22] Nora [pseudonym], interview by author, Chicago, Ill., November 8, 2000.

1993, the suburban descendants wailed in protest. Despite the diminished numbers at Sunday Eucharist, the absence of young people, and the lack of outreach ministries, the mantra, "If it's not broke, don't fix it," became a familiar refrain at any attempt to initiate change. As the processes evolved during the next few years, it became clear that a small pocket of people maintained the facility as a monument to their grandparents and the Italian Catholic subculture that nourished them.

A Great Folding Together of Ethnic Cultures

The "second wave" of immigrant experience for Catholic America was identified by Jesuit Allen Figueroa Deck as the migration of millions of Latin American and Asian Pacific peoples to the United States after World War II. It occurred just as the first wave's memory and meaning was fading into mainstream American culture. Figueroa Deck's metaphor is helpful in understanding the folding of one immigrant population into another during this era. But it failed to grapple adequately with the other movements of now indigenous ethnic communities across the landscape of the U.S., most especially the African American and Puerto Rican communities.

The "first wave" in the nineteenth or early twentieth century achieved acceptance in a predominantly Protestant and rather anti-Catholic country. Notre Dame historian Jay P. Dolan remarks in his *The American Catholic Experience*, that when immigrant Catholics came to the United States, "the vast majority of them headed for the neighborhoods of urban America. The city was their best opportunity for finding employment; it was also where they could link up with the extended community of relatives and friends."[23]

Ethnic parishes and concurrent with them, the "national parishes" of the late nineteenth and early twentieth century, were designated to provide a social and church life with familiar liturgical and devotional patterns from the immigrants' home countries.[24] They provided a center for the lives of the newly arrived communities, serving them as a "way station"[25] between one country and another, this world and the next. They afforded a diversity of religious and liturgical services, educational and social life, a

---

[23] Jay P. Dolan, *The American Catholic Experience: A History from Colonial Times to the Present* (Garden City, N.Y.: Doubleday, 1985) 195.

[24] Ibid.

[25] Ellen Skerrett, Edward R. Kantowicz and Steven Avella, *Catholicism, Chicago Style* (Chicago: Loyola University Press, 1993) 7.

place of acceptance, and familiarity and sanctuary in their new surroundings. After a long and often bitter struggle, World War II gave these immigrants an opportunity to demonstrate their Americanism.[26] By and large, many ceased speaking their native languages. The election in 1960 of John F. Kennedy to the presidency is often used as the marker of this Catholic "mainstreaming."[27]

The Irish, German, Italian, and Slavic ethnic groups were becoming less identifiable from dominant American society. By the late nineteenth century, bishops and pastors were stressing the significance of this adaptation. They perceived a need for the Church to Americanize, to demonstrate that they could be authentically Catholic and American. In several generations whole cultures from Western Europe folded into one another. The cost of this migration was the cohesiveness and intimate community of "urban villages" that had once formed to welcome them.

Just as U.S. Catholics and their bishops, priests, and men and women religious were becoming comfortable with their hard-earned status, a second wave began to fold into the first. In some respects the difficult conditions and demands of a century before were once again on the American Church. Included in this wave were large numbers of African Americans and Hispanics moving to the northern urban cities and occupying the same neighborhoods built by the first wave of Catholic immigrants.

John T. McGreevy's 1997 book, *Parish Boundaries,* posited that when the African-American communities began moving north in large numbers, their encounter with the "white" world was filtered through a distinctly Catholic focus on parish and place.[28] The neighborhoods to which they moved had been "created not found" around a Catholic parish by the previously assimilating immigrant groups. McGreevy attempted to show how the civil rights movement in the early sixties was both assisted and impeded by Catholic urban parochial life. The lynchpin of his argument was connection to neighborhood. The Catholic urban neighborhoods of the late nineteenth and early twentieth century were heterogeneous collections of distinct ethnic, yet Catholic cultures and they were meant to last. Church, convent, rectory, and school were large dominating institutions. Even the architecture of these structures reflected influence and permanence. The language, art, music, and devotional and liturgical practices

---

[26] Figueroa Deck, *The Second Wave,* 1.

[27] Ibid.

[28] John T. McGreevy, *Parish Boundaries: The Catholic Encounter with Race in the Twentieth Century Urban North* (Chicago: University of Chicago Press, 1996) 17.

reflected identity for a population with few other alternatives for expressing it. Parishes increasingly became sources of helping services, education
adapted to the needs of the newly arriving European immigrants, and
social life. In little more than a single generation, all of this facilitated one
of the most rapid cultural assimilations in human history.

Ethnic and religious prejudice was also a major influence in the cultural
isolation of large urban neighborhoods. Adjoining enclaves of Irish, Italian,
Polish, and German peoples reflected a culture of poverty and guaranteed
competition for scant resources. Many immigrants had emerged from long
histories of conflict with their nations of origin. With the sheer numbers
of new Catholic "foreigners," anti-Catholicism was the way a primarily
Protestant dominant culture tried to protect its turf.[29]

A cluster of studies from that era demonstrated that American Catholic
immigrant groups invested a significant percentage of their resources in
property. Working-class immigrants were often more likely than middle-
class natives to own their own homes. These studies suggested that home
ownership was less an American than an immigrant dream.[30] The shadow
side of this investment could be seen in the active opposition to the movement of African Americans into the Irish enclaves of Chicago's Garfield
and Englewood districts in the late fifties. Some of the participants in this
study spoke of hearing Sunday sermons encouraging people not to move
away and sell their homes. White Catholics were warned to close their
blinds when "those people" walked by, meaning the newly arriving African
Americans. Chicago's "white flight" of the early sixties was infamous for its
exposure of the racism inherent to the turf mentality of Catholic ghettos.

Icons of a Catholic Culture

Priests supervised the Catholic world of that immigrant era. Typically
one of the most educated persons in the community, the pastor's role
stretched from "ombudsman" to "guardian of culture"[31] within a dense
social network around the boundaries of his parish church. A pastor stayed
in one area for long periods of time, with his influence often extending

---

[29] Dolan, *The American Catholic Experience,* 201.

[30] McGreevy, *Parish Boundaries,* 18.

[31] Dolan, *Transforming Parish Ministry,* 7–23. For a careful description of the
Americanization of the Catholic clergy of the U. S. in the urban environment of the
nineteenth century, see John Tracy Ellis, ed., *The Catholic Priest in the United States*
(Collegeville, Minn.: Saint John's University Press, 1971), especially "The Formation
of the American Priest: An Historical Perspective," 3–110.

over several generations. He alone was responsible for the care of souls. His own soul was marked with an indelible charism that forever separated his identity from the person in the pews. Within the boundaries of his parish or national group, nothing escaped his attention or advice. As a person who represented a large constituency, he spoke with some political clout. His strongest role, however, was anchored ritually. He welcomed children into the church at baptism, witnessed their weddings and officiated at their funerals.

Every aspect of the parish's life, including cult and sacraments, fund-raising, education, and social life, fell under the eye of its pastor or his curates. "All things to all people," characterized his role in the hearts and minds of his parishioners. Tremendous social services emerged from this setting—youth recreational programs of incredible magnitude (such as the Catholic Youth Organization), orphanages, and social services like Catholic Charities. Together with the religious sisters or brothers affiliated with the parish school, he directed the institutions where most of the children of a neighborhood were educated. The term, "brick and mortar" frequently described priests of this era. They were church builders, often finding the resources to build, pay off mortgages, and sustain large institutions in very meager times. Perhaps, as a reward for their labors, they would collect the title and vesture of "domestic prelate" or more familiarly a "monsignor." They were a unique breed of religious leadership: "Father," elder parent, and statesman to the community of clans and neighborhood families.

Besides the use of the Latin language in liturgy, the point of unity be-tween these groups was what Jay P. Dolan calls, "a Catholic ethos"—an umbrella culture under which many different immigrant groups defined themselves.[32] Some elements of this ethos continued to appear in the con-solidation era of those same neighborhoods. These included that peculiar Catholic docility to authority with its unbending delineation of roles be-tween priest and laity. A prominent document of Pope Pius X noted that the Church was an unequal society "comprising two categories of persons, the pastors and the flock."[33] A second aspect of this Catholic ethos was an emphasis on sin and confession, a sense of the world as a negative, secular society. A third aspect was ritual. The way to the sacred was mediated through the ceremonies they performed, most especially the Mass and

---

[32] For more on this "Catholic ethos" see Dolan, *American Catholic Experience*, 221–40. See also, Mark R. Francis C.S.V., *Liturgy in a Multicultural Community* (Collegeville, Minn.: Liturgical Press, 1991) 43–47.

[33] Quoted in Dolan, *American Catholic Experience*, 222.

other sacraments. The culture of devotional Catholicism reflected a Tridentine popular religiosity: processions with the Eucharist and images of saints, novenas, communal praying of the rosary, as well as faithful attendance to the official sacraments.

The final consequence of this unique Catholic immigrant religiosity was an openness to the miraculous, a sense of mystery in the ordinariness of life. David Tracy dubbed this an "analogical imagination," a way of seeing life that blurs customary distinctions between the secular and sacred. It assumed a God present in the world, disclosing God's self in and through creation. The world and all its events, objects and people were perceived as sacramental, icons of the divine.[34] This ritual imagination dims the distinctions between "Church" and "church," people and building. Catholics in the United States tended to identify with their buildings. Threaten or adjust one, and the other was deeply affected. Hence, as the landscape changed in the late sixties, and it became necessary to cluster and close some of these parochial structures, the loudest voices in protest were often those relatives of the Irish and German immigrants who now lived in the suburbs. A legacy enshrined in glass and stone suddenly appeared to be at risk.

Many parish plants in the northern cities reflected competition among Catholic ethnic communities for prominence among their neighborhood churches. They were often built on a tremendous, even grandiose scale, including a church, parochial elementary school—sometimes even a sec-

---

[34] David Tracy's *Analogical Imagination* posited that Catholic imagination is "analogical" while Protestant imagination is "dialectical." The Catholic spiritual classics assume a God is present in the world, disclosing Godself in and through creation. The world and all its events, objects and people tend to be somewhat like God. Traditional Protestant classics, on the other hand, paint a God who is radically absent from the world and who discloses Godself only on occasion. Andrew Greeley studied why Catholics stay in the Church. He argues that only two out of thirteen reasons given emerged as statistically significant. Those were "faith to pass on to children and the sacraments." Sacraments emerge as uniquely Catholic along with the quality of their liturgical performance. According to Greeley, sacraments likewise impeded defection from the Church when there was an inclination to do so because of failures of religious leadership. Catholic liturgical imagination is rich, dense, multivalent, and rich with metaphor. This cannot but influence the way these generations of Catholics felt about their church buildings. See David Tracy, *Analogical Imagination: Christian Theology and the Culture of Pluralism* (New York: Crossroad, 1981) and Andrew Greeley, *The Catholic Myth: The Behavior and Beliefs of American Catholics* (New York: Collier Books, 1991) 34–64. See also Greeley's *The Catholic Imagination* (Berkeley: University of California Press, 2000).

ondary school—a convent, rectory, and occasionally an ancillary gymnasium or auditorium. The churches themselves held saints' relics lodged in
altars of marble or fine stonework, and they had towering bell towers and
statuary of medieval saints—all of this reflecting a timelessness and sense
of safety. The buildings and fences around the plant protected the school-
yard almost like a circled wagon train. Even the architecture pointed to
the notion that American Catholics frequently defined their surroundings
in religious terms.[35] It spoke of safety and permanence.

One of the most prominent accomplishments was the parochial school.
An elementary school and even high school system was established either
in conjunction with parishes or under the sponsorship of one of the religious orders as an alternative to public education. Catholic colleges and
universities became part of the urban scene. Total education under Catholic auspices was a distinct possibility in these settings. What was achieved
through this era was the establishment of a virtually separate and self-
sufficient Catholic society within the larger urban society. From cradle to
grave Catholics of that era could live out their lives in a Catholic environment. These parochial schools were available to nearly every Catholic
family, "Every Catholic child to a Catholic school," was the prevailing
catechesis. The labor force for this system consisted of members of
Catholic religious orders, primarily women, whose history was also linked
to the parish. (The number of religious sisters in the United States peaked
in 1963 at 104,441.) After 1968, lay teachers began to outnumber the
religious, forever altering that dream of universal Catholic education.[36]

As the ethnic Euro-Americans moved out of their urban neighborhoods at the end of World War II, and the African American community
moved in, the schools that had cradled them there were experiencing the
first crisis of faith. The ranks of vowed religious who had staffed the
parochial school systems had thinned tremendously. As lay teachers were
hired to fill in the ranks, it was finances that provoked the first crisis.

> The Catholic school was a great institution for Blacks. Many joined
> the Catholic Church through the schools. But these same schools
> now cost more to maintain. People were not joining the church from
> them anymore. We had to challenge Black Catholics to maybe a dif-
> ferent identity. School and church together was what most of them

[35] McGreevy, *Parish Boundaries*, 11.

[36] Jay P. Dolan, R. Scott Appleby, Patricia Byrne, and Debra Campbell, *Transforming Parish Ministry: The Changing Roles of Catholic Clergy, Laity, and Women Religious* (New York: Crossroad, 1989) 172.

knew. It challenged the larger Black Catholic community at a time when about thirty parishes closed. What does church look like without a school connected to it? What does the ministry of education look like in a parish when it does not have a school?[37]

The first wave of parochial consolidations appeared in the late sixties in Chicago. The word consolidation meant closure of the parish with the recommendation by the archbishop that the remaining people join one of the neighboring parishes. The sacramentals, school records, properties and territory (if the parish was a territorial) were then transferred to the receiving parish. By 1988, when the archbishop of Detroit announced the closing of forty-six urban parishes, an era came to a close for American Catholics. The pattern of extraordinary growth in population and institutions had ended. An era of consolidation replaced the age of expansion.

Closure and consolidation were synonymous prior to the new canon law of 1983. When a parish was closed, its records and territory were transferred to a receiving parish. The years 1969–75 saw a reduction in the number of (formerly) national parishes in Chicago neighborhoods and the closures or mergers of their schools. The closing rituals in these "receiving parish" consolidations often took place at Sunday Eucharist and included a reception. The focus seemed to be the reading of the archbishop's letter and the gathering with alumni and former parishioners. In a May 20, 1976 letter to parishioners of St. Mary of Mount Carmel, John Cardinal Cody expressed deep awareness of the history of American Catholicism etched on the face of a single parish community:

> I speak in the name of the Church of the past and present—in the names of Archbishop Feehan, Archbishop Quigley, Cardinal Mundelein, Cardinal Stritch, Cardinal Meyer and my own name—when I express a deep word of thanks to the priests, the religious, the good people of your parish now and in years gone by.
>
> But there is ever the need to face reality. The Church must always ask when is a parish to be born and when it must recognize that it is no longer a living parish community. Regrettably, yet with pastoral appreciation for the judgment made at your local community level, I accept your recommendation that the parish of St. Mary of Mt. Carmel be closed.[38]

[37] Fr Donald [pseudonym], interview by author, Chicago, Ill., February 19, 2000.

[38] Harry C. Koenig, ed., *A History of the Parishes in the Archdiocese of Chicago: Published in Observance of the Centenary of the Archdiocese, 1980,* vol. 2 (Chicago: The Archdiocese, 1980) 1662.

The Cardinal's letter raised the question that would be at the center of diocesan planning processes for more than the next two decades: "[W]hen is a parish born and when must it recognize that it is no longer a living parish community"? What would be the criteria for a thriving vibrant parish? The emergence of the post-Vatican II Church against the major fluctuations of U.S. Catholic demographics forever altered the image of the Euro-immigrant church. In Los Angeles, Cardinal Mahony's pastoral letter on ministry in April of 2000 presented a definition of local church in marked contrast to the immigrant brick and mortar parish. He located vibrancy in ministry, in the flourishing of service rooted in the Baptismal call: "The parish church is no longer seen as the place where people go simply to have their needs met. Rather, the parish is where one and all are challenged to exercise their baptismal calling."[39]

[39] Roger M. Mahony, "As I Have Done For You," *Origins* 29, no. 16 (May 4, 2000) 746.

Chapter 2

Traditions of Reconciliation
Conflict, Communion, and Sacred Remembering

It was a fiasco, people wanting everything. Someone had to stick it out and take the blows. The challenge was to face opposition and negativity and ride it out . . . more prayer was necessary to get the wisdom to find the answers. Being an example yourself, especially in the situation of opposition is most important—letting go of wanting to be right . . . and "finding another way to reframe your thinking." It is best to stick together; let go of "this is mine" mentality. Letting go says nothing belongs to you. "If we have to leave and go somewhere else, we go somewhere else!"[1]

Decision-making processes around parish restructuring tended to release powerful energies. This reflection of a woman deeply engaged in the turmoil surrounding the five parish consolidation that formed Chicago's St. Benedict the African East gives witness to a struggle with foundational gospel values. Her perceptions of conflict and reconciliation in the decision-making processes of those years speaks powerfully of a Christian experience deeply imbedded with theology and history. What the Wayne State study called "one of the most extensive efforts at religious reorganization in American history" was more often than not a situation laden with conflict.

[1] Jeannie [pseudonym], interview by author, Chicago, Ill., November 19, 2000.

19

Conflict is messy and painful. Oftentimes, religious people cope with this messy uncertainty by giving the blame for it to "sin." We move away from conflict rather than toward it, often suggesting that the solution to it is more prayer or spirituality. Yet, the above participant's reflection talks about a turning to directly face opposition, about "letting go" of a sense of personal righteousness and turf, to a reframing of perspective. She anchors reconciliation finally in a sense of Church—a particularly expansive relationship of people not necessarily dependent upon buildings.

Reconciliation rests on several anthropological points of reference that emerge from the collected stories and wisdom of the Judeo-Christian Scriptures. People harm each other (the authors of the sacred texts place this fact under the rubric of sin) and yet they are inherently social and cannot flourish in isolation. The consequence is that forgiveness of hurt is crucial to the ability to flourish as persons. In *No Future without Forgiveness* South African Archbishop Desmond Tutu posits that the very survival of human community is linked to the act of forgiveness.[2]

Forgiveness is a "person to person response to unfairness"[3] that leads the offended person to release resentment and claims to requital. Dr. Robert Enright from the University of Wisconsin's International Forgiveness Institute defines it as a process characterized by the willingness to relinquish one's right to resentment, negative judgment, and indifferent behavior toward one who unjustly injures, while fostering the undeserved qualities of empathy, generosity, and compassion.[4] Forgiveness is thus a component of reconciliation, but only a first step. It is one of the most frequent of miracles, says John Patton. It is one among the most unexpected and seemingly impossible of human choices. It is a direction of the will, yet has a dimension

[2] Desmond Tutu, *No Future Without Forgiveness* (New York: Doubleday, 1999) 196–98.

[3] Robert D.Enright, Julio Rique, and Catherine T. Coyle, *The Enright Forgiveness Inventory [EFI]: User's Manual* (Madison, Wis.: The International Forgiveness Institute, 2000) 1.

[4] Robert Enright and Joanna North, eds., *Exploring Forgiveness* (Madison: University of Wisconsin Press, 1998) 46–47. See also Avery Dulles, S.J. "When to Forgive," *America*, October 7, 2002, 6–10. Enright and North further outline the complex range of definitions of forgiveness and their relationship to reconciliation. The simplest definition of forgiveness in this literature is the abandonment of resentment. There are three different drifts in current studies: (1) A gift of self alone: forgiveness is not a gift to the offending person and to others, but to the victim. It heals and restores a sense of self and safety. (2) Subjective perceptions are primarily responsible for the pain we feel: forgiveness is equated with correcting faulty perceptions of suffering and responsibility. (3) The offer of moral love and acceptance to those who offend is a way of contributing to human altruism and expanding the horizons of one's world. Ethicist

of discovery that almost runs against human nature.[5] Reconciliation in this context is more than forgiveness; it is the much larger category of the restoration of human communion after a breach of relationship. The social and interpersonal dimensions of reconciliation remain a fundamentally religious enterprise. In Christian reflection, the source of that pervasive and overarching drive to human reconciliation is God the Creator.

Forgiving is intrinsic to the Christian legacy and traces its roots from the First Testament Prophetic Books and Wisdom Literature directly to the teachings of Jesus. Perhaps the writings of St. Paul reflect the clearest expression of this tradition. Reconciliation is first of all the work of God, who initiates and completes it in human beings through Christ. It is not a human accomplishment, but the work of God within and among us. Only God can restore the magnitude of damage done to children and families by the horrors of violent conflict. Only God can restore "the disappeared" dead or a culture brutally wrested from oppressed native peoples in many of these settings. God begins this mission not with the wrongdoer but with the victim.

Second, the restoration of shattered or compromised humanity is at the very heart of the Christian understanding of reconciliation. Restoration of a damaged humanity is one of the most succinct consequences of "grace," or that life-giving relationship with God. In this perspective, there is no victimization that cannot be healed. The victim experiences healing by reengaging the image and likeness of God within (see Gen 1:26). A paradox of the Christian understanding of reconciliation is that the notions of repentance and forgiveness are not "the preconditions for reconciliation, but are the consequences of it."[6]

Donald Shriver notes that the Christian biblical tradition sees both forgiveness by the victim and repentance by the perpetrator as necessary components of complete reconciliation. Forgiveness by the victim includes (1) openly naming the wrong, (2) drawing back from revenge-in-kind, (3) developing empathy for the perpetrator, and (4) extending to the offender a tentative hand toward renewed community in the future. Repentance for the perpetrator parallels this process including (1) offering repentance for the wrong, (2) feeling gratitude that revenge in kind is not in the offing, (3) developing empathy for the victim's suffering, and (4) hoping for reconciliation with the victim. Donald W. Shriver, Jr., "Is There Forgiveness in Politics?: Germany, Vietnam, America," in Enright and North, 136.

[5] John Patton, *Is Human Forgiveness Possible?* (Nashville: Abingdon Press, 1985) 176.

[6] Robert Schreiter, C.P.P.S., "Entering the Healing Circle: The Practice of Reconciliation," in *The Healing Circle: Essays in Cross Cultural Mission*, ed. Steven Bevans, S.V.D., Eleanor Doidge, L.o.B., and Robert Schreiter, C.P.P.S. (Chicago: CCGM Publications, 2000) 178.

The invitation to repentance or conversion of life, which is at the heart of the preaching of Jesus, emerges more often through the victim, rather than the wrongdoer. Through the victim, the wrongdoer can be called to forgiveness and repentance. In the final account, the experience of reconciliation transforms both victim and wrongdoer into "a new creation" (2 Cor 5:17).[7] This has deeply personal, interpersonal and social implications. Reconciliation transforms a traumatic event from a weight that binds to the past, into a force that moves toward a very different kind of future. It restores broken relationships but in a new configuration. The story of the passion, death, and resurrection of Jesus paints a picture of that new restored humanity created in a reconciled world. This image has great power in facilitating and giving meaning to that enterprise in a specific human situation like the conflicts around the restructuring of local church.

There is a mystery to the very nature of reconciliation. One can identify the psychological components and variables of interpersonal forgiveness as have several contemporary schools of research. Their paradigms identify logical phases and units of the forgiveness event, but the sequences tend to be "invariant" or cyclical. The forgiver may skip over some steps and move back and forth over others. The process has an element of grace—it is out of control of anyone but the victim. Still, there is a moment in both individual and social reconciliation when the boundaries between the wounded individual and their offender undergo a substantial change. Without condoning or excusing an injury, the forgiver begins to view the offending event in context—to include within their own narrative of the event the stresses and personal history of the offender.

This cognitive reframing of perspective is where the stresses inherent to parish restructuring and reconciliation particularly intersect. Inclusion,

---

[7] Pope Paul VI's 1975 apostolic exhortation, *On Evangelization in the Modern World (Evangelii Nuntiandi)* brings a further nuance to this paradox. He calls evangelization "bringing the Good News into all the strata of humanity from within and making it new." He links evangelization to conversion; to the "personal and collective consciences of people." Effecting humankind's "criteria for judgment, determining values, points of interest, lines of thought, sources of inspiration and models of life." When the Church is the perpetrator of the source of trauma, this turns evangelization upside down. The limits of its conversion expose the whole Church as penitent among the human family. It is constantly seeking a sense of conversion that is authentic and recognizable. See Pope Paul VI, *On Evangelization in the Modern World (Evangelii Nuntiandi)* (Washington D.C.: United States Catholic Conference, 1976) 15–16.

[8] Eric F. Law, *Inclusion: Making Room for Grace* (St. Louis, Mo.: Chalice Press, 2000) 42.

from the work of multicultural theorist Rev. Eric Law, is a graced discipline of extending a boundary around the needs, interest, experience, and
perspective of another, resulting in a clearer understanding of oneself,
fuller description of the issues at hand, and a newly negotiated boundary
of a community.[8] In the context of parish restructuring, this sense of
graced inclusion locates reconciliation as the end product of the task.

There is likewise a mystery about human woundedness. The complexity
of social and individual trauma demonstrates that recovery is often never
really finished. Reconciliation can be completed only with the consum-
mation of the whole world, "when every tear will be wiped away" (see
Rev 7:17 and 21:4).[9] The magnitude of the task of reconciliation leads to
acknowledgement ever more deeply that it is the work of God. There is a
sense that human efforts toward reconciliation of any breach can never
completely restore what was lost. The initiative and guidance of God is
fundamental to any hope of complete restoration of any breach. Belief in
the paschal mystery, at the core of Christian faith, extends another notion
of grace as God's solidarity and the consequent restoration of humanity.
What began for the human community in the death and resurrection of
Jesus will somehow be completed at the end of time, when Christ makes
the final "peace by the blood of his cross" (Col 1:20).[10]

Since at least the sixteenth century, much of the Christian ritual tradition of reconciliation has focused on the individual. Its perspective, in
Roman Catholic sacramental practice, began with the wrongdoer, who
changes heart and asks forgiveness for sinful acts. Social reconciliation, in
the work of Chicago's Fr. Robert Schreiter, focuses more upon the reconstruction of a moral order to society, insuring that the wrongdoing of the
past will not be repeated. It has three important dimensions. First of all,
it tells the truth about the past. Second, on the basis of that truth, it seeks
what justice can be done to remedy the wrong perpetrated. Third, it
struggles to create a new future for both victims and wrongdoers.[11] It is

---

[9] The expression is found in the Sacramentary in the special insert for Eucharist
Prayer III in Masses for the dead.

[10] Schreiter, "Healing Circle," 181. Harold Wells makes use of this notion of divine
solidarity as "atonement"—restored harmony and peace between God and humanity.
This solidarity of God, perhaps realized in a new way and location, I prefer to call
grace. It is that mysterious and graceful indwelling of God that makes a restored
humanity for both victim and wrongdoer possible. See Harold Wells, "Theology of Reconciliation: Biblical Perspectives on Forgiveness and Grace" in *The Reconciliation of
Peoples: Challenge to the Churches*, ed. Gregory Baum and Harold Wells (Maryknoll,
N.Y.: Orbis Books, 1997) 9–12.

[11] Ibid., 181–82.

"a locus and a focus," says John Paul Lederach, a prominent Mennonite leader in the area of peace education and conflict transformation. Social reconciliation is a locus—a place where people and things come together, where the diverse inner-connected energies and issues driving conflict can meet, most especially the paradoxes of truth-telling, mercy, justice, and peace. Reconciliation is likewise a focus—a way to reframe human conflict: to address, integrate, and embrace the breach of a painful past and a necessary shared future as a means of dealing with the present.[12]

The basic paradigm of reconciliation embraces a paradox. It suggests, for example, that a focus on relationship will provide new ways to address impasse as it appears on issues. Reconciliation provides a space for grieving the past that permits a reorientation toward the future. Inversely, the envisioning of a common future creates new lenses for dealing with the past.[13]

Individual and social reconciliation are interrelated. The first focuses upon the restoration of damaged humanity, while social reconciliation focuses upon the reconstruction of a moral order. Individual reconciliation looks more toward the human dimension of healing, while social reconciliation centers its efforts upon its ethical dimensions. Both engage in actions that lead to restoration. They both draw upon the resources of truth-telling, the revision of narratives, and the refashioning of relations to the past. Interpersonal forgiveness focuses more resolutely on the past while social reconciliation as moral reconstruction directs itself more toward the future.[14] Healing depends for its success upon an agent and a community of safety to guide the social reconciliation process. A certain quality of imagination likewise is required to envision a new social configuration in continuity with its past. This is the key to the dream of Gospel-based reconciliation.[15]

Conflict Transformation:
A Model from the First Testament

The term reconciliation does not appear frequently in the Scriptures and in fact is not a major preoccupation in the First Testament. Yet, the

---

[12] John Paul Lederach, *Building Peace: Sustainable Reconciliation In Divided Societies* (Washington, D.C.: Endowment of the United States Institute for Peace, 1997) 31.

[13] Ibid.

[14] Schreiter, *Healing Circle*, 183.

[15] Ibid.

story of salvation as God reconciling the world to God's self runs like a thread through all the sacred texts. The word is not used at all in the Hebrew Scriptures, although it appears within other major themes of the ethos of Judaism, like the notion of atonement. A vision of a reconciled people of Israel as sculpted by the authors of the Hebrew Scriptures likewise includes other themes that build a foundation to human reconciliation as it will emerge in the writings of Paul of Tarsus. Justice and *shalom*, the universalism of the prophetic literature, especially the images of reconciliation of opposites in the poetry of Isaiah and Jeremiah, likewise build a foundation for this vision. The notions of sin and redemption, with roots in the Genesis creation story, add to what Harold Wells calls an evolving sense of "divine solidarity."[16] The task of restoring the right relationship of Creator and creatures emerges again and again from the texts, as ultimately the plan of God.[17]

Lederach, from the context of contemporary religious-based conciliation, uses the Jacob-Esau story and Psalm 85 as a lens to look at conflicted relations and their restoration after breach. Through them some important distinctions emerge between the notions of conflict resolution, conflict management, and conflict transformation.[18] "Conflict resolution" is a field of study focused on understanding how conflict evolves and ends. It looks for strategies and skills for dealing with the volatile and often destructive outcomes of conflict. Its underlying presupposition is that conflict is undesirable and should be eliminated. "Conflict management" entered professional circles in the mid-seventies with the idea that conflict follows certain predictable patterns and dynamics that can be understood and regulated. Management of conflicted relationships recognizes that conflict is never resolved, but rather emphasis is placed on affecting the destructive consequences of it. The notion of "conflict transformation" emerged in the early nineties in the search for adequate language to describe the peacemaking venture. It recognizes that social conflict is a phenomenon of human creation lodged in relationships. It is a phenomenon that transforms the event, the relationship in which the conflict occurs, and often times its very creators. It looks to what is constitutive for transforming individuals, relationships, and social organization.

---

[16] Wells, "Theology for Reconciliation," 9–12.

[17] Ibid., 10.

[18] John Paul Lederach, *Preparing for Peace: Conflict Transformation across Cultures* (Syracuse, N.Y.: Syracuse University Press, 1995) 16–19.

The Jacob-Esau myth (Gen 25–33) offers a metaphor with which to view the process of conflict transformation. The breach between the brothers is described with language and images profoundly familiar to those interviewed from the closure consolidation processes of parishes studied for this work. When Esau returns from hunting and realizes with his father that Jacob and his mother have tricked the bestowal of the blessing reserved for the first born, he is enraged. He is hurt, hateful, and hungry for revenge. The trauma of a stolen generational blessing affected the whole clan, leading many to choose behavior that called their identity as children of Israel into question. Jacob flees in fear and the brothers are bitter enemies. Esau pleads with Isaac for blessing. "Father, bless me too! . . . Have you only that one blessing, father? Bless me too!" (Gen 27:34, 38). This notion of blessing enough only for one sibling resulted in competition that turned violent.

The nature of blessing and the loss of it were likewise pressing questions to those attending the closures of parish communities where the generations of memories and legacy dwelt. Competition between formerly related communities added additional levels of loss and disorientation in many of the stories gathered from consolidating local communities. People in both the San Francisco and Chicago parochial consolidations spoke of feeling "second class" to the now primary worship site of their parish. If one community appeared to get more resources or be the locus of too many parochial activities, the other became angry. The choice of St. Justin's as the worship site for the three merged parishes in Chicago's West Englewood resulted in closure for two others. A town hall meeting format was selected to make the final choice some months after the Archdiocese of Chicago had formally announced consolidation. When the results were read from the paper ballots, people from the site chosen for the new parish stood and cheered—embittering those from the other two. A discernment process had deteriorated to a win-lose situation! Many of the former Sacred Heart and St. Rafael's congregations were hurt and outraged. Professional conciliators admitted being overwhelmed. The final outcome left behind suspicions that the vote had been manipulated. A group went from St. Justin the next Sunday and publicly apologized. Still, it left a bitter taste for many and weekend Mass attendance significantly declined.[19]

The experience of consolidation of parishes in the U.S. for many has been a conflict-laden experience. Intense conflict among religious people,

---

[19] Br. Lauren [pseudonym], interview by author, Chicago, Ill., February 27, 2001.

especially among clergy and members of religious communities, scandalized some. That winner-take-all mentality, familiar to American politics, left people in a church setting embittered and isolated. Some moved to other parishes, taking their wound with them despite numerous personal invitations for them to return. How to work through the intricacies of conflicted decision making and reflect on it afterwards has been an ongoing difficulty for church people.

Throughout the Hebrew Scriptures, major moments of deep religious insight and transformation often take place in and through intense interpersonal and social conflict. Conflict is a sacred space, often revelatory of God's presence. Several foundational principles can be gleaned from the Jacob-Esau story as noted in the work of John Paul Lederach:

1. Reconciliation after any breach is a journey ultimately toward and through conflict. Jacob and Esau separate after the manipulation of the generational blessing from Isaac. For Jacob the separation is driven by fear; for Esau, it is driven by rage and desire for revenge. At some point, years after both have established their own families, the voice of God sent Jacob back to the breach: "Return to the land of your fathers, where you were born, and I will be with you" (Gen 31:3). In other words: God's presence requires the journey toward the one perceived as enemy. Relationship is the basis of both conflict and its long-term solution. Relationship is built on mechanisms that engage each side of a conflict with the other in a person-to-person relationship as opposed to seeking innovative ways to disengage or minimize the conflicting group's affiliations. This method takes time, sometimes lavish amounts of it, to work through the conflicted issues.

2. Reconciliation assumes encounter, not only of people, but also other different and highly interdependent streams of activity. It must find ways to address the past without getting locked into a vicious cycle of revenge or mutual exclusiveness. People need opportunity and space to express to and with one another the trauma of loss and their grief at that loss. They must find a way to vent the anger that accompanies the pain and the memory of injustices experienced. Acknowledgement is a key to this. Hearing and knowing another's story validates experience and feelings. It is the first step toward restoration of the person and the relationship. Reconciliation envisions a future in a way that enhances interdependence. It involves a turning toward the breach, toward the source of conflict. It is an encounter with self, with God, and with the other.

3. Reconciliation involves the creation of a social place to wrestle with an intricate human paradox.[20] Jacob's turn toward his brother meant a wrestling with blessing and ultimately himself. Jacob spent the night before his meeting with Esau wrestling an angel until daybreak. Even though wounded, Jacob finally receives his own blessing. He gives the place a name—"Peniel, 'Because I have seen God face to face'" (Gen 32:31)—so it would be remembered.

Remembering and the sanctity of place are keys to social reconciliation. They wrestle in a paradox mutually shaping one another. Lederach articulates the parameters of this wrestling using Psalm 85:10. The psalmist refers to the return of people to their land and the opportunity for safety and order. "Truth and mercy have met together; peace and justice have kissed" (translation from the Lederach work).[21] The four perspectives of this psalm and their interactions—truth, mercy, peace, and justice—are a tremendous resource for breaking deadlock or impasse in highly charged conflict negotiation. By asking participants from both sides of a conflict to address their conflicted reality from these four perspectives, a definition of reconciliation appropriate to a very particular situation emerges.[22]

"Truth," suggests honesty, revelation, clarity, open accountability, and vulnerability, a seeing the other as created in the image and likeness of God. Without the perspective of truth, no conflict could ever be resolved. Yet, truth alone leaves human beings naked, vulnerable, and often unable to measure up to elevated standards. The notion of ultimate, universal truth can separate as well as draw people together.

Mercy is constitutive of the message of Jesus with deep Hebraic roots in *hesed*, the loving kindness that is one of the primary characteristics of God. It highlights the compassion, forgiveness, acceptance, and space adequate for a new start. Mercy is the bestowing of grace, the safety and trust for restored relationship. Without the flexibility and tolerance implied by mercy, human relationships deteriorate. Without compassion and forgiveness, the restoration of community is beyond human capacity. Yet,

[20] Lederach, *Building Peace*, 26–29.

[21] John Paul Lederach, *The Journey Toward Reconciliation* (Scottsdale, Pa.: Herald Press, 1999) 53.

[22] St. Augustine's "Commentary on Psalm 85" no. 9 noted a similar dialectic with the images of peace, justice, mercy, and truth. He pointed out that justice and peace kiss one another in this psalm, they do not quarrel among themselves.

mercy alone is superficial. It can obscure and even cheapen relationships if it is granted too quickly.

Reconciliation is not possible without a turn toward the demands of justice. Justice raises powerful images of right relationship, of equal opportunity, rectifying wrong, and restitution. Without justice, the brokenness continues and festers. And yet there is no such thing as complete justice. None of the losses that accompany human life can ever be completely restored. The cry for justice, however, needs to be attended critically. It can be a smokescreen for revenge that eases anger at an injustice for a while but perpetrates cycles of violence. Schreiter distinguishes several forms of justice: Punitive justice punishes the wrongdoers to assert that such behavior will not be tolerated again no matter what legitimization perpetrators attempt to give. Restorative justice, while admitting that justice can never undo what has been done, tries to make amends for the evil of the past while dealing with its consequences in the present. Third, structural justice tries to address the inequities in society, which fostered the violent trauma in the first place, i.e., economic and social imbalance. While difficult to address and usually only partially achieved, structural justice tries to get at the roots sometimes stretching back generations deep into culture and even religion.[23]

With peace comes images of biblical *shalom*, that harmony, unity, and well being of a right relationship to God, others and the earth. It is the feeling and prevalence of respect and security. But, peace is a farce if preserved for the benefit of some and not others. *Shalom* is the consequence of God's indwelling with Israel, in the temple with the ark and the cult, in the voice of the prophet who announced God's presence and in the moral demands of covenant fidelity. Reconciliation involves the creation of a social place where truth and forgiveness, justice and mercy meet, are validated and joined together, rather than being imposed into an encounter in which one wins and another loses.[24]

The Jacob-Esau story blends elements of conflict and reconciliation with aspects of blessing, dedication, and memorial—the symbols of interpersonal restoration. It leads to an intense mysterious moment of grace, or changed perspective. "[T]o see your face is like seeing the face of God" (Gen 33:10; NRSV). The story does not have a fairytale conclusion with the clans living happily ever after. Restoration of relationship does not necessarily mean social configurations remain the same. After several days

[23] Schreiter, "Healing Circle," 182–83.
[24] Lederach, *Building Peace*, 29.

together, the brothers and their respective clans separate again to live in different valleys.[25]

Resurrection Models of Forgiveness

A woman walked into the parish office at the end of the first year of Immaculate Conception's consolidation in San Francisco. Millie was a somewhat severe, Italian survivor who pressed her lips firmly together against any church innovation. She was a regular lector and led one of the most verbally charged public meetings of ministers against the consolidation. She was an outspoken critic of the whole process. And once the specifics of the Immaculate Conception consolidation began, she led the troops from the morning 7:30 Mass and rosary group against any change. She wrote anonymous letters concerning a half-hour change in Mass schedule and the merger of the two Sunday bulletins. Her grandson was in the school, and she angrily added her voice in parent meetings. I was a bit nervous when she called one morning out of the blue and asked for an appointment. All she wanted was to briefly tell me that she had decided to forgive me for all I had done to the "Immaculate." She died less than a month later.

The Gospels attest to one fact with extreme clarity: Jesus forgave. His was a forgiveness that manifested the beginning of a new era, the beginning of the reign of God. Jesus embraced sinners and called them to an internal repentance and reconciliation for the sake of the kingdom.[26] The Christian understanding of reconciliation emerges from the experience of the risen Christ. It has individual and social dimensions synonymous with the Gospel message itself and forms an essential component of living the Gospel. In the words of Franciscan theologian Fr. Kenan Osborne, "Christian life as such is a life in and through reconciliation. Were one to remove every aspect of reconciliation from the life of a Christian, there would be no Christian life at all."[27]

From within the covenant perspective of the Christian Scriptures, all human beings corporately are related to God and one another. As members of God's people, sin is always a communal rupturing or breaking of

[25] Lederach, *The Journey*, 26.

[26] Joseph A. Favazza, *The Order of Penitents, Historical Roots and Pastoral Future* (Collegeville, Minn: Liturgical Press, 1988) 69–70.

[27] Kenan Osborne, O.F.M., *Reconciliation and Justification* (New York, Paulist Press, 1990) 16.

life-giving and loving relationships. Therefore reconciliation must have a communal dimension. The Church participates in the covenant of Christ by living obediently according to the law of love. The inseparability of the love of God and love of neighbor in the teachings of Jesus makes apparent that reconciliation with God is inseparable from reconciliation with others. The Church participates in the reconciliation of Christ and makes it visible and tangible through the ages by its ministry of reconciliation. We participate in this ministry by meeting the daily challenges to mutual forgiveness, individually and corporately.

Part of the mission of the Church, as alluded to in the resurrection accounts of the Gospels, is to extend the reconciling presence of Christ to the world. Sustaining peace through mutual forgiveness was the way envisioned by the Church of extending the reign of God. The early Christian community took seriously its pastoral mission to preach the saving power of faith in Christ that called all persons to turn away from sin and believe in the gospel. The call to radical conversion involved personal sorrow for sin and a willingness to be created anew. For the believer, this was accomplished through participation in the two experiences that defined the limits of membership in the early Church: baptism and Eucharist.

The Second Testament writers, especially the Synoptic Gospels, saw Jesus through the experience of forgiveness. In the Gospel of Luke, during Jesus's public ministry, he announces forgiveness to those who show sorrow for their sins (5:18-26; 7:36-50). He visits with sinners on the margins of his society (19:1-9) and speaks in parables about the Father's love for those who stray (chap. 15). It is Luke's Christ alone who prays forgiveness from the cross. He does not forgive his executioners, however he asks God to forgive those who "know not what they do" (23:34). Matthew's Gospel sees the death of Jesus through this limitless mercy in a pouring out of his blood "for the forgiveness of sins" (26:28). When asked how many times to forgive one another, the response extends limitlessly: "seventy-seven times" (18:22). Theologian Edward Schillebeeckx posited that the experience of forgiveness is intimately associated with the experience of the resurrection of Jesus.[28] The first accounts of resurrection

---

[28] Edward Schillebeeckx, O.P., *Jesus: An Experiment in Christology* (London: Collins, 1979) 390–92. The Japanese novelist Shusaku Endo entitles the final chapter of his novel on the life of Christ, "The question." Jesus's forgiveness to the disciples from the cross (most of whom were in hiding) forms the root and beginning of the resurrection experience from a Japanese perspective. See Shusaku Endo, *Life of Jesus*, trans. Richard A. Schuchert (New York: Paulist Press, 1978).

in nearly all the New Testament accounts include a sense of personal reconciliation. This sense of restored relationship emerges from the disciples' realization that Christ had forgiven them from the cross for a betrayal that perhaps exceeded the scant evidence of the Gospel narratives. The stories testify to a precious legacy of interpersonal forgiveness in the early Church. Jesus's own consistency with his own teachings on forgiveness, even to his own death, may have contributed to the transformation of fearful disciples to fearless apostles.

There is no single proclamation about the identity and mission of Jesus that more shocked and scandalized the religious leaders of his day than his claim to forgive sin. "Who but God alone can forgive sins?" was the astonished cry in Luke 5:21. Jesus offered the physical healing as proof that he did indeed have the power to forgive sin. The removal of sin was a function of the healing of illness; a connection still made in Roman Catholic sacramental practice with the ritual for anointing of the sick. Likewise, there is still no single proclamation about the identity and mission of the community of believers that would continue to shock and give scandal, than that they too bear that power. Yet an enduring challenge of the Gospel has been how that mission and power of the Christ is passed on to his followers.

The question of how the disciples came to be convinced that the crucified Jesus was alive has preoccupied theologians and storytellers for centuries. The Synoptic and Johannine literature connect it to forgiveness. The appearance of the risen Jesus in the Gospel of John concludes with empowering words: "Whose sins you forgive are forgiven them, and whose sins you retain are retained" (20:23). The Easter experience in Luke crescendos in the disciples' proclamation of the forgiveness of sins (24:47). St. Paul says, "if Christ has not been raised . . . you are still in your sins" (1 Cor 15:17). As Schillebeeckx notes, "the forgiveness of sins is a gracious Easter gift."[29] The abandonment by Simon Peter and the apostles left the group isolated and traumatized. The experience of the risen Jesus gave rise to a profound peace, because in and through this encounter, the experience of their betrayal was wiped away. This very experience of being forgiven counted as evidence that Jesus was alive. It is foundational to the ongoing legacy of Jesus of Nazareth.

Paul of Tarsus is the principal resource of the theological paradigm of reconciliation in Christian praxis and tradition. Some form of "to reconcile," occurs thirteen times in the authentic and Deutero-Pauline writings.

---

[29] Schillebeeckx, *Jesus*, 396.

Paul identifies the Church's mission—its very reason for gathering—with reconciliation. Second Corinthians identifies the community of disciples as "ambassadors" of reconciliation (see 2 Cor 5:18-20). The quality of Christian community is an announcement to the world that all enmity between God and humankind is at an end. The peace that marks the life of the early Christian community is a sign of that mystery. Combining the references in Romans and 2 Corinthians with the usages in Colossians (Col 1:22-23) and Ephesians (Eph 2:12-16), there is some suggestion that a theology of reconciliation can be discerned on three levels. At the level of grace, Christ is the mediator through whom God reconciles the world to God's self. Jesus lays down his life, as servant of God's reconciling will from the beginning of creation. And only God can restore the fabric of human community from the multiple levels of human wounding and sin. At the ecclesiological or church level, Christ reconciles Jew and Gentile, bringing them together in a communion deeper than clan and culture. Maintaining community even in the face of betrayal witnesses to power greater than self. Finally, at a cosmic level, the Christ event—the radical laying down of a life in love— reconciles all the powers in heaven and on earth, all human institutions and potentials, to a single purpose: the reign of God.[30]

> Indeed, if, while we were enemies, we were reconciled to God through the death of his Son, how much more, once reconciled, will we be saved by his life. Not only that, but we also boast of God through our Lord Jesus Christ, through whom we have now received reconciliation. (Rom 5:10-11)
>
> And all this is from God, who has reconciled us to himself through Christ and given us the ministry of reconciliation, namely, God was reconciling the world to himself in Christ, not counting their trespasses against them and entrusting to us the message of reconciliation. (2 Cor 5:18-19)

From the two central verses of Paul's theology, several ideas appear that are central to the early Church's sense of its place in the reconciling mission of God. (1) God is the ultimate agent of reconciliation. (2) The reconciliation that Christians have to offer in overcoming the enmity

---

[30] Schreiter notes the work of two other writers in this convergence of reflection on reconciliation: Cilliers Breytenbach, "Reconciliation: An Exegetical Response," *Journal of Theology for Southern America* no. 70 (1990) 64–68, and Jose Combin, "O tema de reconcilia, cao e a teologia na America Latina," *Revista Eclesiastica Brasileira* 46, no. 182 (1986) 272–314. Schreiter, *Reconciliation*, 43.

created by suffering is not something we find in ourselves but something we recognize as cosmic right relationship to God. (3) Reconciliation is something more often discovered rather than achieved, prompting then a larger process of human repentance.[31] Forgiving (not counting the trespasses against a wrongdoer) and being forgiven are inextricably interrelated. Anglican bishop and theologian Rowan Williams spoke of the almost holistic complexity of the choice toward forgiveness: If forgiveness is liberation, it is also a recovery of the past in hope, a return of memory, in which what is potentially threatening, destructive, despair inducing in the past is transfigured into the ground of hope.[32]

Restoring Communion: Resources from the Early Church

The term *koinonia* or communion is a rich theological concept rooted in the primitive Church. It refers first of all to the participation in the life of God, and thus, through sacramental baptism and Eucharist, the communion fellowship shared among the disciples of the Christ. One of the greatest challenges faced by the New Testament Church was working out the implications of this new reconciliation for Jews and Gentiles in the same community of disciples. Paul states in Galatians 3:27 that by baptism, Christians are "clothed" with Christ, as are the neophytes in the Easter liturgies. Eucharistic *koinonia* shapes the formation of a new people who transcend differences of race, social status, or gender. This communion excludes "neither Jew nor Greek," "neither slave nor free person," "male" nor "female"—"for you are all one in Christ Jesus" (Gal 3:28). The ritual of Christian Eucharist celebrates and at the same time affirms steps toward that communion.

The primary sacrament of reconciliation is the event of the Church itself. Eucharist, therefore, is the fullest ritual expression of that event. It is the ritual sacrament of reconciliation that constitutes the Church as the Body of Christ.[33] The Eucharistic assembly is founded on the imagination of Jesus, an intuition about an inescapable human unity. Community is not made to happen. It is both discovered and called into being.[34]

[31] Schreiter, *Reconciliation*, 42–45.

[32] Rowan Williams, *Resurrection* (London: Darton, Longman and Todd, 1982) 32. First Timothy 5:22 is perhaps the earliest reference to an actual reconciliation ritual through the imposition of hands on the penitent sinner and the welcome back into Eucharistic communion around the table of the Lord.

[33] James Lopresti, in Favazza, *Penitents*, xxii.

[34] Ibid., xxiv.

Eucharist was the most common reconciling ritual employed by the San Francisco and Englewood consolidations. People spoke with great fondness of the "Unity Masses" used during the early years of the ten-parish Englewood cluster. These liturgies joined all the parishes of the cluster in a monthly Sunday afternoon gathering of their best: song, vesture, youth ministry, and leadership. Fr. Peter Scholtes's *They'll Know We Are Christians*,[35] a popular hymn written while the author was associate at St. Brendan's in the 1960s, reminded participants that they were about doing church, "one in the Spirit . . . one in the Lord." Yet at times of internal church conflict the role of the Eucharistic liturgy was notably problematic. People at odds with one another after conflicted meetings of the planning commissions found it difficult to share a potluck, let alone a Eucharistic liturgy. Yet these worship events could soothe and point out what unity a fractured local church still had in common and could build upon.

In the ritual of Eucharist, believers can experience themselves intimately or spiritually bound to one another. "The cup of blessing that we bless, is it not a participation in the blood of Christ? The bread that we break, is it not a participation in the body of Christ?" (1 Cor 10:16-17). In the act of consuming the one loaf of bread, distinct human beings are linked together in an intense social relationship. There are two other extensions from this notion: first, the cosmic inclusion of all the saints—past and present and in the future *eschaton*—and second, the notion of excommunication. Paul asks in 1 Corinthians 5 that a man be excluded from the table for an incestuous relationship. Its purpose was not however punitive so much as it was medicinal. Exclusion from Eucharistic *communio*, in its origins, was at the service of conversion. The hope was that a change of heart would bring the excluded one back to the table.

Communio is so much of the focus of the Gospels and teachings of the early Church, yet it was a term seldom included in the dialogues within settings devoted to reconfiguring local parish. To forgive is to restore communion. Forgiveness in the context of parish restructuring, according to Patricia Kelly, "is to join God in co-creating and re-creating the communion which is our legacy within the body of Christ."[36] It invites a community back to life and shares in a mystery intensely holy. The injunction in Matthew 5:24 to leave the gift at the altar and go first to reconcile with an

---

[35] Peter Scholtes, *They'll Know We Are Christians* (Chicago: FEL Publications, 1966) assigned to The Lorenz Corp., 1991.

[36] Patricia Kelly, phone interview by author, Chicago, Ill., October 16, 2000.

errant brother or sister takes on new significance in this context. There is no time to lose.

The notion of the local church as a communion has important implications for the processes of parish merger and closures. Participants noted that this communion needed to be based on honest relationship and ritual integrity. When church is less than the ideal of this rich *communio*, worship must somehow speak the desire to know again its richness.

During the first two centuries, there really was no standard way of restoring communion after serious breaches. A multiplicity of reconciliation practices and rituals are alluded to in the literature of the early Christian community. Ritual creativity marked the era. Different communities in their own settings highlighted different things. Mutual confession of faults and segregation from the community remained two consistent innovations. James 5:16 reads, "confess your sins to one another and pray for one another, that you may be healed." This tradition had echoes in other early writings (1 John 1:9 and the *Didache* 4.14 and 14.1). The discipline of truth-speaking and the acknowledgement of oneself as sinner had a privileged place in early New Testament spiritualities. Church—honestly grappling with its own sinfulness—serves as an impetus for conversion and a graced containment for working through conflict. Theologian Doris Donnelly notes this from a contemporary context:

> What we need, above all, is a community in which we can all tell the truth, in which there are no cover-ups, in which we can be ruthlessly honest. We are sinners. We need a Church in which the climate is accepting and supportive enough for the call to conversion to pierce us all.[37]

Chapter 18 of Matthew comes closest in the New Testament to looking at a methodology of conciliation. Together with the Acts 15 account of the Council of Jerusalem, it also gives us a lens to view conflict within the community of the early Church and the application of the *kerygma* of Jesus to these concrete internal situations. For the community of Matthew, recently excluded from the synagogue, this item was of crucial importance.

> If your brother sins [against you], go and tell him his fault between you and him alone. If he listens to you, you have won over your

---

[37] Doris Donnelly, "Reconciliation and Community," *Repentance and Reconciliation in the Church*, ed. Michael J. Henchal (Collegeville, Minn.: Liturgical Press, 1987) 30.

brother. If he does not listen, take one or two others along with you, so that 'every fact may be established on the testimony of two or three witnesses.' If he refused to listen to them, tell the church. If he refuses to listen even to the church, then treat him as you would a Gentile or a tax collector. (Matt 18:15-17; see also Luke 17:3-4)

The injunction to attend to one who "sins against," alluded to conflict between members of the church. One of the few references to the *ekklesia* in the Gospels indicates that sin always had an ecclesial dimension and hence a need for definite procedures to handle an erring brother or sister. It also alluded to the power of binding given to the Twelve and extended into the community of disciples. The early Church employed two pastoral responses for members convicted of sin: (1) to "go directly" in distinct stages to the one who had "sinned against" and enlighten them of the sin that separated them from the community; (2) to segregate the sinner— noting Jesus's particular affinity to the Gentile and tax collector. Personal sin, after all, isolated from community. Honest acknowledgement of the separation was often the first step to bringing the sinner back, or stepping away and saying goodbye in the face of continued resistance to return to conversion.[38]

Going directly, taking one or two witnesses along and finally taking the matter to the whole assembly is reflected in other Pauline letters[39] and reflects how consciously and seriously the primitive Church took the task of internal relationships. References to the conflict over requirements for Gentile converts at the Council of Jerusalem in Acts 15 and Paul's account of his confrontation of Cephas in Galatians 2:11-14, likewise reflect that threefold pattern. One can almost see the paradox of reconciliation reflected in the process—balancing truth, mercy, justice and peace in each concrete situation.

In the third century, confessing one's sins to "someone of God," most especially confessors or those who survived imprisonment or torture for the faith, created a controversy of authority in the early Church. The "companioning care" of returning sinners by those members of a church who accompanied the penitents back into communion was reflected in divergent traditions of reconciliation practice and ritual. Likewise they testify to a variety of ministries in the Church giving flesh to the larger "ambassadorship" of reconciliation given to the whole Body by the writings of Paul.

---

[38] Favazza, *Penitents*, 79.
[39] 2 Thess 3:6, 14-15; 1 Tim 5:19-22; Titus 3:10-11.

Study of the history of this sacrament has shown that few areas of Christian ritual have changed as much as the sacrament of penance (reconciliation). The variety and flexibility of ritual practices are a testimony to the creativity of local churches over the decades responding to conflicted pastoral situations in a multiplicity of ways. In the third century, Origen outlined seven ways that Christians have for obtaining the forgiveness of sins: baptism, martyrdom, almsgiving, the forgiveness of others, the conversion of sinners, "great love" (see Luke 7:47), and the more arduous way, which is penance.[40] Recent historical writings on this ritual sacrament have confirmed the social and ecclesial character of its most ancient forms. The third-century institution of an order of penitents and the practice of *exomologesis* (to bear witness or to confess) describe a segregated penance crafted to draw those who had abandoned their baptismal commitment back into conversion and communion.[41]

The public ritual confession of fault demonstrates another strand of the repertoire of pastoral care for the sinner. In the North African church of that period, Tertullian described this ritual revelation of oneself as a sinner that so consistently marked early Church ritual practice. It marked prayerful context for public apology and confession of faith:

> Exomologesis is a discipline that leads you to prostrate and humble yourself. It prescribes a way of life, which, even in the matter of food and clothing, appeals to pity. It bids you to lie in sackcloth and ashes, to cover your body with filthy rags, to plunge [your] soul into sorrow, to exchange sin for suffering. It requires that you habitually nourish prayer by fasting; then you prostrate yourself at the feet of the priests and kneel before the beloved of God, making all the brethren commissioned ambassadors of your prayer for pardon.[42]

---

[40] Owen F. Cummings, "Reconciliation and Penance: Some Needed Distinctions," *Chicago Studies* 34, no. 2 (1995) 154–55. Fr. M. Francis Mannion would see the first six under the notion of penance and the seventh related to the restoration to communion after post-baptismal sin. This distinction ignores the reality of social reconciliation and the Pauline vocation of the Church (including the local church) to channel that reconciliation grace of God into the world (2 Cor 5:17-21).

[41] *Exomolgesis* or confession was not a private confession to a bishop or presbyter. In Tertullian's *agere penitentiam* or post-baptismal penance, it is a public or ritual avowal of one's faith in God's mercy and of one's sinful life. After an unspecified period of time in public penance and confessing one's sinfulness, there was a public ritual of reconciliation. The ritual confession of sinfulness *(exomologesis)* does not seem to have been a confession of specifics, but of the mercy of God and one's sinfulness. See Osborne, *Reconciliation and Justification*, 61–62.

[42] The process included the wearing of some sort of sordid clothing, fasting or restriction of diet, lamentation, prostration before the presbyters, and kneeling before

The North African bishop, Cyprian, more narrowly defined three moments to the penitential process: (1) the doing of the penance, which included the penitential actions described by Tertullian above as well as other personal penances, done under the supervision of the clergy; (2) the liturgical or ritual confession of faults *(exomologesis)*, without necessarily the disclosure of individual sins; and (3) the reconciliation of the penitent through prayer, the laying on of hands and re-admittance to the Eucharist.[43] With Cyprian, an identifiable process of penance emerges. These notions of process with identifiable stages, ritual expression, and the ritual time to attend to the very human aspects of conversion are new venues of the Church's tradition to be applied to social reconciliation.

Medieval penance shifted its focus from reconciliation and conversion to forgiveness of sins. Slowly, confession to someone of God shifted to annual private confession to a priest. The Fourth Lateran Council in 1215 canonized this, obliging all who had reached the age of discretion to annual confession and began the transition to modern notions of penance. It defined four ritual actions or moments of sacramental penance as: contrition, confession of sin, penance-satisfaction, and absolution. Despite the presence of other strategies—canonical penance as described by Cyprian, individual works of mercy, pilgrimage to special shrines, and even military service in the Crusades—this remained the traditional Roman Catholic reconciliation pattern for the next eight hundred years. The *conversi* or penitents continued as an identifiable group giving rise to a series of medieval penitential movements. Among those eventually regularized by Church authorities was the thirteenth century's Francis of Assisi who became a *conversus*, later establishing rules of life for orders of penance—vowed men, cloistered women, and lay associates.[44]

Monastic orders would give the determining shape to medieval and modern Roman Catholic sacramental practice. Anglo-Saxon and Celtic monks began to extend a more informal penance, spiritual direction, and a counseling tradition that they borrowed from Eastern monasticism. This

---

the entire assembly; found in *De Paenitentia*, 9, 3–4, as quoted in Joseph Favazza, "Reconciliation: A Journey, A Process, A Little Hang Time," in James Dallen and Joseph Favazza, *Removing the Barriers: The Practice of Reconciliation* (Chicago: Liturgy Training Publications, 1991) 36.

[43] Ibid., 36–37.

[44] James Dallen, "History of the Reform of Penance," in *Reconciling Embrace Repentance and Reconciliation in the Church*, ed. Robert J. Kennedy (Chicago: Liturgy Training Publications, 1998) 83–84. See also Raffaele Pazzelli, *St. Francis and the Third Order: The Franciscan and Pre-Franciscan Penitential Movement* (Chicago: Franciscan Herald Press, 1989).

non-public practice, which did not segregate penitents into an identifiable group, provided no ritual of reconciliation or ministry in public liturgy. The emphasis came to be on the absolution.

What began as a manifestation of conscience for the sake of spiritual guidance evolved to a private confession of sins so that a confessor could assign an appropriate penance or satisfaction. By the fifteenth century only private confession survived as the official means of forgiveness for sins committed after Baptism.[45] From the vantage point of social reconciliation, the ritual and pastoral care traditions of primitive Christianity are a wealthy vein of new resources for the conflicts internal and external to church.

Modern Penance and the Vatican II Reform

The contrition, confession, penance, and absolution pattern given official sanction in the Council of Trent and enumerated again in the 1973 renewal of the sacramental rite was a familiar one to the American Catholic imagination.[46] Those socialized on the Baltimore catechism could speak it from memory. Confession lines on Saturday afternoons, the privacy of the darkened confessional, the seal of confidentiality, and the words of absolution were one of the identifying marks of American Catholic culture.

When the Second Vatican Council's *Constitution on the Sacred Liturgy (Sacrosanctum Concilium)* called for the reform of the ritual sacraments, penance was one of the most complex and the last of its tasks. The implementation of Vatican II liturgical principles with its full, conscious, and active participation of the assembly (14), clashed with strong cultural impressions of the sacrament of penance: "rites which are meant to be celebrated in common, with the faithful present and actively participating, should as far as possible be celebrated in that way rather than by an individual and quasi-privately."[47]

Reform of the rite in "the light of sound tradition"[48] and "growing somehow out of the forms already existing,"[49] called to memory the more

---

[45] Ibid., 86.

[46] Joseph A. Favazza, "The Eucharistic Table, a Reconciling Table? Our Belief, Our Experience, Our Dilemma," *The Many Presences of Christ*, ed. Timothy Fitzgerald and David A. Lysik (Chicago: Liturgy Training Publications, 1999) 94.

[47] Nos. 26–27 in *The Liturgy Documents*, vol. 1 Chicago: Liturgy Training Publications, 1991) 15.

[48] Ibid., no. 4.

[49] Ibid., no. 23.

ancient communal and ecclesial roots of penance. The reformed 1614 ritual of Paul V had focused almost entirely on the juridical, rather than the liturgical role of the priest. Scholastic theology's preoccupation with confession and absolution minimized praise, prayer, and almost all social and ecclesial references.[50] The drafting of the new Rite of Penance, with over six years of commissions and schemas, brought into focus the disagreement between those who wished to hold onto the Council of Trent's more juridical vision and those who wanted the new rite to be informed from the more primitive tradition of reconciliation.

The 1973 renewal of the rite, essentially a compromise and hybrid of these two visions, attempted to recover a theology of reconciliation rooted in baptism, Eucharist, and sacramental penance—the third reconciliation sacrament for "those who fall in to sin after Baptism."[51] The three forms of the Rite of Penance attempted to recapture the sense of public worship with the inclusion of prayer, Scripture, and the pattern of the Liturgy of the Word. Public examination of conscience and the use of large numbers of priest celebrants in Lenten and Advent communal penance services have begun to adjust the cultural image of sacramental confession for the American church. But crisis around the reform of this sacrament continued to linger.

The initial renewal documents had began to recognize the variety, change, and historical development of the rite. Reference to the social nature of sin revitalized a literature on penance and penitential practices, initiatives for communal celebrations of the sacrament, the penitential rite of the Eucharist, and grass roots interest in a new order of penitents.[52] Calls to restore the individual form of the rite as the normative form of reconciliation by consequent papal and U.S. episcopal documents have failed to derail that movement. Fears of cheap forgiveness have resulted in a tight restriction on the sacrament's third form, general absolution. What perhaps will be remembered with greatest poignancy from the papal documents of this era and even the literature of the great jubilee year of 2000 are the public apologies of the pontificate of John Paul II. His public examination of conscience on the Eastern Schism, the case of Galileo, the Crusades, the Inquisition, Jews, and women has resulted in more public acknowledgements of past wrongdoing than any religious leader in modern

---

[50] Dallen, "Reform," 86.

[51] *Penance and Reconciliation in the Church* (Washington: United States Catholic Conference, 1975) 12.

[52] Dallen, "Reform," 87.

history.[53] At the risk of oversimplifying a complex evolution of recent ritual history, it is becoming increasingly clear that future expressions of reconciliation in both sacramental and non-sacramental forms must be "multi-strategic."[54]

Few other venues of church life have exposed the inadequacies of the current sacramental practice of reconciliation with its emphasis on individual and personal sin as the conflicts around the consolidation and reorganization of parishes. Together with the most recent sexual misconduct and authority scandals of U.S. Catholicism, the need for alternatives to current reconciliation ritual practice have been further highlighted. In the context of social divisions, a more complex rite is needed. It is not likely that a series of individual private confessions can effect the turning of a conflicted group in a new direction or assist the forgiveness of hurt and insults made to one another in the heat of a conflict. Another form is needed.

When events tear at the now classic Tridentine pattern of reconciliation in the Catholic sacramental imagination, the consequences are often profound. One of the priests from the Chicago consolidation noted that these are intensified exponentially by confusion as to the agent of the reconciling action when "the church" is the cause of the breach:

> [C]urrent sacramental practice presumes a mutuality. It is face to face. This pattern is woven into our beings as Roman Catholics but it doesn't work in this situation. The perpetrator (in the ritual) asks forgiveness of the church (who is the proposed victim) and God. And the celebrant says the absolution. Who says the absolution when the perpetrator is the church itself? How do you forgive the institutional church that used . . . or abused its own middle management when no one admitted guilt or asked to be forgiven?[55]

---

[53] See Luigi Accattoli, *When a Pope Asks Forgiveness: The Mea Culpa's of John Paul II*, trans. Jordan Aumann, O.P. (Boston: Pauline Books and Media, 1998). The Jubilee "Service Requesting Pardon," March 12, 2000 at St. Peter's Basilica listed seven areas for apology: sins in general, sins in the service of the Church, sins that have harmed the unity of the body of Christ, sins against the people of Israel, sins against love, peace, the rights of peoples and respect for cultures and religions, sins against the dignity of women and the unity of the human race, and sins related to the fundamental rights of the person. See "Service Requesting Pardon," *Origins*, March 23, 2000, 646–48.

[54] Joseph Favazza, "The Eucharistic Table, A Reconciling Table?: Our Belief, Our Experience, Our Dilemma" in *The Many Presences of Christ*, ed. Timothy Fitzgerald and David A. Lysik (Chicago: Liturgy Training Publications, 1999) 95–96.

[55] Fr. Bundy [pseud.], interview by author, Chicago Ill., February 24, 2001.

Rituals crafted by local communities to address the disintegration of parochial relationships particularly highlighted a need to expand the repertoire to address a variety of social breaches. Psychologist Denis Woods assists in understanding the nature of social reconciliation by noting an array of conflicted settings. Distributive divisions result from basic human competition for resources, such as those of ethnic groups competing for meager jobs and scant resources, or those resulting from collective bargaining. Ideological divisions are those that result from groups struggling for apparently divergent values. Right-to-life and pro-choice groups are often further isolated from dialogue for lack of basic common ground at the level of values. Finally, structural divisions result from conflict where the structure determines that the decision maker will be winner and the winner takes all.[56] The task of responding to each of these breaches of human relationship requires distinctive pastoral and ritual resources.

In the course of its history, confession's manner and minister have varied. Experience has shown that if one is to proceed on the path of conversion, sin must be named and consciousness of sin must be shared in some public forum, beyond mere self-acknowledgement.[57] The repertoire of reconciliation practice from the store of the early Church offers ritual options to assist in the admission of culpability, especially in settings such as corporate structures where it is difficult to locate personal guilt.[58]

Ritual cannot carry the full weight of healing for the wounds of group conflict. One Englewood priest attempted to engage the conflicted staff of the combined parish in some prayer services adapted from the style of charismatic renewal. He feared his attempt to draw them together was ridiculed. But colleagues noted that the timing and substance of the prayer itself did not address the systemic and perhaps justice issues that caused the rift. Any rites adapted from current sacramental practice need to be a link in a chain of pastoral care that gradually bring the members of a group to recognize the reality of their social situation and (without denial or excuse) to take responsibility for it. It needs to assist participants to see the reality of their division from a new perspective.

Effective reconciliation ritual might require the presence of adversarial groups to face one another, weep together, begin again to trust each other, and swear cooperation for the future. Public witnessing of a "purpose of

---

[56] Denis J. Woods, "Reconciliation of Groups" in Peter E. Fink, S.J., *Alternative Futures for Worship*, 4 (Collegeville, Minn.: Liturgical Press, 1987) 38–39.

[57] Ibid., 88.

[58] Ibid., 38.

amendment" as in the *exomologesis* of early Church practice, could be an important moment in any reconciliation process. The role of public apology to groups wronged by church mission practice or policy has shown itself to be a powerful way of marking stages of social reconciliation.[59] Effective reconciliation ritual needs to help penitents see and feel the distance between themselves and those victimized being lessened.

Churches Bearing Sorrow: Reconciliatory Remembering

The restoration of baptized believers to the communion of the church after a serious breach has shown itself to be a comprehensive and ongoing process. It involves every feature and practice of Christian life by which believers more fully convert themselves to Christ.[60] At its best, it attempts to juxtapose the experience of breach within a community against the story of the life and teachings of the Christ. Through this juxtaposition something new is created—disciples healed and reintegrated into the life of a community, and a community tasting anew the depth of its unity in Christ.

In wrestling with the mystery of God's action in church ritual and liturgy, Lutheran theologian Rev. Gordon Lathrop notes an almost archetypal power to juxtaposition. Liturgy takes a concrete situation and joins it with a memory of what God has done in the past, to create a third new thing.[61] The sacraments of the Church are enacted in *anamnesis*, in remembrance of Jesus the Christ juxtaposed with a concrete reality.

Liberation theologians posit two main postmodern alienating human dilemmas affecting the quality of this remembrance: domination and difference. The reflection of churches caught in the violent political regimes of South Africa and Latin America in the past few decades has evolved a whole new literature on social reconciliation. The recovery of humanity for the victim and perpetrator of violent oppression in these contexts has

[59] See Walter Wink, *When the Powers Fall: Reconciliation in the Healing of Nations* (Minneapolis: Fortress Press, 1997) 54–59.

[60] M. Francis Mannion, "Penance and Reconciliation," in *The New Dictionary of Sacramental Worship*, ed. Peter Fink (Collegeville, Minn.: Liturgical Press, 1990) 934–35; see also Mannion's "Penance and Reconciliation: A Systemic Analysis," *Worship* 60, no. 2 (March 1986) 98–118, and Robert J. Kennedy, "Baptism, Eucharist, and Penance: Theological and Liturgical Connections" in *Reconciliation: The Continuing Agenda*, ed. Robert J. Kennedy (Collegeville, Minn.: Liturgical Press, 1987) 47–49.

[61] Gordon W. Lathrop, *Holy Things* (Minneapolis: Augsburg Fortress, 1993) 54–56.

become a central precept of this literature. The recovery of humanity is the result of remembering a greater master narrative in which the story of one's life can fit.

Reconciliation in the context of great polarities and fragmentation of the human family, also happens in the context of remembering. The healing and vision sought by the churches to the scandal of the divisions within Christianity occur within a praxis of transformation, what Toinette Eugene has called "emancipatory anamnesis," or reconciliatory remembering.[62] What sets free or transforms in the aftermath of any fracture of relationship is ultimately the encounter with a greater human narrative, a story of redemption that renews, reconciles, and puts us in solidarity with the struggle of God's people for freedom since the beginning of time. The process of remembering must effectively juxtapose what Schreiter calls "narrative of the lie" and the "redeeming narrative" that acknowledges and liberates truth. It must recall the stories of wretched and scandalous sin and evil alongside (and in juxtaposition to) the stories of saving grace. "In forgiving we do not forget . . . we remember in a different way."[63]

Against this legacy, the conflict and emotional upheavals experienced around recent church consolidations take on a new poignancy. There is often an unspoken shame that the institution that inherits this legacy can itself be torn by dissention or a cause of harm to its constituents. The recent experience of churches in settings of violent social upheaval have added new insights to the reconciliation legacy of the risen Christ. Their insights into reconciliation have something to say to those restructuring themselves in other contexts.

Neither of the two settings studied for this work had outright examples of violence. Church restructuring in various parts the country has evoked threats toward those responsible for implementing unpopular strategic

---

[62] Toinette Eugene, "Reconciliation in the Pastoral Context of Today's Church and World" in *Reconciling Embrace*, ed. Robert F. Kennedy (Chicago: Liturgy Training Publications, 1998) 13.

[63] Herbert Anderson and Edward Foley, Capuchin, *Mighty Stories, Dangerous Rituals* (San Francisco: Jossey-Bass, 1998) 182. Anderson and Foley use Schreiter's notion of "narrative of the lie" and "redeeming narrative" in the context of their presentation of the mythic and parabolic nature of story. Narrative comforts and gives identity while parable stirs up and challenges the comforted. Bishop Tutu noted that forgiveness does not mean amnesia, most especially in the community, national or international level. "Those who forgive and those who accept forgiveness, must not forget in their reconciling. If we do not deal with our past adequately, it will return to haunt us." See the forward to Enright and North, *Exploring Forgiveness*, xiv.

plans, as well as the more subtle kinds of violence—illegitimate uses of manipulative force that violate reputation and basic human civility.[64] The social phenomenon of human forgiveness is a process of reconstruction of the moral order of society. St. Paul, in particular, noted that the ultimate source of that pervasive and overarching drive to reconciliation is God the Creator. To forgive, to choose "to let go," of recrimination looks in hope forward to a future where one can remember without bitterness. This is a *confessio* of most profound faith.

Overcoming the suffering caused by violence's most subtle expressions involves wrestling with evil and distortions of a basic human intuition to goodness. It means confronting that "narrative of the lie" which coils itself around basic senses of security and self within the wounds of individual and collective psyches. The discovery of a greater redeeming narrative is a complex, difficult task. A victim works his or her way through a trauma by acknowledging the violence and finally wailing out in protest. Giving voice to pain and calling others to one's side eventually restores a sense of a social network. Awareness of helplessness and the limits of one's ability to cope begins the process of reconstructing a more authentic and accurate narrative of one's life after a traumatic hurt.

Anglican Fr. Michael Lapsley lost both of his hands and part of his sight to a mail bomb in 1990 as apartheid was being dismantled. The power of shared memory, a story acknowledged, reverenced, and recognized is particularly critical in forgiving one who has not asked for pardon:

> The question is not one of forgetting but rather it is the problem of how do we heal our memories. How do we stop our memories from destroying us? Forgiveness, yes—that is always the Christian calling— but no one should suggest that forgiveness is glib, cheap, or easy. What does it mean to forgive those who have not confessed, those who have not changed their lives, those who have no interest in making it up to the relatives of victims and the survivors of their

---

[64] For more on the distinctions of human violence see R. Scott Appleby, *The Ambivalence of the Sacred: Religion, Violence, and Reconciliation* (Lanham, Md.: Rowman & Littlefield, 2000) 15. He notes that violence is the illegitimate—extralegal—use of force. Noting the work of David Little, he characterizes four types of behavior: (1) Violent intolerance is the use of illegal force against the outsider. (2) Civic intolerance is the use of legal force or "legitimate violence" against the outsider. (3) Civic tolerance occurs when laws are enforced that forbid the use of force against the outsider. (4) Nonviolent tolerance is a form of militancy that rejects the use of force or violence in opposing the intolerant.

crimes? . . . It is important for all the relatives of victims and for all survivors to tell their story—and for that story, often for the first time, to be acknowledged, reverenced, and recognized. This will help us to begin to create shared memory.[65]

Suffering to transformation is relearning a fundamental trust at the same level and intensity as events that shaped the self in the early developmental stages of life. Faith in a new narrative—often with scars that last a lifetime—allows victims a new sense of their own humanity. Violence is most often aimed at stripping away humanity, leaving a twisted sense of reality that isolates, paralyzes, and subdues fundamental trust. Even in its more subtle forms, violence attempts to position and adjust memories in a radical fashion to reconstruct reality and meaning. Attempts to go back to a previous memory are often met with the threat of more violence. The loss of memory is fundamentally the loss of identity. The reconstruction of memory is one of the most critical tasks to overcome the suffering of violent trauma. An older memory must be disengaged from the acts of violence that created it, and a boundary be put around the violence to separate it within the psyche. The Christian ethos addresses the question of how to suffer and how to regain humanity. It juxtaposes a larger narrative to serve as a framework to rebuild a shattered one.[66]

Reconciliation does not mean a simple harmonizing of conflicting groups. It is never a hasty process or an attempt at managed conflict where oppressor and victim yield some of their interests to bring about a cessation of the hostilities. The complexity of human reconciliation defies easy solutions to victimization. In very different but also in very real ways both oppressor and oppressed are robbed of some of their humanity. Reconciliation is about restoring that humanity. And only God can ultimately bring it about, albeit in the *eschaton*.[67]

Truth commissions from countries like El Salvador, Chile and South Africa have demonstrated how time consuming and expensive the demands of reconciliation are. The stories of victimization need to be told again and again before the narrative of the lie is exorcised and a new, credible human

[65] Michael Lapsley, "My Journey of Reconciliation in South Africa: From Fighter to Healer," *New Theology Review* 10, no.3 (1997) 21–23. See also Michael Worsnip, *Priest and Partisan: A South African Journey* (Capetown: Ocean Press, 1997) and David J. Bosch, *Transforming Mission* (Maryknoll, N.Y.: Orbis Books, 1991) 514.

[66] Schreiter, *Reconciliation*, 38–39.

[67] Ibid., 48–49.

story constructed. One is humbled by the wrongs that often cannot seem to be repaired by any human means.

The Cross—the principal icon of the Christian heritage—is the "epicenter" of the Church's response to violence in whatever form.[68] Death on the cross was a horrible, inhuman form of torture, an outrage and a blasphemy. Reconciliation takes disciples to the limits of human possibility.[69] The Cross represents a return of trust and a confession "that loving is worthwhile, whatever it may cost in self-giving and even death."[70] The love of enemies remains intrinsic to Christian discipleship (see Luke 6:35). The literature around Christian forgiveness is still fairly recent. Much more needs to be articulated in terms of a psychology and spirituality for those seeking to apply the resources of that tradition to the experience of victimization of whatever kind.

This willingness to forgive reflects a world restored to meaning, a humanity connected in a solidarity that makes life worthwhile. Archbishop Tutu calls this the "bundle of life" originating in the Genesis creation accounts, the roots of a moral universe constructed in such a way that one's humanity is linked to that of all others. A key motive for forgiveness of any breach of relationship in the South Africa experience was the care and restoration of this bond:

> We are human beings because we belong. We are made for community, for togetherness, for family, to exist in a delicate network of inter-dependence. Truly, it is not good for [people] to be alone, for no one can be human alone.[71]

How a community's past is remembered is key to its future flourishing. Its health is related to its memory. When the seam of a local faith community appears fragmented by a conflict like those provoked by decisions for parish closure, a moral order must somehow be restored to the bad blood, soiled reputations, and, often, broken friendships. A rediscovery of a moral cosmos that can hold people together often occurs in the review of its epic stories, in the deeper older narratives of the Church's very foundation.

---

[68] Ibid., 47.

[69] Ibid., 46–47.

[70] Juan Luis Segundo, *The Humanist Christology of Paul* (Maryknoll, N.Y.: Orbis Books, 1986) 82.

[71] Tutu, *Forgiveness*, 196.

Chapter 3

The Negotiation of Crisis
Forgiveness, Trauma, and Sacred Space

They tried to include all the different languages: English, Spanish and Tagalog . . . We had a Eucharist at the beginning and the end, and that was important . . . They did have a retreat . . . There was a symbolic gesture there. If you design something with good organization and good ritual, there still has to be a certain space for freedom, for a certain something to emerge. It would be like you're sailing in a balloon; everything is ready to go up. You're looking for a current; you have to allow something to go. You have to be open to whatever emerges. When the bishop from [a neighboring diocese] was doing the liturgy, there was a couple there involved in the process since the beginning and they announced that they had decided to be married. To me that was a sign that this was going to happen—being blessed by their presence there. Aside from the retreat, this was a sign that we were on the right road and moving in the right directions.[1]

There are rituals that tell us we are on the right road and push us in the right direction. The above participant in the San Francisco consolidation struggled to articulate the way ritual worked or did not in the service of that process. Language, place, symbolic gesture, "hang time"[2] (an open

[1] Edward M. [pseudonym], interview by Dinah P. Shaw, San Francisco, Calif., February 23, 2001.

[2] For more on this notion of "hang time" see Joseph Favazza, "A Journey, A Process, and A Little Hang Time," in James Dallen and Joseph Favazza, *Removing The Barriers: The Practice of Reconciliation* (Chicago: Liturgy Training Publications, 1991) 33–39.

space for something to emerge), bread, wine, and familiar prayer all mingle in a way that can draw people together and perhaps reconcile conflicted relationships. The description presumes things about the functioning of human ritual, what makes it effective or not in marking social transitions like a parish consolidation. It either draws individuals and communities into new relationship or not. There is a mystery to it and an ongoing element of surprise. That same San Francisco participant challenged the processes to a deeper reflection on the interaction of church and ritual:

> [A] thorough analysis of what ritual is, the meaning of church and the experience of the church is needed . . . because people aren't on the same page as to what church means and what ritual is. The premise is you're merging two churches. But if they aren't clear on what church is, then how can they agree on a change?[3]

In another real sense new understandings of church require new ritual expression. An examination of prevalent literature on trauma, grieving, and forgiveness provides some new frames to the experience of recent U.S. church closures and consolidations.

The Sanctity of Place and Reconciliation

In 1947 a German-speaking liturgical commission published some basic principles for the construction of church buildings. They formed a popular compendium of church practice with dedicated space and how people felt about these spaces at the time of the American-German immigrant church. Church buildings were "consecrated" without noting the Reserved Eucharist, "to celebrate and make new the sacrificial offering of Christ for our redemption and to receive the fruits of Christ's redemptive sacrifice in the holy sacraments." A parish church was a ritual epicenter, "to hear the Word of God," to pay one's devotions to Christ, present in the Eucharistic bread, and participate in extra-liturgical devotions. Churches had significance and dignity shared with no other building, a "tabernacle of God amongst men, the place where God guarantees that He may be found by His faithful, our Father's House and God's royal palace."[4]

---

[3] Edward M. [pseudonym], interview by Dinah P. Shaw, San Francisco, Calif., February 23, 2001.

[4] See Theodore Klauser, "Guiding Principles for Designing and Building a Church in the Spirit of the Roman Liturgy," in *A Short History of the Western Liturgy: An Account and Some Reflections*, 2nd ed. (Oxford: Oxford University Press, 1979) 162.

The pre-Vatican II ritual prescribed for the restoration of a building profaned by some malevolent act made a connection between worship space and the experience of reconciliation. The rite began with a gathering at the doors of the desecrated building, followed by procession and psalmody. The washing and a sprinkling with blessed water connected the restoration of dedicated space to worship with eucharistic and baptismal symbols.

Reflecting ritual practices from the Middle Ages, the 1917 Code of Canon Law drew a connection between sacred space and reconciliation. When sacred space is altered, distorted, or destroyed, something deep in Catholic imagination reacts. The rage and intense emotion of people years after the closing or consolidation of a parish church testifies to the deep anthropological significance of dedicated space. The notions of consecrating and desecrating worship space, although not used in the new Code of Canon Law, have profound consequences for people. The rituals presumed by these words change the meaning and significance of geographical space.

There is a similarity between what people experience when sacred space is threatened, altered, or destroyed and the sense of violation often associated with deep psychological trauma. The descriptions employ similar works and images. For many these symptoms endure for years afterwards. After the upheaval of a parish merger or closure, one of the most recurrent observations of the clergy, religious, and lay leadership is that people stay angry a long time. Often up to a decade after the fact, many involved with this task reacted with the same intensity of emotions as if the event were recent. Words like hurt, chaos, sadness, grief, intrusion, disillusionment, violation, anger, fear, and powerlessness were common responses as people described the consolidations in both San Francisco and Chicago. Acknowledging the death of a community or the withdrawal of blessing to a sacred place felt for some nearly unthinkable. It was not uncommon to lash out at those judged responsible. In a culture of geographic mobility, the loss of a parish church seemed to point beyond itself, at a greater American loss of "the local" with its intimacy and identity. Powerful emotions are attached to one's place, to that "latitudinal and longitudinal" locale "entwined with personal memory, known or unknown histories, marks made in the land that provoke and evoke."[5]

[5] Lucy R. Lippard, *The Lure of the Local: Senses of Place in a Multicentered Society* (New York: The New Press, 1997) 7.

Traumatic events "overwhelm the ordinary systems of care that give people a sense of control, connection and meaning." There is disorientation and rage, "intense fear, a sense of helplessness, loss of control and threat of annihilation."[6] People with dense ritual memories of liturgies performed in closed church locations report also experiencing these symptoms at times when they are near the now-closed space. Even clergy and local leaders charged with implementing changes to space formerly dedicated to worship noted experiencing intense feelings around the task. One priest interviewed for this study spoke of an ongoing and pervasive sense of sadness whenever he passed the vacant lot that had been the parish church of his childhood. He could still feel on his skin the ritual that had once filled that space: "Eucharist had been celebrated there, after all. Funerals and weddings had been performed there."[7]

Dedicating and Un-dedicating Sacred Space

> Where do you go and let go and God comes in? I learned to take my holy spot with me, and I learned with mobility to bring it where I went. The people who get hurt most are those in the neighborhoods who aren't so mobile, those for whom the neighborhood church is a stable anchor for the security of their spirituality.[8]

The current 1983 Code of Canon Law notes in that "sacred places lose their dedication or blessing if they suffer major destruction or if they have been permanently given over to profane uses, de facto or through a decree of the competent authority."[9] This mandate also reflected in the preconciliar ritual as well as the current Episcopalian ritual prescribed in the *Book of Occasional Services*, terminates a building's blessing by a simple declaration of the local Bishop.[10] This reflects good ecclesial order but perhaps an unbalanced ritual mathematics—an inflated sense of the per-

---

[6] Judith Herman, *Trauma and Recovery* (New York: Basic Books, 1992) 156.

[7] Fr. Tom [pseudonym], interview by author, Chicago, Ill., December 21, 2000.

[8] Fr. Nick, interview by author, Chicago, Ill., February 14, 2001.

[9] James A. Coriden, Thomas J. Green, and Donald E. Heintschel, eds., *The Code of Canon Law: A Text and Commentary* (New York: Paulist Press, 1985) 849.

[10] The Episcopal Church, U.S.A., "Secularizing a Consecrated Building," *The Book of Occasional Services, 1994* (New York: Church Hymnal Corp., 1995) 205. See also Byron D. Stuhkman, *Prayer Book Rubrics Expanded* (New York: Church Hymnal Corp., 1987) 206. His remarks presume other rites that acknowledge the loss inherent to the situation. These include the removal of altars and consecrated furnishings, prayers, blessings, and the peace.

formance power of an official declaration. With all the ritual prescribed for the dedication of a building, a ritual density during its lifecycle, the accomplishment of its closure with a simple episcopal declaration lacks a ritual sense. Major levels of ritual make a parish; so little is required to unmake it.

Matters Liturgical was published in the late fifties by Fr. Joseph Wuest as an almanac of U.S. parish liturgical life with suggestions for pastors on regulations for ritual and custom. The book likewise noted that no special ceremony was prescribed to reduce a church to some profane, non-sordid use but a decree of reduction by the local ordinary. He nonetheless made some ritual suggestions that inventory some of the primary stations of a building's ritual life and the meaning connected to them.

1) The reservation of the Blessed Sacrament was to be discontinued and the sacred oils and sacred vessels removed.

2) The relic of a saint enshrined in the church, particularly its patron, was to be removed with a public and solemn ceremony. "A priest in surplice and stole shall recite the Antiphon, Verse, and Oration from the first Vespers of the Saint. The relic shall then be removed from its shrine and shall be transferred in accordance with the directions of the Ordinary."[11]

3) Any fixed altars in the church were to be carefully "desecrated." A priest in surplice and stole recited the antiphon, verse, and oration from the first Vespers of the title of each altar, then striped the altar, removed the relics from the sepulcher, and with the aid of a workman separated, at least momentarily, the table of the altar from the base. He could then wash the table and pour the water used into the *sacrarium*.

4) Portable altars in the church were likewise to be stripped. The sacred stones were not to be desecrated, but disposed of according to the directions of the ordinary.

5) If the church was consecrated, the twelve crosses on the inside walls and the two on the posts of the main entrance were to be removed by a priest, with the assistance of a workman, if necessary. The priest then would wash the crosses and pour the water used into the *sacrarium*.

---

[11] Rev. Joseph Wuest, C.SS.R., *Matters Liturgical: The Collectio Rerum Liturgicarum* (New York: Frederick Pustet, 1959) 71.

6) If there were any sacred images in the church having great value or esteemed and venerated by the faithful, they were to be removed and transferred to another church according to the directions of the ordinary and the permission of the Holy See.

7) If there were burials in the church, a priest in surplice and black stole would recite over them the *De profundis* with the customary verses and prayers. The bodies were to be removed and reburied in another place, according to local custom.

8) Finally if possible, a cross was to be affixed at some suitable place from which it could not easily be removed in memory of the once sacred character of the edifice.[12]

The rituals suggested here were public and familiar. The discontinuance of eucharistic reservation and the stripping of the altars have peculiar resonances to the liturgies of Holy Week. The washing of the crosses and altars somewhat reverses the anointing of the original dedicating rituals and has a resonance of cleansing, acknowledging that painful memories could linger in and about a place. The attending to the dead and the fixing of a permanent memorial cross (reminiscent of its symbolic use in a funeral) attempts to facilitate closure for generations of worshipers, not simply those in the remaining community. It recalls that in God's ritual time, no detail and no one is extraneous. Nothing is lost.

In 1996, Sr. Rita Fisher from the Office of Worship for the Diocese of Columbus (Ohio), wrote one of the first articles to address the consolidation-closure issue from the perspective of liturgy. Her reflections and ritual suggestions were a welcome resource for many of us looking for suggestions on how to accompany parishes through consolidation or closure. The experience, she noted, calls for "remembering, grieving and, above all, giving thanks." If the decision to close a church provoked "great pain and anger," she recommended a "listening session or town hall meeting" to allow people to speak out their anger and hurt. A professional therapist or facilitator, she continued, might likewise be helpful before celebrating any ritual closing.[13] For many involved in this task on the local level, Fisher's

---

[12] Ibid., 72.

[13] Rita Fisher, I.H.M., "The Grace of This Place: Closing a Church," *Liturgy 90* 27, no. 2 (February–March 1996) 9.

suggestions, although on target, bordered on understatement. In the presence of conflict, ritual has to work much harder.

Canon 1212 §1 recognizes that it is the diocesan bishop who has the authority to determine that a place once used exclusively for divine worship can be given over to another use. He is after all a "corporation sole" in U.S. legal parlance, one who can do what he wants with his property. A local bishop can issue a decree allowing a parish to build a new church and use the former church for a parish hall. From the perspective of the canons a declaration is sufficient to recognize the change in status of a place and no other ritual is needed. Canon 1212 §2 further states:

> Where other serious reasons suggest that a church no longer be used
> for divine worship, the diocesan bishop, after hearing the presbyteral
> council, can relegate it to profane but not sordid use with the consent
> of those who legitimately claim rights regarding the church and as
> long as the good of souls is not thereby impaired.[14]

The responses of people who have seen their parochial churches closed or consolidated in recent years would seem to point in another direction. The decree of the local bishop may satisfy the needs of canon law, but "the good of souls," although not a strict category of canonical jurisprudence, raises some other questions. The closure or consolidation of parochial churches frequently creates situations of intense conflict. Ritual, time, and attentive pastoral care can bring closure to a space formerly relegated to worship. This closure can be, in a broader sense, a reconciliation. A proclamation alone often seemed to add to an additional sense of violation alluded to by pastors and local leadership alike.

Some closed parishes testified that a bishop's presence at the end of a pastoral planning process often made a parish intensely angry, especially if he had no personal presence to a community of people to that point. In one case the local dean of the region was a bishop who had grown up in the school of the closing parish. It was interesting that many people in remembering the event years later did not recall whether the presider was a bishop, the more important detail seemed to be the relationship of alumnus.

---

[14] Coriden, Green and Heintschel, *Canon Law,* 849. For a more detailed description of the appeals process for diocesan decisions for parish closure, see Thomas J. Paprocki, "Recent Closings and the Administrative Recourse to the Apostolic See: Recent Experiences of the Archdiocese of Chicago," *The Jurist* 55 (1995) 875–96.

Patterns of Forgiveness

Patricia Kelly has noted that the successful negotiation of the conflict around a major church restructuring requires forgiveness. She defines it as "a drawing closer together . . . a remembering without bitterness." Eventually a decision, a movement of the will, is made that reframes an individual or group's perspective to include more than their own pain, inconvenience, or discomfort: "Forgiveness is a subset of the merger/closure process. It will never be entirely over. As a clinical psychologist, regression and digression are part of any adjustment to change. It is to be expected and attended to."[15]

This process of adjusting to any loss, most especially a church building or worshipping community, is not linear. It is normally a cyclical working through of the experience in memory, entering it a bit deeper at each cycle. One way anthropologists access the various cultural ways that people resolve conflict, grieve loss, and reconcile relationship after a breach or trauma is by studying ritual. It is a window into human behavior. All cultures have rituals surrounding major lifecycle transitions—the fear-creating experiences of birth, marriage, and death. Ritual patterns emerge from these rites of passage. They accompany individuals and groups as they move from one social status to another. More than eighty years ago Dutch anthropologist Arnold van Gennep observed a pattern in the rites of passage of traditional cultures. He identified three movements to rituals marking human transition: (1) separation from an existing state of affairs, (2) the liminal or in-between stage of transition, and (3) reaggregation or a reintegration to a new state.[16] This pattern can be located in a broad spectrum of rites of passage whether found in egocentric or highly individualistic cultures like those in Western Europe or the more sociocentric cultures of Asia or Africa.

Gerald Arbuckle identifies this pattern as a basic anthropological fact of life.[17] Human history, he notes from the works of Paul Ricoeur and Walter Brueggemann, is written in the struggle between chaos and the yearning for belonging and identity. Once this collective and individual identity has

---

[15] Patricia Kelly, phone interview by the author, Chicago, Ill., October 16, 2000.

[16] Arnold van Gennep, *The Rites of Passage* (Chicago: University of Chicago Press, 1960). See also Mark Searle's application of van Gennep's insight to the process of change and conversion particularly in context of the rites of the RCIA (Rites of Christian Onitiation of Adults) in "The Journey of Conversion," *Worship* 54 (1980) 35–53.

[17] Paul Ricoeur, *The Conflict of Interpretations: Essays in Hermeneutics* (Evanston, Ill.: Northwestern University Press, 1974) 468–81. See also Gerald A. Arbuckle, *Change, Grief, and Renewal in the Church* (Westminister, Md.: Christian Classics, 1991) 68.

been established in what he called the "orientation stage," almost any action will be employed to avoid losing it, even to denial if it is destroyed. He noted that within the human psyche are two identifiable movements that are in dialectical tension: (1) to cling to what has been lost as a source of belonging and (2) the ability to adapt and grasp revitalized identity in new circumstances. In time of crisis or "disorientation," these two movements are especially in tension. The nostalgic urge to hold on to the past is generally stronger than the desire to embrace the new at this stage. Ricoeur's countermovement of reorientation occurs when the pull to escape into the past is overcome by the surprise of a new reality. Though links to the past remain important, the emphasis is on newness. The three stages as defined by van Gennep and Ricoeur deeply enrich the understanding of human change and conversion.

Reconciliation can be seen in a broad way as a life-crisis ritual. The psychological patterns for resolving relational breach emerge from somewhere deep in the relation of psyche and culture.[18] Anthropologist Victor Turner took the tripartite pattern of van Gennep and sought to articulate further the nature of the liminal space in the center of rites of passage. This "betwixt and between" space is one of danger and yet imagination and great healing promise. Much depends on the efficacy of the ritual. He theorizes in fact that liminality is the generating source of culture and structure. Turner's research focused on the unfolding identity of persons involved in the ritual process, rather than upon the process itself. He pointed out a distinctive kind of antistructural bond, *communitas*, that emerges in liminal situations and unites persons in an intense, almost ecstatic sense of solidarity and connection.[19]

Life crisis rituals usually involve a liminal phase of seclusion from the centers of social life. Novices are initiated into adulthood or into the mysteries revealed in this dark and complex time. It is often the time of emergence of a society's deepest values in the form of sacred dramas and

[18] Anthropologist Richard Shweder notes that culture and psyche intimately influence one another. In point of fact they "make each other up." Richard Shweder, *Thinking through Cultures* (Cambridge, Mass.: Harvard University Press, 1991) 2.

[19] Turner defines *communitas* as "social antistructure." Its bonds are, "undifferentiated, egalitarian, direct, nonrational, existential. It is spontaneous, immediate, concrete, not abstract. . . . It does not merge identities; it liberates them from conformity to general norms. . . . It is the font and origin of all structures and at the same time their critique." Victor Turner and Edith Turner, *Image and Pilgrimage in Christian Culture* (New York: Columbia University Press, 1978) 250. See also Nathan D. Mitchell, *Liturgy and the Social Sciences* (Collegeville, Minn.: Liturgical Press, 1999) 50.

objects or the reenactment of cosmological narratives and the deeds of saints and ancestors. It has the function of establishing a "distanced replication and critique of the events leading up to and composing the 'crisis.'"[20] Ambiguity reigns in the liminal. People and public policies may be judged skeptically in relation to deep values. Life crisis rituals stress these deep values often exhibited to initiands as sacred objects or stories. The liminal is a privileged place where people are allowed to think about how they think, about the terms in which they conduct their thinking, or to feel about how they feel in daily life. Ritual acts as a frame, a metaphorical border within which the facts of experience can be viewed, reflected on, and evaluated. It recreates a place where members of a given group strive to see their own reality in new ways and to generate a language (verbal or nonverbal) to talk about "what they normally talk."[21] The ritual structures create a frame of safety around which chaos is contained, holding individuals and groups until resolution or reaggregation can emerge.

Human rituals and narratives are contextual and fragile. Yet they give meaning and structure to chaotic events. The weaving and presentation of a "fine mat" is a time-honored ritual of reconciliation from Samoa. It exposes the consequences of a relational shame to a breach in a community's life and the restoration or reweaving of family honor. A year-end mudslinging and "scapegoating" rite of the Ijaw of Nigeria discloses those resentment-evoking events of a brief frame of history, heightens them, ridicules them, and sends away the river mud on the back of a pack animal.[22] The three hybrid rites of the current Roman Catholic sacrament of penance reveal a praxis of interpretation about breaches of relationship and prescribe a pattern of rite to contain and restore them. The private individual priest-to-penitent form remains normative. Still these rites are fragile and incomplete. They function as agents of restoring human relationship and yet at the same time are in constant need of reconciliation themselves.[23] Ritual both influences and reflects the ways conflicted human relationships are restored. It is both descriptive and prescriptive of social relationships.

---

[20] Victor Turner, *Ritual Process: Structure and Anti-structure* (Ithaca, N.Y.: Cornell University Press, 1969) 166.

[21] Victor Turner, *The Anthropology of Performance* (New York: PAJ Publications, 1987) 102–3.

[22] Kathleen Hughes, R.S.C.J., "Reconciliation: Cultural and Christian Perspectives," in *Reconciliation: The Continuing Agenda*, ed. Robert J. Kennedy (Collegeville, Minn.: Liturgical Press, 1987) 115.

[23] Herbert Anderson and Edward Foley, *Mighty Stories, Dangerous Rituals* (San Francisco: Jossey-Bass Publishers, 1997) 167.

Exploring this same pattern from the experience of those recovering from any form of intense trauma, Dr. Judith Herman raises several key issues to its efficacy: the establishment of safety, remembrance and mourning, and the reconnection with ordinary life.[24] Trauma recovery in this context has profound parallels to forgiveness—anamnesis—the disciplined remembering of a hurtful event without compulsively "rerunning" the details to use the past as a weapon against the perceived wrongdoer. It involves ultimately remembering up against a larger redeeming master narrative of the human community that places it in a new context.

This liminal remembering and grieving is a frightening and dangerous time. The sanity of the perceived victim is often at stake. Yet, it makes possible the relinquishment of isolation and a renewed human solidarity. This is often noted as a key moment of healing for those recovering from a simple traumatic event to those experiencing the symptoms of full post-traumatic stress disorder. It is a growth or expansion of awareness that allows one to move from victim to "survivor." Many of those interviewed noted that this remembering and the experience of solidarity with other communities in similar transition were integral to coming to grips with the closure of a neighborhood parish church.

Trauma and Ritual

One of the major keys to the understanding of forgiveness-reconciliation is the notion of "trauma." According to leading trauma recovery expert Bessel A. van der Kolk, the experience of trauma is an essential part of being human. Human history is a story written in blood and suffering. Some people quickly adapt to shattering life events with flexibility and creativity. Others become fixated on the event and lead "traumatized and traumatizing existences."[25] "The essence of psychological trauma is the loss of faith that there is order and continuity in life. Trauma occurs when one loses the sense of having a safe place to retreat within or outside oneself to

---

[24] Judith Herman, *Trauma and Recovery* (New York: Basic Books, 1992) 156. See also J. Lebron McBride in *Spiritual Crisis: Surviving Trauma of the Soul* (New York: Haworth Pastoral Press, 1998) 16–22 where he names these phases as (1) risking and revealing, (2) responding and releasing, (3) reflecting and reconciling, (4) resurrecting and rebuilding.

[25] Bessel A. van der Kolk as quoted in Patricia Mathes Cane, *Trauma, Healing and Transformation: Awakening A New Heart with Body Mind Spirit Practices* (Watsonville, Calif.: Capacitar, 2000) 14.

deal with frightening emotions and experiences."[26] Early work in the field defined trauma as a rift causing an "abrupt disintegration of our inner world."[27] When in danger, a "fight-flight" or "freeze" response engages the whole physiology and psychology of a person. The strong physiological reactions and powerful surges of energy connected to this response are the body's normal mechanisms for self-protection in time of danger. When danger is prolonged, the bodily response to traumatic reaction can take years to disentangle. Post-traumatic stress disorder (PTSD) was the clinical name finally given to this in 1980. It is a form of anxiety triggered by memories of a traumatic event that directly and personally impacted one or that one may have simply witnessed. Most people live with some degree of traumatic life experiences. But the inability to cope after being overwhelmed by some extreme stress affects some with particular ferocity based on factors that include family history, personality, emotional makeup, culture, age, relationships, support systems and coping abilities.

Symptoms of post-traumatic stress include emotional numbness and sleep disturbances (including insomnia), depression, irritability, or outbursts of rage. External stimuli or dreams can trigger feelings of intense guilt or shame. Some survivors call this "intrusive memory,"[28] direct playback with little in the way of symbolic mediation. The past invades. It continually re-enters the present without being invited. The "traumatic memory" of an event preoccupies or possesses one.[29] Most of the literature around this definition came from studying war veterans of World War

[26] "The Psychological Consequences of Overwhelming Life Experiences," in *Psychological Trauma*, ed. Bessel A. van der Kolk (Washington, D.C: American Psychiatric Press, 1987) 2–3. Robert Grant gives further breadth to this definition. Events are experienced as traumatic when they overload an individual's capacity to cope, protect self and others, and make sense of overwhelming experiences. Robert Grant, "Trauma in Missionary Life," *Missiology: An International Review*, 23, no. 1 (1995) 73.

[27] Ronnie Janoff-Bulman, *Shattered Assumptions* (New York: Free Press, 1992) 63, as quoted in Beverly Flannigan, "Forgivers and the Unforgivable" in Enright & North, *Forgiveness*, 99.

[28] Andrew M. Jefferson, "Remembering and Re-storying: An Explanation of Memory and Narrative in Relation to Psychotherapy with Torture Survivors," *Torture* 10, no. 4 (December 2000) 108. Not everyone involved in a traumatic event experiences post-traumatic stress disorder. According to studies, it appears that from seventy to ninety five percent of people involved in traumatic events do not experience the disorder. Factors that may increase the likelihood of developing PTSD are previous history of emotional disorder, previous history of physical or sexual abuse, family history of anxiety, early separation from parents, dysfunctional family systems, and alcohol or drug abuse.

[29] Herman, *Trauma and Recovery*, 33–42.

II and Vietnam, and women victims of sexual abuse. But as a category of human experience, it is still in its infant stages of study.

Every person exposed to prolonged trauma responds uniquely. Worlds come undone in the wake of torture, childhood abuse, spousal infidelity, betrayal, etc. People may experience hyperarousal, reliving of the trauma by intrusive flashback, avoidance, or numbing. Assumptions about personal control and rules of justice, self and world, self-worth, the meaning of life, and assumptions of goodness are shattered. Experiences of this magnitude assault people's fundamental bedrock, assumptive beliefs about life that include: the world is benevolent; the world is meaningful; the self is worthy.[30]

The degree and scope of the damage caused by a trauma's magnitude determine how complete the forgiveness process can be.[31] At the core are disempowerment and disconnection. "Psychological trauma is an affliction of the powerless." At the moment of trauma, the victim is rendered helpless by some overwhelming force.[32] Recovery then has a reverse quality "based upon the empowerment of the survivor and the creation of new connections."[33]

Restoring the connection between survivors and their community requires literally a "re-storying"—the psychic processes of recalling and revising a hurtful event.[34] Narrative therapists note that adequate recalling of a trauma is critical to making new meaning from it. Through the body, where memory is stored, the past can be re-enacted and reconstituted to make memory real in the present experience. But first the terror and intense emotion around the event in memory need to be contained.

A community of safety is required to provide this container and place for putting words and meaning to a traumatic event.[35] The ancient notion of church as sanctuary indicates its place in the imagination as the traditional locus of safety and healing. Intense group process and ritual together integrate and give meaning to individual and social experience of trauma. Given lavish amounts of time, basic capacities of human trust, autonomy, initiative and competence, identity and intimacy can be recreated and

---

[30] Ibid.

[31] Beverly Flanigan, "Forgivers and the Unforgivable," in Enright and North, *Forgiveness*, 101.

[32] Herman, 133.

[33] Ibid., 33.

[34] Jefferson, "Re-storying," 108.

[35] Robert Schreiter, C.P.P.S., "Creating Circles of Listening in a Parish," *Initiative Report* (March 2001) 3–6.

reclaimed. The way that traumatic experience is handled can be a catalyst for growth and transformation. But healing requires tremendous restructuring of the whole person, physically, emotionally, psychologically, spiritually and socially. Bringing new perspectives and/or creating new realities around the traumatic memories can facilitate depth transformation.[36] But this can occur only after the tremendous releasing of the energy that holds these in the body. A key to recovery is empowerment. Simply discovering and expressing old wounds can often just re-stimulate their pain and the accompanying memories held oftentimes in the very cells and tissues of the body. These memories need to be resolved and restructured around a new understanding.[37] This notion appears in the context of reconciliation as "reframing."

Ritual Performance and Forgiveness

Interpersonal forgiveness in any culture is a social encounter fraught with ritual. We express regret, apology, shake hands or embrace, offer restitution in formal ritualized patterns often determined by our culture. Thus rites or ritualized action have the potential to give intense meaning to the lives of those who perform them. Doris Donnelly in her 1986 presentation to the Federation of Diocesan Liturgical Commissions suggested that the Roman Catholic Church is in need of a new ritual climate with regard to hurt and sin, conflict and forgiveness. In particular, sacred safe space must be created in which people can give vent to their more messy emotions: anger, frustration, betrayal, conflicts, pains, and agonies—thus creating a climate in which the truth of human brokenness and sin can be spoken. Ritual that is not big enough to embrace the complexities of human relationships is of little service to a world increasingly at interpersonal, intercultural, and international impasse.[38]

Victor Turner's schema refers to the processes of human reconciliation as social drama. Ritual performs this human drama. It frames and directs grief and human conflict toward greater, more foundational cultural and human values:

---

[36] Cane, *Trauma*, 17.

[37] Aminah Raheem quoted in Cane, ibid.

[38] Doris Donnelly, "Binding Up Wounds in a Healing Community," *Repentance and Reconciliation in the Church*, ed. Michael J. Henchal (Collegeville, Minn.: Liturgical Press, 1987) 18.

Turner understood that society is a process punctuated by performances, that rites are not rubrics, that ritual frames must always be
re-framed, that ritualizing is a group's collective autobiography, that
human beings invent their lives as they go along, playing games, performing their being.[39]

There are identifiable stages or moments to these dramas or life crises,
each with its own characteristics and time span. Turner noted four: a social
breach-breakdown, ensuing crisis, resolution-schism, and reintegration.[40]
In a breakdown of social relationships within a particular group or society,
the relational status quo is lost. This breach is "signalized by the public,
overt or deliberate non-fulfillment of some crucial norm regulating the
intercourse of the parties."[41] This disturbance could at times be something
intensely positive and dynamic for a community, and other times dramatic
and cathartic.[42] Some anthropologists posit a "displacement of aggression
theory"—that ritual is the place in the fabric of human culture where
aggression can find some form of release in favor of human sociality.

Cathartic ritual permits the shedding of pent-up, potentially destructive feelings to emerge cleansed and reshaped.[43] The ritual agent—an individual, a collective, or one who acts (or believes he or she acts) on behalf
of others as a representative—dramatizes the breach. By heightening or
mirroring the breech ritually, there is communication that something is
not in right relationship and in need of attention. Something is tearing at a
community's social fabric.

The second movement of ritual social drama is crisis. If there is no
quick resolution of the breach, there is a subsequent intensification of the
crisis insuring that the situation provoked by the breach is handled. A phase
of mounting urgency supervenes. Unless the breach can be attended and
contained quickly within a limited area of social interaction, there is a
tendency for it to expand within the widest set of relevant social relations

[39] Mitchell, *Liturgy*, 53.

[40] Fr. Mark Hay's 1997 doctor of ministry thesis project, from the South African
perspective gives a particularly succinct synopsis of Turner's thought in this regard.
Mark Hay, O.M.I., "Ukubuyisana: Reconciliation in South Africa" (doctoral thesis,
Catholic Theological Union, 1997) 201–3.

[41] Victor Turner, *Dramas, Fields, and Metaphors: Symbolic Action in Human Society*
(Ithaca, N.Y.: Cornell University Press, 1974) 38.

[42] Ibid., 35.

[43] Signe Howell and Roy Willis, eds., *Societies at Peace: Anthropological Perspectives*
(London: Routledge, 1989) 16.

of the antagonistic parties. The "escalation of crisis,"[44] can be of particular significance to the healing process. It prevents any denial of the need for change in the status quo and confirms that there is a rupture of relationship. The energy released pushes toward some resolution to the problem.

In the third stage of redressive action and integration, "mechanisms" are employed to restore equilibrium. These mechanisms vary in type and complexity. Such factors as the depth and the shared social significance of the breach, the social inclusiveness of the crisis, the nature of the social group within which the breach took place, and the degree of its autonomy with reference to wider or external systems of social relations, influence this complexity. These mechanisms range from personal advice—informal mediation or arbitration—to formal juridical and legal machinery, or to the performance of public ritual.

Reintegration or schism, the final stage of the restorative process, resolves the rupture either by reintegration or by a "social recognition and legitimization" of the separated group. This latter social recognition can be a "recognition of irremediable or irreversible breach or schism."[45]

The ritual agent plays a pivotal role in the movement of an individual or group after a breach in relationship. Leading or structurally representative members, who have credibility and recognition by the community, play an important function in the birth of a restored or even changed social order. They can reenact the rites for themselves or in the name of others. Within this paradigm the idea of "escalation" could be seen both positively and negatively. This stage is critical to the good resolution of the conflict. If a society does not have the necessary variety of mechanisms available for a return to the peace of the status quo, there is serious danger of splintering or fragmentation.

When redress fails there is usually regression to crisis. At this point direct force becomes a serious option in various forms of war, revolution, intermittent acts of violence, repression and rebellion. Where the disturbed community is small and relatively weak, regression to crisis tends to become a matter of endemic, pervasive, smoldering factionalism, without sharp, overt confrontations between consistently various parties.[46]

It is important to note the heightened nature of ritual performance within Turner's social drama.[47] In the midst of the crisis there is a sense of

---

[44] Turner, *Dramas*, 38.

[45] Victor Turner, *On the Edge of the Bush: Anthropology as Experience*, Edith Turner ed. (Tucson: University of Arizona Press, 1985) 292.

[46] Ibid., 41.

[47] Hay, "Ukubuyisana," 203.

the "liminal," often involving the cessation of everyday commerce and human sociality to discover renewed or even radically new structures of relationship. Symbolic action and the concrete mechanisms arrive at their fullest expression in this phase. Healing rites, exorcisms, and ceremonies of prayer are sometimes employed. In modern societies, redressive rituals are most likely to belong to the judicial system, conflict management, or the processes of legislative inquiry. The restoration of order or equilibrium does not, however, necessarily imply reconciliation. The space between the action of restored community and the ritualizing of that event varies according to the culture and gravity of the situation. It is dangerous but holy ground.

Framing, Reframing, and Forgiveness

The notion of framing as taken from the work of anthropologist Gregory Bateson, is to discriminate a sector of sociocultural action from the general ongoing processes of a community's life. It is a reflexive, bordered space and a privileged time within which images and symbols of what has been sectioned off can be "relived," scrutinized, assessed, revalued, and, if need be, remodeled and rearranged.[48] Within the context of the forgiveness process, "reframing" plays a graced and somewhat mysterious role.

Research from groups like the International Forgiveness Institute at the University of Wisconsin and the Templeton Foundation is giving some new theoretical frameworks to the patterns of human reconciliation in a Euro-American context. The psychological phases of interpersonal forgiveness form a backdrop of cultural practice for restoring broken relationships. The paradigm of Robert Enright, Suzanne Freedman, and Julio Rique identifies a four-phase pathway that many victims follow when they forgive a wrongdoer:

1. In the "uncovering phase," a victim becomes aware of the emotional pain associated with an injury. Complete honest acknowledgement

[48] Turner, *Anthropology of Performance*, 140. See also Gregory Bateson, *Steps to an Ecology of Mind* (New York: Ballantine, 1978) 179–89. In another work, Turner describes the paradoxical relationship of frame to ritual. The rules frame the ritual, but the ritual transcends the frame. The word performance is from the Old English *parfournir*—to furnish completely or thoroughly, to perform or bring something completely about, to consummate something. In the carrying out of a play order or project, something new is often generated. "Traditional framings have to be reframed—new bottles made for new wine." Victor Turner, *From Ritual to Theater* (New York: Performing Arts Journal Publications, 1982) 79.

that harm has been inflicted from one party to another is required. Along with this is a further acknowledgement of the sense of injustice and (implicitly), preoccupation with the offender, cognitive rehearsal of the offence, and recognition of the desire for revenge.

2. The "decision phase" is marked by the victim putting aside the desire for revenge and considering forgiving the offender. A change of heart with an emerging willingness to forgo prolonging the hostility through acts of revenge marks a tremendous psychic shift.

3. In the "work phase," the victim works on the process of forgiving the offender. The development of understanding and empathy from the victim toward the perpetrator takes place with a cognitive "re-framing" of the story to identify emotionally with the offender and to commit morally not to pass on the pain of his or her injury to the one who caused the injury. Reframing is an attempt to build up a complete picture of the wrongdoer and his or her action by role taking or by viewing him or her in that person's own context. This expands the victim's narrative to include the context of the perpetrator's life and action. As a result, the victim is able to build up positive feelings of empathy and compassion toward the wrongdoer.

4. The final or outcome stage is a deepening of this process. It is accompanied by the insight that one is not alone, a finding of meaning in the suffering and the forgiveness process, and the offer of renewed community to the perpetrator in the future. The victim experiences improved psychological well-being as a result. Paradoxically, when the gift of mercy and compassion is extended to the offender, the victim likewise experiences healing.[49]

Most western paradigms on forgiveness speak from only one side of the breach of relationship, from that of either the victim or the sinner-perpetrator. Philosopher Joanna North, who co-edited the publication of the above study, noted that forgiveness is an active endeavor, a matter of willed change of heart that is "multiperspectival."[50] Reframing of perspective is central to this willed change. She notes a strong parallel between

[49] Robert Enright and Joanna North, eds., *Exploring Forgiveness* (Madison: University of Wisconsin Press, 1998) 53.

[50] Joanna North, "The Ideal of Forgiveness: A Philosopher's Exploration," in Robert Enright and Joanna North, eds., *Exploring Forgiveness* (Madison: University of Wisconsin Press, 1998) 20.

the pattern of forgiveness for the victim and repentance for the offending party. Ritual that serves reconciliation in any context would need likewise to engage and reflect this pattern.

Human stories or narrative frames are dynamic and are constantly in revision; they are always being reframed. Ritual narrative repetition can untangle the distortions of reality or a "narrative of the lie" caused by the traumatic breach of betrayal or the gross violation of human rights. This process requires and creates a liminal time and place. A major task for a change agent in any therapeutic reframing, from the perspective of family systems theory, is convincing participants that reality as they have mapped it out can be expanded or modified.[51]

Leadership on the individual or a group level most often achieves this task by ritualizing, by creating a space where people tell their stories—over and over again if necessary—until wounded stories begin to change and open up new perspectives. The grace of repetition often comes in this way. The ritual retelling of stories at anniversaries and commemorative moments is a way of reinforcing identity and reaffirming that a change has taken place, a new window of perspective. The way ritual does this is key to an anthropological understanding of forgiveness. The social drama employs mechanisms, what Michel Foucault called "technologies," to re-inscribe the self with a new narrative, a bigger redeeming one, one that can even include the context of the perpetrator.[52] Recovery from trauma and the process of social or interpersonal forgiveness require a re-inscribing of the body. A conscious effort is needed to replace rituals of denial—that lead to aggression and the fragmentation of human community—with rituals of remembrance.[53]

Kairos: *Ritual Action, Ritual Time*

Effective ritual allows one to experience past events in the present and anticipate what is hoped will happen in the future. The timing of steps in the process of forgiveness is difficult to manage or predict. Appropriate

---

[51] Salvador Minuchin and H. Charles Fishman, *Family Therapy Techniques* (Cambridge, Mass.: Harvard University Press, 1981) 76–77.

[52] Mitchell, *Liturgy*, 88. Tom Driver speaks of the *techné* as a method for accomplishing something in the real world. The *techné* of ritual is a field of action for divine, human, animal, and vegitative cosmos of mores, moralities, and mutual relationships. See Tom Driver, *The Magic of Ritual: Our Need for Liberating Rites That Transform Our Lives and Our Communities* (San Francisco: HarperSan Francisco, 1991) 47.

[53] Ibid., 76–77.

intervention of ritual and/or accompanying pastoral care requires particular discretion, respect for the element of mystery, and the structure and movement of healing unique to each situation. Key to healing is the ability to escape the tyranny of traumatic past events, relating to them in a way that respects the integrity of memory, yet free from a painful bondage of it. On the part of the victim or victimized community, the ability to transcend or to stand away from the intrusion of the past into the present, determines the shape of the future. Reconciliation is folded into a *kairos* sense of time.

The notion of reconciliatory emancipation of Toinette Eugene gives another nuance of meaning to ritual time. She posits that the practice of anamnesis or the "great remembrance" is a focal point for authentic human liberation, lest the past be repeated.[54] The writers of the South African Kairos *Document* called for reconciliation before the fall of apartheid. The resistance by some of the major religious players of that country testified to the paralysis of a call to reconciliation if it is offered out of time and without attention to the changes of justice and liberation. Systemic change must occur as a condition of authentic human reconciliation.[55]

Remembering takes time. It does not happen simply by willing it or scheduling it. Reconciliation occurs in God's good time, "that intersection of God's many faceted grace, the free cooperation of individuals, the church's action and the particular circumstances of time and place."[56] It requires allowing individuals and groups the time to tell their stories fully and at the same time, to honor the diverse communication styles of cultures.

> [T]he early church came to realize from pastoral experience what sociologists, psychologists, anthropologists and others in the human sciences are saying in our own day—that lasting change in life-style and life attitudes takes time, that the movement from alienation to reconciliation demands work, and that there are no "quick fixes" when it comes to personal re-formation and transformation.[57]

A constant critique of the processes used for parish reorganizing across the United States in the last decade was that they did not give people ade-

---

[54] Toinette Eugene, "Reconciliation in the Pastoral Context of Today's Church and World," *Reconciling Embrace*, ed. Robert F. Kennedy (Chicago: Liturgy Training Publications, 1998) 6.

[55] Ibid., 12.

[56] Ibid., 16.

[57] James Dallen and Joseph Favazza, *Removing the Barriers: The Practice of Reconciliation* (Chicago: Liturgy Training Publications, 1991) 29.

quate time to adjust to the significant change being asked. More specifically, participants wanted time to grieve and internalize the reasons given for the consolidation or closure. Many asked for leadership to repeat (sometimes again and again) the criteria for the closure decision. Finances did not seem to be an adequate reason to close a parish church. Turner noted that with the life-crisis social-drama paradigm, ritual could be replayed over a considerable period of time, with the final formal ritual of reconciliation happening years later.

The formal nature of ritual helps to give public common shape to experience. Its formal character creates a safe space in which to grapple with sometimes difficult and conflictual pasts, and bring closure to an experience of breach that has been named and confronted. Redressive action must be taken, often employing dialogue, intermediaries, and ritual. Behavior is changed, apology spoken, and reparation is offered. There is a need for closure and ritual to indicate a change in relationship. Even though the focus of the ritual in this context is the past, social reconciliation is directed toward the future.[58] Funeral rituals accomplish their power in these ways.[59] The Christian celebration of Eucharist likewise operates within this defined "liminal space," that threshold condition of persons in process of social transformation, to use Turner's concepts. The theological notion of "grace" can be seen as a holding environment for growth and a place of empowerment[60] in the midst of ritual reframing.

Trauma and the Benevolence of the Church

Traumatic experiences assault fundamental assumptive beliefs.[61] In situations of internal ecclesial strife these general groupings take on deep religious undertones: the world is meaningful, the world is benevolent, and the self is worthy. One of the principle sources of trauma around the clustering of the San Francisco and Englewood parishes appeared to happen with a clash of ecclesiologies and the authority structures inherent to them. When conflict escalated around these structures and the models of

[58] Hay, "Ukubuyisana," 157.

[59] Robert Schreiter, C.P.P.S., *The Ministry of Reconciliation: Spirituality and Strategies* (Maryknoll, N.Y.: Orbis Books, 1998) 92–93.

[60] McBride, *Spiritual Crisis*, 35.

[61] Three basic assumptions that when shattered, constitute trauma: (1) the belief in personal invulnerability, (2) the perception of the world as meaningful and comprehensible, and (3) the view of oneself in a positive light. J. Jeffrey Means, *Trauma and Evil: Healing the Wounded Soul* (Minneapolis: Fortress Press, 2000) 68.

decision making were inconsistently applied, "church" lost some of its benevolence, safety, meaningfulness, and moral legitimacy in the imagination of its perceived victims.

The decision-making processes gathered about conference tables implied an image of church with facilitated leadership and shared decision making. This model emerged as a kind of egalitarian church; what one bishop feared was a more "congregational model" at variance with more traditional church structures. It presumed that consensus among participants was the goal. Success was a decision everyone could live with and to which everyone would participate. Butcher paper and marking pens were the predominant symbols of that process of group dynamics borrowed from community organizing. Effective leadership was facilitation toward consensus and the small group was the cell within which most conversation took place. Leaders and agenda emerged from the group rather than being appointed from higher authority, and therefore were ultimately accountable to the group for its functioning.

The hierarchical Church, with the weight of final decisions falling to the local bishop, was a second ecclesial model implied by decision-making processes used in local parish restructuring. As the ultimately accountable "corporation sole," the local bishop is responsible for final oversight. The final arbiter between the universal Church and the local church, he is at the center of all the administration and pastoral outreach. He pastors and links the communities of the diocesan church, sets the leadership agenda for his regional infrastructure, and passes it through structures of its administration. Success, especially in the mind of episcopal peers, is faithful translation of the tradition into the structures and cultic life of his diocese. A bishop consults, but his office, invested with a sacred character, is accountable for the most part only to the authority structure above him, i.e., the Holy See.

The corporate world provided the third operative church model. When Chicago and San Francisco began looking at the possibility of financial collapse, accountants from corporate America were a primary resource to handle the crisis. The criteria for parish viability in most cases, were the October Mass count, volume of programs, the status of buildings, and balanced budgets. The chancery of the diocese was easily perceived as corporate offices with the parish serving as a franchise. Insurance and litigation were cultures only understood by professionals who controlled access. This church model, with its centralized planning processes, represented church as efficient bureaucracy, a cost-efficient business with managed risk.

Sometimes the rules would get confused. Several operative models would be functioning at the same time. Groups of people would presume one image of church when another (or combination of several) was operative. The initial recommendations of the Catholic Community of Englewood during its first wave of cluster planning in the late seventies provided the earliest example of this conflict. After nearly a year of work, informally initiated by Cardinal Cody, the cluster leadership presumed that he would implement the recommendations from the grass roots processes. The Cardinal's plan was significantly at variance to theirs. When he reminded participants through the news media that the authority to open and close schools and parishes was his alone, those involved in the processes were demoralized.

The processes and symbols of the conference table gave the impression that all parties in the discussion were equal partners. Town hall meetings, open microphones, and small group process were the rituals of a new dynamic of church. "Small Group dynamics gave voice to the people. It wasn't done in church. The ritual was done around tables with newsprint and markers. It worked toward consensus and grabbing people at the fringes or margins of the process. It gave people a chance to talk and to listen."[62]

Even if reminded from the beginning that their discussions were "only consultative," the symbols of the conference table spoke otherwise. Power often appeared to be given to the local church, only to be taken back. After table "votations" with colored cards, prioritized values, and reams of butcher paper notes taped to the walls, the rites of the conference table clashed with the powers structures of the eucharistic table. When bishops announced decisions at variance with the final group processes, participants noted feeling used. "The Catholic Church is not a democracy," was a painful repeated mantra throughout the San Francisco consolidation because it felt so antithetical to the rites of the conference table.

Another Chicago priest spoke about a sense of almost multivalent levels of betrayal in experience of his consolidation process. When trauma is involved, a basic sense of trust appears violated.

> The diocese . . . [having] asked to join two parishes that did not want to join together had betrayed me. There was a sense of additional betrayal from staff and other parishioners for my not fighting hard

[62] Fr. Donald [pseudonym], interview by author, Chicago, Ill., February 19, 2001. For a complete summary of these rites as used in processes around parish consolidations see David James Schnier, "A Process Model for Top Management to Evaluate and Define A Mission Statement for Consolidated Roman Catholic Parishes" (master's thesis, Webster University, 1997) 32–37.

enough for them. The process did not have a spirituality. Its main purpose appeared to be economics. There was a feeling of not being listened to and manipulation. It was a death, not only of two parishes, but part of my idealism, my trust of church and diocese.[63]

The key variable here seems to be the sense of violation. The greater the perception of violation, the greater was the susceptibility of survivor symptoms: psychological numbing, depression, rage, isolation, and shame. David Noer's 1993 work, *Healing the Wounds: Overcoming the Trauma of Layoffs*, studied the effects of corporate downsizing on employees. He coined the term "layoff survivor syndrome" to describe the trauma to especially long-term employees who experienced job loss. In his estimate, the root cause of this personal devastation is the "profound shift in the psychological employment contract that binds individual and organiza-tion."[64] The consequence of significant employment trauma is a shattering of the sense of the benevolence of the work world and of one's basic trust in the cooperate organization. In a church context, trauma causes disillu-sionment to the sense that the church structures and community are benevolent and therefore trustworthy. One of the first issues of trauma recovery is the establishment of a community of safety. When the item on the table is the ongoing existence of that local community, itself a ritual source of safety, recovery becomes further problematic. This sense of safety must be delineated in a different way.

Forgiveness, conflict resolution, and recovery from trauma require an awareness of a human solidarity, some form of "universality" that crosses communities and cultures. When conflicting parties do not share at least portions of the same worldview, moral community, or ritual-religious tradition, the chances of finding some conciliation is minimal. There is no common ground. Interpersonal and social healing occur with the articula-tion of common ground, a shared social place of safety, a locus and a focus.

The consolidation and closure of parishes has functioned like a micro-cosm of the major issues facing the Church in the United States. For some impacted by the clash of church models in this context, the experience has proven traumatic. A variety of factors have influenced this. In an ecclesial setting, this often provokes a crisis of faith that parallels trauma in other contexts.

---

[63] Fr. Bundy, interview by author, Chicago, Ill., February 24, 2001.

[64] David Noer, *Healing the Wounds: Overcoming the Trauma of Layoffs* (San Francisco: Jossey-Bass, 1993) 3–6.

Trauma: Meaning and Cultural Fit

Trauma assaults another assumptive belief—the sense of the world as a meaningful place. Schreiter's *The New Catholicity* defines culture from the work of Jens Loenhoff as having three dimensions of meaning. It binds peoples together by embodying beliefs, performing those embodied histories and values, and symbolizing identity:

> Culture embodies beliefs, values, attitudes, and rules for behavior. Second, culture is performance—rituals that bind a culture's members together to provide them with a participatory way of embodying and enacting their histories and values. Performance also encompasses embodied behaviors. Third, culture is material—the artifacts and symbolizations that become a source for identity: language, food, clothing, music, and the organization of space.[65]

Marist anthropologist Gerald Arbuckle, who has written prolifically on the refounding of vowed religious life, comments that most mergers fail because leaders give insufficient consideration to the human or cultural dimensions of change. He points out the need for cultural compatibility or what he coins as "cultural fit" between the beliefs, histories, and sources of identity of organizations that seek to consolidate. He further claims that if there is insufficient cultural fit, then cultural collisions will destroy efforts to unify those communities.[66] Arbuckle defines culture from the much broader perspective of affect—the feelings expressed in symbols and myths; the complete set of feelings affecting for the most part unconsciously all specific behavior patterns of individuals and groups. Examples specific to organizations include interiorized systems of authority, modes of communications, and the understanding of mission and strategies.

---

[65] Robert J. Schreiter, C.P.P.S., *The New Catholicity: Theology between the Global and the Local* (Maryknoll, N.Y.: Orbis Books, 1997) 29.

[66] Gerald A. Arbuckle, S.M. "Merging Provinces," *Review for Religious* 53, no. 3 (May–June 1994) 353. In a pertinent article on the "Learning Cultures" of U.S. religious life, Fr. David Couturier identifies several distinct learning cultures or "diverse patterns of understanding, emotions, rituals and practice that assist religious men and women to mediate the world, interpret their experiences and make appropriate decisions. These include the Essentialist culture, Existentialist culture, the Socialization culture, the Behavior culture, the Liberation culture and the Professional culture. The polarization of religious life and practice in the U.S. can be seen through this lens with some new search for common ground between the groups." David B. Couturier, O.F.M. Cap.

Cultural interaction calls people to new ways of acting and being. Familiar patterns of behavior must often be left behind. Any attempt at cultural change is stressful for the people involved. Since culture provides people with a sense of order and security, a "felt sense of order" is often undermined or threatened when cultures interact. People often feel uprooted, lost, disillusioned, angry or sad. Fears and prejudices about the culture with which they must interact come to the surface. Efforts to merge cultures often lead to varying degrees of overt or underground resistance. Reactions to cultural change in individuals often stockpile and consequently appear out of proportion to the provocation of the moment. Definitions given to the notion of culture can sometimes themselves resist change. A participant from the San Francisco consolidation defined culture as a primary reason to resist further pastoral overtures initiated by the staff. His reflection reveals a parent's fears of integrating suburban and inner city children.

> It [the consolidation] blended two very different cultures which was very difficult. "The culture at _____ seemed to have a little more money at times and maybe a broader view of the world, about how to do things. And that is not to slight anybody at _____. It was almost like Inner Mission-Outer Mission, inner city-outer city, inner urban-suburban.[67]

When people resist change, in Arbuckle's perspective, it is often for one of several reasons; either the loss of the known and tested or concern over the implications of personal and group loss. The loss of meaning and identity is felt most keenly around the experience of myth—that narrative tradition that claims to reveal to people in an imaginative way a fundamental truth about the world and themselves. Myths are stories that "inspiringly or feelingly"[68] tell people who they are, what is good and bad, how to organize themselves to maintain their feelings of unique identity in the world. The consolidation of a faith community powerfully impacts the world of people who hold a collection of common foundational myths as authoritative.

Challenges to a community's foundational myths affect people in various emotional ways like anxiety, numbness, sadness, or anger. The public

---

"The Learning Cultures of Religious Life," *InFormation* 6 (November–December 1998) 1–10.

[67] William B. [pseudonym], interview by Dinah P. Shaw, San Francisco, Calif., January 25, 2001.

[68] Arbuckle, "Merging Provinces," 355.

myth is a set of stated ideals that are acknowledged and bind a group together. In practice these may have little if any cohesive force like the Ten Commandments for Christian churches. The operative myth is what in actuality gives a group their cohesive identity. An operative myth can sometimes differ dramatically from the public one. Finally, a residual myth is a story normally not conscious and with no daily impact on a group's life. However, it will often appear as a powerful operative myth in a time of stress.[69] The San Francisco Italian community kept alive the memory of their exclusion from the local German parish and the consignment of their worship to the basement nearly a century previous. At the time of their consolidation to the parish responsible for the dishonor, the story emerged again but in a surprising venue. A Filipino woman narrated the story as if it were her own at the time of the merger. It began again at that point to function as an operative myth, holding people together with a sense of common victimization and powerlessness.

The consolidation of two parishes is a consolidation of two cultures and two myths. If they are not compatible or cannot function together, the groups will undermine the amalgamation and slip apart. One parish in Chicago closed a second worship site and school in the early nineties. They found that the two former parish communities gravitated to separate Sunday Masses, forming for all practical purposes two separate parishes in the same building. Even though both were primarily Spanish-speaking communities, ongoing attempts by staff to bring them together for common activities were resisted for years afterwards.

The place where individual and collective myths are most engaged is in ritual. Grieving actual or perceived losses can reflect the best of the former cultures in an ongoing respectful and egalitarian way. It can likewise reflect the worst. Effective ritual depends on leadership with skills for addressing the uncertainties, anxieties, and risks that emerge in cultural change. These ritual leaders often need to be culturally fluent themselves, with an ability to credibly move from one community to the other in a respectful way. The vision of a new area presence of church in the Englewood clustering was best articulated in its regular Sunday afternoon "Unity Masses." One of the priests involved with the Catholic Community of Englewood said that the value of those liturgies through the most turbulent years was their ability to encompass varied and even divergent approaches to church: "The vision of Church needed to be in common. There were multiple visions and multiple ecclesiologies. It wasn't just personalities that

[69] Ibid., 356.

brought the conflict. It was conflicting structures and visions."[70] The symbols of the liturgy—its music, vesture, rhythms, and proclamation—had to be ambiguous and rich enough to carry the weight of divergent styles and theologies and build bridges between them.

Trauma, Esteem, and Wounds to the Soul

The third assumptive belief assaulted by trauma is worthiness of the self. Canon law permits a diocesan bishop to close a church and relegate it to profane use "as long as the good of souls is not thereby impaired."[71] "Traumatic events inflict wounds to the soul," in the sense that value and meaning systems that undergird life are shattered. Survivors of the Nazi concentration camps like Elie Wiesel spoke of loss of faith, God and the soul. Soldiers returning from the horrors of Vietnam spoke of having left their souls behind them in the jungles. Severe trauma with the resulting spiritual crisis and chronic psychological problems are often spoken of as "soul" loss.

In the 1986 documentary *Facing the Truth with Bill Moyers*, a number of survivors of the South Africa apartheid holocaust were interviewed, including a Soweto woman who was tortured while in detention. She said she survived the repeated rape and torture by taking her spirit out of her body and putting it in the corner of the cell. She could then, disembodied in this manner, look on, as horrendous things were done to her body. By doing this she could then imagine that it was not she herself but a stranger suffering this violation. With tears in her eyes, she noted that she had not yet gone back to that room to fetch her soul and that it was still sitting in the corner where she had left it.[72] One of the priests interviewed from Chicago used similar words to express the impact of the consolidation process on his own sense of self and priesthood:

> The defense mechanisms used by victims of trauma vary. But objecti-
> fying or demonizing was prevalent for us. Disassociation is the way
> trauma victims cope. They leave their bodies. I am not present to my
> body. The body is present. I just was not really there. I then could not
> be present to the Body of Christ. I felt "dead by friendly fire."[73]

---

[70] Fr. Eugene [pseudonym], interview by author, Chicago, Ill., February 2, 2001.

[71] Coriden, Green, and Heintschel, *Canon Law*, 83.

[72] *Facing the Truth with Bill Moyers*, VHS, directed by Gail Pellett (United States: PBS, Films for the Humanities & Sciences, 1999).

[73] Fr. Bundy, interview by author, Chicago, Ill., February 24, 2001.

The notion of soul is integral to any anthropology of forgiveness. The truest self, among the many personas of a human being, is closest to what Thomas Moore means by soul. He refers to it not as a thing, "but a quality or dimension of experiencing life and ourselves. It has to do with depth, value and relatedness, heart and personal substance."[74] Soul appears then to be a concept of the personality that speaks of the whole person integrated in his or her own unique way. Trauma disrupts or destroys the integration of the whole person.[75] The soul is the dynamic center of initiation and free choice: "the spirit, the transcendental ego, subjectivity, the free will, or the "atman." It is the bond of connection with things beyond and with others, as real to each human being as it is immaterial. Lose it and one feels dead, cut off, alone, "dispirited" or "depressed."[76] The essence of psychological trauma is the loss of faith that there is order and continuity in life. Trauma occurs when one loses the sense of having a safe place to retreat within or outside of self, to come to grips with frightening emotions and experiences.[77]

It is as if soul has drained away. The connectedness between self and others appears broken. The victim is left with a distorted view of the self fragmented or contaminated by the humiliation, pain, and fear that the event imposed. Difficulty integrating the event into the personal belief system, or complete alienation from the former belief and value system is often the result. A severe crisis of faith results that sometimes makes it difficult to distinguish the boundaries between good and evil.[78] People on

---

[74] Thomas Moore, *Care of the Soul: A Guide for Cultivating Depth and Sacredness in Everyday Life* (New York: HarperCollins, 1992) 5.

[75] McBride, *Spiritual Crisis*, 13.

[76] Shweder, *Thinking through Cultures*, 257.

[77] From the field of addiction studies, Charles Whitfield calls that divine consciousness within each person a "higher self." What happens to this higher self as a result of trauma is a blocking of the energy and creative force for living that is often associated with spirituality. The notion of "abandonment depression" describes the longer term consequences of unresolved trauma. Charles Whitfield, *Alcoholism, Attachments, and Spirituality* (New York: Perrin, 1985) 88.

[78] A larger issue within the anthropology of human forgiveness is evil. Croatian theologian Miroslav Volf's recent works struggle with this issue from the context of the Balkans. His conclusion that the best way to rid the world of the violent sacred is to "reject it into transcendence." The only means of diminishing human recourse to violence, quoting Jewish scholar Henri Atlan, is to insist that violence is legitimate "only when it comes from God. The theologization of violence is a pre-condition of the politics of non-violence." Miroslav Volf, *Exclusion and Embrace* (Nashville: Abington Press, 1996) 303.

both the San Francisco and Englewood consolidations spoke of being surprised by hatred. One man referred to the pastor facilitating his consolidation as an "enemy" whom he sought to unseat by almost any means. Staff members, even members of religious communities, spoke of competitive feelings of envy and suspicion bordering on hatred for those who previously were friends or colleagues. It has not been uncommon in parish consolidations for the agents of these changes to receive threats of violence.[79]

Liturgist Mark Searle defined conversion as "the successful negotiation of crisis or change," a "passage" to which a person may pass to a new lease on life entering a new set of relationships with himself, the world around him, and with life itself. The journey of conversion, then, passes through crisis, not just moments of alarm and anxiety, but in the broader sense of any turning point or moment of change.[80] Research on life transitions in the early seventies such as that of Daniel Levinson made reference to the notion "marker events."[81] These incidents associated with the onset, turning point, or conclusion of a crisis do not cause or facilitate the conversion. They are, however, so closely associated to the event that the imagination invests them with the power of symbol. Their meaning goes beyond any common or objective meaning they may have had for others who have not shared the experience. They stand at powerful junctions of reconciling ritual.

The experience of conversion is marked or grasped by symbols, drawn either from a person's inner life, from the conventions of language or events associated with the changes taking place for an individual or a group.[82] Every life crisis is an opportunity for conversion or transformation. The humbling fact is that not everyone or every group can successfully negotiate every passage of life. The reasons for this are often complex: fear of the unknown, fear of the loss of identity and change, or ultimately, fear of dying. Entropy or laziness, the absence of energy, or substantial enough

---

[79] Eric Law uses power perceptions to understand the roots of violence in victimized groups. When a community victimized in the past, is threatened again, there may be distance between its perceived power and the reality of the situation. Justified violence often erupts when a group feels powerless but is not. See Eric H. F. Law, *The Wolf Shall Dwell with the Lamb* (St. Louis: Chalice Press, 1993) 13–27.

[80] Mark Searle, "The Journey of Conversion," *Worship* 54, no. 1 (January 1980) 36.

[81] Daniel Levinson, et al., *The Seasons of a Man's Life* (New York: A. A. Knopf, 1977) 193. See also Gail Sheehy, *Passages: Predictable Crisis in Adult Life* (New York: E. P. Dutton, 1976) which brought Levinson's work to popular attention.

[82] Searle, "Conversion," 44.

insight or desire to threaten the status quo, likewise contributes to the limits of personal and group transformation. The processes of human transformation of crisis are seldom linear. They form "a spiral through which progress is made only in deeper experiences of death and rebirth."[83]

Forgiveness of the trauma's source often requires wrestling with a spiral of experience, multiple levels of consequence that can in some ways only be marked by symbol and ritual. When the agent of the trauma is not clear, this is further complicated. Forgiving an institution is often problematic. In the diocesan processes used for church consolidations, the locus of responsibility for decisions was dissipated. To whom does one forgive or make the offer of forgiveness when a local church is closed apparently against one's will? Nevertheless, the stages of separation, liminality, and reaggregation reflect a basic pattern of human transition or change. Effective ritual in the context of church restructuring needs to respect the movements of that pattern in which soul is recovered. It is ultimately at the service of conversion, rendering an experience intelligible and less terrifying. It enables the journey to be completed from crisis, through encounter with the sacred, toward a certain newness of life and perspective.[84]

[83] Ibid.
[84] Ibid., 47.

Chapter 4

Remembering in a Different Kind of Way
Grief, Lament, and Healing

Most consolations mean a loss of people. There doesn't seem to be any way around it. Some leave the local church and join another parish. Others left the Catholic Church and returned to their Baptist roots. Loss and grief take time. Some can possibly come back after the healing of the loss.[1]

How can major transitions like these be gentled? The question of loss and grief rests against any attempt at human interpersonal or social change. In the situations of local parish restructuring, it became one of the most crucial issues, often anything but gentle. Forgiveness and grieving are intimately intertwined and culturally determined. What to do with what has been lost, especially when it is a place of memories where ethnic Catholic identity has been anchored? Robert Schreiter coined the term "remembering in a different kind of way" to offset the old adage, "forgive and forget." Forgiveness requires full remembering against a greater foundational story. In the Christian context this is the paschal mystery of the life, death, and resurrection of Jesus. Grieving and forgiveness are intertwined. Remembering adequately against time for adjusting to significant

---

[1] Fr. Bernard [pseudonym], interview by author, Chicago, Ill., February 2, 2001.

81

loss has been one of the major issues affecting the success or failure of local parish restructuring.

Detachment from What Is Lost

Human grief is that deeply mysterious process of sorrow, anger, denial, guilt, and confusion that so often accompanies significant actual or anticipated loss by individuals and by cultures. In her work with dying patients, Elizabeth Kübler-Ross articulated the now familiar stages of her dying pattern: denial, anger, bargaining, depression, acceptance or resignation.[2] For the dying, "letting go" is in order to prepare for death. Those who grieve let go of a loss in order to live again.[3] Some of the dynamics of social grief will parallel Kübler-Ross's pattern, and other aspects will be quite distinct.

Anthropologist Gerald Arbuckle had identified three major stages of what he calls "cultural grieving"—a larger collective response to significant loss and of the meaning systems connected to it. He posited that the main reason why religious congregations, parishes, or dioceses resist renewal is a failure to mourn or ritually detach themselves from "that which is lost" or "no longer apostolically relevant."[4] Interviewees frequently linked resistance to new pastoral initiatives in the consolidated churches to a failure to grieve the death of the old parishes and the buildings that housed them. Expressions of sadness, together with symptoms of resistance (denial, repression, and projection) to the reality of the loss marked the first moment of social grief. There is nostalgia for what has been lost, a restlessness, despair, or anger often indiscriminately directed at those facilitating the change.

The second movement of loss is liminal. A community feels both attracted by the security of its past and the call to face the future. This is often a time of anxious reflection, a search into mythological roots to recover a sense of identity or self worth. There are often outbursts of localized nationalism (or in this case parochialism) and delusions of grandeur that mask a widespread repression or denial of what has been lost. This is a time of risk because the temptation is for the culture or organization to cling stubbornly to what has been lost and to refuse to face the future.

---

[2] See Elizabeth Kübler-Ross, *On Death and Dying* (New York: Macmillan, 1969).

[3] Kenneth R. Mitchell and Herbert Anderson, *All Our Losses, All Our Griefs* (Philadelphia: Westminster Press, 1983) 60.

[4] Gerald A. Arbuckle, S.M., *Refounding the Church: Dissent for Leadership* (Maryknoll, N.Y.: Orbis Books, 1993) 180–81.

Often times a spectacular project is initiated by a group to make the "parishioners feel good." The liminal time for a group is dangerous. A chronic form of grief can take over a group's imagination making it difficult for the group to move out of an escapist depression. An adequate sense of identity to carry them through the transition can become distorted. Feverish activity can even be a way that groups use to keep from facing the reality about themselves.

"Reaggregation" is the name given to the third movement of cultural grieving. A bereaved culture is able finally to look with some almost marked detachment at what has been lost. It is able to reassess its story and past, and to speak its pain and perhaps rage at separation. It is able to launch into the future carrying the best of its past with it.

Human symbol making, narrative, and ritual in the face of systemic grief is a way of constructing and reconstructing a sense of safety and selfhood sometimes in the midst of intense emotional reaction to separation from an object of attachment. Different categories of loss—material, relational, intrapsychic, functional, role, and systemic loss—have their own variables and specific patterns of recuperation.[5] They are the ways a culture deals with physical bereavement. It likewise sets the pattern for how individuals within that culture cope with significant loss.

Effective grieving rites formally articulate that the loss affects not only individuals within the culture but the whole culture itself. Without the naming of the loss and the articulation of the new future for the culture in a reframed set of internal relationships, the culture takes the risk of being held hostage to its past or at least being haunted by it. Unarticulated grief encourages a host of culture-destroying behaviors, often including holding on to time-tested ways of living. But holding on strangles; letting go heals.[6] Ritual agents facilitate both individuals and cultures through these stages of grieving. Their task is to model a mastery over anxiety, so that a new and realistic order is achieved that pays adequate respect to the past.

Death rituals of traditional cultures move in two directions. The ritual disengagement-engagement process is first directed at the deceased. The dead are formally disengaged from the living to become engaged in relationships with other spirits elsewhere. They are assigned to a new esteemed and safe status: tradition. The second set of rites is related directly to the living. They are formally disengaged from the negative influences of the

---

[5] Anderson and Mitchell, *All Our Losses*, 36–46.
[6] Ibid., 185.

deceased and engage themselves in forming a new set of social relationships or culture.

Separation rituals vigorously encourage the community to admit that death has occurred. During the liminal stage, the community concentrates over a lengthy period of time on the two processes of disengagement and engagement. Finally, reaggregation rites mark the end of mourning and serve to refocus attention on new configurations of social relationships.[7]

Although any profound loss brings in its wake intense feeling states for the individual, grief is a social phenomenon. In traditional cultures, no member of a clan can be indifferent to the death of any member. In a sense, when one human being dies, the entire group dies. Ritual and narrative are formal ways of acknowledging this loss. A community itself needs to mourn and reform the pattern of its social relationships. Based on the study of traditional cultures, inclusive even of First Testament cultures, Arbuckle names several conclusions about the role of ritual in social grieving. All change is experienced as "catastrophic," even if rationally acknowledged as for the better, because it threatens the established and familiar order of personal and group life. It carries in its wake new attitudes and behaviors, changes in relationships, and a movement outward into an unknown future.

In the processes of grief, ritual is a way of inscribing the body personal (the individual personality), the body politic (social personality) and their interactions with new meaning. Forgiveness implies a ritual reframing and re-inscribing the individual self and body politic, after traumatic breach. Both are linked to the revision of narrative, literally a "re-storying" of a painful event, the telling of it in a different kind of way. The interconnected patterns of grief and forgiveness that one would expect at the death of a loved one are no more dramatically personalized than with the announcement of a parochial closure.

Now You Can Move On

> Between you and me, you can close all of them. We don't need them as they are constituted today. We got each other and we don't need them churches. Church is people not places.[8]

"God can be worshipped anywhere," a parishioner of the San Francisco consolidation had said. People do not need church buildings to worship

[7] Arbuckle, *Refounding Church*, 186–87.
[8] Maryann [pseudonym], interview by author, Chicago, Ill., November 15, 2000.

"in Spirit and truth" as Jesus had invited the Samaritan woman in John's Gospel (John 4:23).[9] The insight radiated a new-found ecclesial sense intently focused on people. "Let's do Church," one of Englewood's pastors had said—Church gathered together, out there, active, hospitable, and rooted in a profound faith conviction. From a highly conflicted internal church setting to this kind of faith conviction is an immense faith journey. It is how one individually or collectively wrestles up against the mystery of human change.

Under affiliation and over affiliation were critical issues for those engaged in parish restructuring processes. For many of those interviewed, moving on meant first to show up. It meant to stay in the process for the duration. This required a unique, often times difficult perseverance by many of those interviewed from the Chicago and San Francisco consolidations. Some became so engaged in the question of their church's survival that they seemed to have little other life. Family and other social affiliations were overlooked or even ignored. Others who dropped out of the processes seemed to be the ones with the ache of it most permanently printed on their imaginations.[10]

One of the Englewood leadership spoke of meeting a woman in the grocery store who had been a member of one of the closed churches in the early sixties when their children were in school. Several years after the church was torn down the woman was still unresolved with it. She said that she wept every time she walked by the closed site of St. Brendan's. The parish leader responded with an angry question, "Where were you when we were fighting to keep the place open? You came looking for it when you needed it, and it wasn't there any more." The conclusion of many in the Englewood consolidation was that those who complained the loudest were people who attended church only infrequently. The woman at the supermarket appeared unreconciled to the closure of the parish because she did not participate in the process. The Englewood leader felt that the sense of church for those who attended only occasionally was

---

[9] For an excellent account of the biblical tension in the early Christian community between worship and sacred buildings, especially after the fall of the Temple of Jerusalem in 70 C.E., see Chris Roland, "Buildings, Cathedrals, and the Gospel," *The Hidden Spirit: Discovering the Spirituality of Institutions*, ed. James F. Cobble, Jr., and Charles M. Elliot (Matthews, N.C.: Christian Ministry Resources, 1999) 52–62.

[10] Minuchin and Fishman's celebrated work on family therapy noted that dysfunction within family systems is often the result of over affiliation or under affiliation. Salvador Minuchin and H. Charles Fishman, *Family Therapy Techniques* (Cambridge Mass.: Harvard University Press, 1981) 69.

perhaps more as social service resource rather than as a people with a mission. They often left the consolidation process with still bleeding wounds.

Another aspect of the moving on seemed to be a looking directly at what was lost, a willingness to embrace without denial a local reality now changed. For some it meant actually watching or participating in the disassembling of their former churches. Dorothy Banks, now a deceased Englewood parishioner, had been quoted in a local newspaper as St. Brendan's Church was torn down. She and the new pastor of the Englewood churches looked on as the wreckers destroyed the church kitchen and removed its stained glass windows for a local historical society museum. "I did all I could for this place," she noted to the reporter, "I'm going to get on with my life."[11]

Others spoke of this moving on as related to conscious choice. At some point in working through what had been lost in a breach of relationship, some participants chose simply not to linger on it further. But, this moving on was always in a particular context and for a purpose. The first movement of Enright, Freedman, and Rique's forgiveness paradigm, referred to in the previous chapter, is withdrawal by the injured party from preoccupation with the offense and the offender. The work phase begins with the decision to let go of reprisal and begin a reframing of perspective.[12] Moving on in this context required that the previous experience of church had to be adequately examined and clearly seen as unworkable. Enthusiasm and conviction emerged in adequate attending to grief: "I had no feelings after the closure. It was time to move on. I put it behind me when I walked out the door. We felt that we had done what had to be for the church to be alive and viable. We were stymied by where we were. We were just separate clans."[13]

For others the vision for a future church had to be adequately crafted and accepted as a viable alternative before one could move on. Other versions of this were related to family and the desire for inclusion in the formation of the new church configuration. One spoke of letting go finally for the sake of children, another of stepping away from paralyzing emotions of powerlessness and rage with the realization that change was inevitable. Without a fundamental resignation to the loss, participation in the formation of a new church was impeded. Fear of being left out ultimately

[11] Grant Pick, "Resurrection," *The Reader* (Chicago), August 9, 1991, sec. 1, 27.

[12] Robert D. Enright and Joanna North, eds., *Exploring Forgiveness* (Madison: University of Wisconsin Press, 1998) 53–54.

[13] Nora [pseudonym], interview by author, Chicago, Ill., November 8, 2000.

pushed some to reengage in the framing of a future church in that locale: "You can't derail it. You can't stop it. You might as well get onboard and manipulate what you can manipulate. A burden left me, and I could mourn the death of Immaculate Conception and move on to the process of putting it back together."[14]

The inability to "move on" by some participants is a challenge to pastoral care. Liminal times are dangerous, yet full of promise and potential. Still people sometimes get stuck. For a new identity or a resolution of conflict to emerge from an impasse, it is often necessary to adequately wait. Ritual storytelling, lament, or the venting of anger and sadness fill the time. Those who over affiliated or discontinued the processes of local pastoral planning remained longest conflicted, some for more than a decade afterwards. An almost permanent kind of liminal state seemed to restrain people in crisis, like these, from entering into a new relationship with the consolidating church or moving on to active participation in another parish or Christian community.

"If It Ain't Broke, Don't Fix It": Disengagement and Reframing

> There was a lot of letting go. There had to be willingness to let go of attachment to one's particular parish. I remember the first "vision" papers where the scenarios were sketched out with the three parishes on the West joined with a worship site. We were told we would be a stronger church, stronger community if we pulled together. It was painful to let go of St. Justin and watch the parishes in our area let go of their places.[15]

Negotiation around the conference table could not happen effectively when staff and leadership were unwilling to release their attachments to parish boundaries and buildings to extend these boundaries around a larger collective. It was an arduous and time-consuming process. As long as the perspective remained turf and survival of the project in that one locale, the individual and group would not embrace the notion of an area Catholic community, with its cluster of communities and their needs.

Fr. Jack Farry had noted that the Catholic Community of Englewood was a successful clustering experience because of a decrease in the

---

[14] William B. [pseudonym], interview by Dinah P. Shaw, San Francisco, Calif., January 25, 2001.

[15] Br. Lauren [pseudonym], interview by author, Chicago Ill., February 27, 2001.

parochialism that had previously marked the identity of the ethnic-national parish. To think in terms of "area ministry" as opposed to the needs of a particular parish was a new experience of church for many. It was the card that attracted a cadre of new religious and clergy to work in the Englewood cluster in the early seventies. As the communities began to close in the late 1980s, one of the priests noted that the competitive parochialism reemerged. The actual surrender of a particular parochial church for a new one required disengagement from a history, identity, and the architecture that expressed it. It became an occasion of tremendous grief and sadness.

Studies of reconciliation indicate that individual forgiveness appears in the mystery of reframed perspective, one that includes the story and perspective of the offending party. When this has begun to happen, the desire to continue holding resentment likewise disappears or lessens. A frame is a border around a piece of reality in memory. Remembering well is a way of reframing this border toward inclusiveness of the offending party and God's Messiah. This happens in a mysterious way in the forgiveness process. It is difficult to pinpoint when or how this happens for a victim. But when it does, the other steps or processes of forgiveness likewise engage themselves.

This choosing to let go is conversion in a traditional sense of the word. It is a glance forward to a future where remembering happens without bitterness.[16] The major task for the change agent in any therapeutic re-framing of a situation is convincing members of the family system that reality as they have mapped it out can be expanded or modified. Family systems theory proposes three phases: enactment, focusing, and achieving intensity. In enactment, participants interact with one another with the coaching of a therapist in order to experience the family reality in alternative ways. In focusing, the therapist organizes the data of the family interactions around a theme that gives them new meaning. In achieving intensity, the therapist heightens the impact of the group's transactions supporting the experience of a new therapeutic reality.[17]

"If it's not broke, don't fix it," became the mantra at the subsequent long series of parish and school meetings to align the two parishes in San Francisco. It indicated that the participants at that site were not convinced that their parish was in any way deficient and in need of affiliation with its neighbor. It was not yet dead and grieved, remembered and

---

[16] Patricia Kelly, phone interview by author, Chicago Ill., October 16, 2000.
[17] Minuchin and Fishman, 76–77.

memorialized; therefore, they were not ready to seek another affiliation. Contrary to the old adage, pastoral theologian Herbert Anderson suggests that change be initiated before what is currently in place "peters out."[18] He notes that in an age of often chaotic and rapid change, constancy is maintained by allowing the past and future to coexist in the present. This is the role of ritual and liturgy. It expresses this expanded or reframed vision of local church, and it evokes it into reality.

Therapists, spiritual directors, and accompanying soul friends become the locus for reconstructing the story in a way that leads a group through the grief to a new vision of self, church, and local worshipping community. Effective ritual and pastoral care can more easily accompany individuals and groups through this journey earlier in the process. Ritual processes for "healing of memories" often employ exercises of active imagination in the safety of prayer and intense group dynamics to work through past traumatic events in a liberating way. With the passage of time adequate to the trauma, effective "remembering, re-storying, and resetting of memories" can occur. Still, only when a narrative has been remembered enough, can active forgetting result and people let go.[19]

Two rituals that particularly exemplify reframing are proposed by Mari West Zimmerman. In her book, *Take and Make Holy,* a resource for abuse survivors, her "Service of Healing for a Congregation" uses prayer around the cross and a mutual signing on the forehead by members of a congregation wounded by a common traumatic situation, like a clergy scandal. Her "Service for Release and Forgiveness" employs a public naming and relinquishment of claim for revenge. A ritual burning of slips of paper inscribed with the names and specific wounding of the perpetrators symbolizes an attempt at conscious surrender of hostility.[20] These rites serve to facilitate the reframing of grief and loss with its letting go or forgetting into new meaning.

---

[18] Herbert Anderson, "Ritual Moment and Pastoral Process: Rethinking Pastoral Theology," *Finding Voice To Give God Praise,* ed. Kathleen Hughes (Collegeville, Minn.: Liturgical Press, 1998) 156.

[19] Andrew M. Jefferson, "Remembering and Re-storying; An Exploration of Memory and Narrative in Relation to Psychotherapy with Torture Survivors," *Torture* 10, no. 4 (December 2000) 111.

[20] See Mari West Zimmerman, *Take and Make Holy: Honoring the Sacred in the Healing Journey of Abuse Survivors* (Chicago: Liturgy Training Publications, 1989) 82–91 and 158–67. The rituals contained in this volume can easily be adapted to a communal context. See particularly chapter 5, "When the Congregation Becomes a Victim," 74–82.

As they sought to put a new border around this experience, partici-pants in the Chicago consolidation referred to a particularly African American sense of detachment that emerged from generations of victimi-zation reflected in gospel music and literature. The familiar maxim, "God does not sleep," put their losses in a new context. At some point in any struggle the results need to be "turned over" to that God whose vigilance will someday make it right. This reference particularly appeared in the language of many conversations around choices made for the closure of worship sites with which they clearly disagreed. A conviction grew that God would work it out one way or another in a justice that assumes to itself any need for vengeance. The resurrection becomes a new frame to the larger context of God's restorative work.

Lament, Powerlessness, and Sacred Space

Changes of sacred space are not a new issue in the Judeo-Christian narrative and ethos. The Scriptures, particularly the Psalms, are abundant with parallels, references, and nuances to a history of changes—some-times violent changes—to the character and geography of sacred space, "the house where you dwell, the tenting place of your glory" (Psalm 26:8). In fact, there seems to be an ongoing connection in the psalms of healing-restoration with changes to sacred space. In the liminal waiting of the lament psalms, slowly new universalizing insight emerged that God could not be contained in buildings. The pattern of these psalms creates another resource for honestly speaking the deep feelings evoked by parish closure.

One Englewood woman described the town hall process used in the decision to close her church with words that spoke lament. It was "an opportunity for people to scream, fight, bite and kick, an opportunity and invitation in safety to vent."[21] Lament is a human expression of grief that needs to be brought to prayer. It is not a prayer form disrespectful to God, rather it honors the God who listens and cares for the sufferings and oppression of people. It is a prayer form anchored in the psalms that confronts powerlessness with trust and intercession.[22]

---

[21] Elizabeth [pseudonym], interview by author, Chicago, Ill., January 18, 2001.

[22] I am particularly grateful to Fr. David G. Caron, O.P., for his conversations with me in this area. His doctor of ministry thesis project on ministry to those with HIV has some particularly enlightening uses of lament. See David G. Caron, O.P., "Liturgy as Pastoral Care for those with HIV/Aids" (doctoral thesis, Catholic Theological Union, 1998) 168–71.

Over one third of the psalms in the Old Testament are prayers of lament. Kathleen Fischer's book, *Women at the Well*, proposes that lament is a way of empowering those facing profound loss. This empowerment is crucial for those working their way through the restructuring of local church, especially when those decisions are made by those outside the local context. She notes that when lament is absent from Christian living and liturgy, prayer can be confused with docility, submissiveness and passive silence.[23]

A number of the psalms, like Psalm 74, lament the loss and desecration of the Jerusalem Temple. The pattern reflects an almost disciplined articulation of personal and communal pain into the heart of God, the loss of sacred space, its resulting identity, and a sense of abandonment by God.

> Why, God, why have you cast us off forever?
>> Why does your anger burn against the sheep of your pasture?
> . . . .
> Turn your steps toward the utter ruins,
>> toward the sanctuary devastated by the enemy.
> . . . .
> They set your sanctuary on fire;
>> the abode of your name they razed and profaned.
>
> (vv. 1, 3, 7)

The prayer of lament is also one of profound hope and faith. It acknowledges that God hears the cry of the poor, is with the individual or group in their suffering and will be faithful to them as is promised in the Scriptures.

Since lament expresses the assurance of being heard by God, prayers of lament can serve as a profound source of healing for those in the midst of the particularly conflicted deliberations around the closure of a parish church. Strong language and protest were spoken in the interviews from San Francisco and Chicago's Englewood. Lament allows individuals and communities to name in the context of worship the emotional content of their losses as well as the inconsistencies, failures, ambivalences, and ambiguities of the contemporary religious situation.[24]

---

[23] Kathleen Fischer, *Women at the Well: Feminist Perspectives on Spiritual Direction* (New York: Paulist Press, 1988) 102.

[24] David Couturier, O.F.M., Cap., "A Spirituality of Refounding," in *Religious Life: Rebirth Through Conversion*, ed. Gerald A. Arbuckle, S.M., and David L. Fleming, S.J. (New York: Alba House, 1990) 85–87.

Walter Brueggemann posited that the now-familiar grieving pattern of Elizabeth Kübler-Ross (denial, anger, bargaining, depression and acceptance) was an effort to structure ritual for a culture that has misplaced the art of relating constructively to significant loss.[25] This general pattern moves from an experience of chaos or turmoil to a resignation and peace, requiring the accompaniment of a trusted group or person.

Anger is a liminal moment paralleled in both grieving patterns. The danger, as with any liminal experience, is getting stuck. In a culture like that of the U.S. that encourages the denial of loss, anger is often directed in an almost random array. More often than not, it falls on the accompanying change agent who is not comfortable with the expression of anger either. This was frequently the experience of those facilitating the recent consolidations and closure of Catholic parishes. Projection of rage at midlevel management assigned to facilitate these often-unpopular decisions was frightening and confusing. Local pastors in these roles often attempted to smooth over people's feelings with reassurance and promises of limits to the change. This often was interpreted as lies, a reason for further anger and mistrust. Pastoral care tended then to leave people at the stage of anger or Stoic resignation.

The praise at the end of the lament pattern attests to a movement from resignation to acceptance and peace.[26] Unlike the Elizabeth Kübler-Ross pattern, Hebrew psalmody supplements the grief and anguish with

---

[25] Walter Brueggemann, "The Formlessness of Grief," *Interpretation: A Journal of Bible and Theology* 31, no. 3 (July 1977) 267–75, quoted in Gerald Arbuckle, S.M., *Change Grief and Renewal in the Church; A Spirituality for a New Era* (Westminster, Mass.: Christian Classics, 1991) 65–67. Psalms of lament (musical compositions in their original context) embodied a general pattern that could be helpful in preparing rituals or liturgies acknowledging desolation or anguish.

[26] **Lament Psalms**

Lament Psalms	Kübler-Ross
Address to God	Denial and isolation
Complaint or lament	Anger
Confession of trust	Bargaining
Petition for help	Depression
Words of assurance	Acceptance
Vow of praise	

See Frank J. Henderson, *Liturgies of Lament* (Chicago: Liturgy Training Publications, 1994) 16–17. Despite clear consensus among scholars about the lament classification, the author assembles a comprehensive list of psalmody that falls under the general lament pattern helpful to ritual planners. See also pages 54–56.

confidence and petition.[27] Denial becomes a turning to God and confession of trust supplants bargaining. Body posture and movement were connected to the wailing, the music, and the pattern of the lament psalms: One crouched to the ground. Dust was strewn on the head. There was the tearing or renting of clothes. One donned coarse apparel, and abstained from food and drink (see Psalms 35:13-14 and 69:10-12 for examples).[28] The reaching out of hands is an image of lamentation that expresses deep longing and human desire.

Sacral processions are also a lament resource from Christian worship with roots deep in the Hebrew Book of Psalms. Pilgrim psalms, such as Psalm 85, mentioned in chapter 2, with its famous "kindness and truth shall meet, justice and peace shall kiss," reflected a longing for the restoration of Jerusalem and the Temple cult;[29] for "the glory that dwelt in our land." That glory of YHWH, the Shekinah,[30] was that sense of the Holy that hovered about the tent or in the Jerusalem Temple precincts where the ark of the covenant was enthroned. It said that YHWH was with his people. God's Spirit was said to withdrew from Jerusalem when the Temple was destroyed. The psalm spoke a hope that the glory, quenched by terrible sin, violence, and desecration, would return. Virtuous living out of the covenant, kindness (mercy), truth, justice and peace are linked to the fruitfulness of the land. Slowly Israel became aware of a new insight in this longing for God's presence. They became aware that it hovered about social relationships in right order, in almost the same way that it once was sensed in the Temple cult. God's presence could not be reduced or contained to buildings.[31]

---

[27] Walter Wink posits that intercession is spiritual defiance of what is in the name of what God has promised. It visualizes an alternative future to the one apparently fated by momentum of current forces. History in his framework belongs to intercessors who believe the future into being. It is an act of co-creation with God. It is an act in which one small sector of the universe rises up and becomes translucent, incandescent, a vibratory center of power that radiates the power of the universe. Walter Wink, *The Powers That Be: Theology for a New Millennium* (New York: Doubleday, 1998) 185–87.

[28] Othmar Keel, *The Symbolism of the Biblical World*, trans. Timothy J. Hallett (New York: Seabury Press, 1978) 319.

[29] John Paul Lederach's translation. See also Haggai 1:5-11, 2:6-9 and Malachi 3:13-21.

[30] See Exodus 40:34-38.

[31] There are at least two procession types in these psalms, the procession in which YHWH seems to participate and the pilgrimage in which the people solemnly advance to the sanctuary. The "going up" to the temple had resonance of the original transfer of

Closure Rituals:
Remembering in a Different Kind of Way

> They brought pieces from the other churches. Little treasures . . .
> the bells from St. Martin, the crucifix from St. Carthage . . . other
> icons and treasures. The baptism font idea came from St. Martin's
> (which had been newly renovated before its closure). It had a magical
> effect, the most prominent thing in the church . . . It was the first
> structure built in the new church. It established our identity around
> the font. Many of us were baptized in pools like that one as Baptists.
> It makes us think about our own baptism. The Church was literally
> built around baptism. There was not a church at St. Bernard's for
> many years, so the building meant even more. It was a gift.[32]

The Greek word, *anamnesis*, references a crucial ritual moment from
the most ancient Eucharistic prayer traditions. The great remembering
builds and expresses the most precious values of the Christian experience.
The way to remember, what to hold and of what to "let go," is a crucial
aspect of worship "in Spirit and truth" (John 4:23). As noted earlier,
Schreiter coined the notion of "remembering in a different kind of way"
as integral to processes of human reconciliation, making memorial up
against the life, death, and resurrection of Jesus.

The closing liturgy is the end of a parish history. These liturgies across
the country attempted to bring gentle closure to a noble history of Catholic parochial community life. But, at times they served to make people
more angry. In these situations, the closing liturgies became more like an
angry funeral than a final celebration of a noble era of Catholic cultural
life. It is interesting to note that the majority of those interviewed from
the Englewood consolidation could not remember the details of their
closing liturgies.

No specific closure ceremonies were employed by the St. Anthony-
Immaculate Conception consolidation in San Francisco. Interviewees for
that site mentioned that perhaps this would have been helpful. Other
parishes in the San Francisco twelve-parish restructuring had formal
closure rituals, most especially a final Sunday Eucharist in the presence of
the archbishop. But since Immaculate Conception was allowed to remain

---

the ark of the covenant to Zion. It is the "pro-type" of the YHWH procession. YHWH
was not always present there. He moved to Zion in triumphal procession over the local
rival gods and hostile peoples with his people. The visits to the Temple and annual
pilgrimage retained resonances of this. Keel, *Symbolism of the Biblical World*, 323.

[32] Elizabeth [pseudonym], interview by author, Chicago, Ill., January 18, 2001.

open under the care of St. Anthony's, there appeared to be no reason to ritualize a closure. In the perspective of the parish staffs, nothing, after all, had changed. The reaction indicated that something had been profoundly altered in the fabric of that local community and the rites crafted for the occasion seemed to falter. Some of those interviewed questioned whether any closure rites would have helped people cooperate more with pastoral initiatives over the subsequent few years. Without some kind of assent to the new configuration chosen for the locale, rites of closure or consolidation may have had little impact on the imaginations of those most affected by it.

When the people of the eight Englewood parishes merged into Chicago's St. Benedict the African in 1989, it was with a more apparent consensus. A single parish was to be formed with multiple worship sites, quickly reduced to two. The Catholic culture that built the original churches had abandoned the neighborhood for the suburbs. Many of the parishioners most active in the consolidation process had moved into Englewood at the front of that "white flight." Members of the Catholic African American culture had a different take on this loss. They lost autonomy and the ethnic roots of the groups who built their facilities and neighborhoods. They lost small intimate communities of people who supported each other as both African American Catholics in the midst of a primarily Baptist African American culture. They lost institutions that provided worship, social services, Catholic education, and youth services—resources to protect their children from the ensuing violence and poverty of urban Chicago.

The closure ceremonies of those five East Side parishes included Sunday Eucharist with receptions for former parishioners, religious, and staff. The presence of staff from the former St. Bernard's was the more important item in their reflections. An article from a local newspaper had described the closure of St. Brendan's in September of 1988 with the specifics of this ritual. Most of the Englewood interviewees remembered a few details: a Sunday Eucharist, homily, gospel singing and reception. Music, especially combined gospel choirs, preaching, personal invitation to join the new parish and the reception welcoming former parishioners were the key parts of the ritual.

The parishes that formed St. Benedict the African's West Side (Sacred Heart, St. Rafael, and St. Justin) experienced their loss through an additional level of turmoil. The closure decision at the end of their process was marked with suspicion that they would be eventually subsumed by the East Side of the new parish. Further, fears that the choice of St. Justin as their worship site had been manipulated by fellow parishioners left a lingering angry tone as they came together at the end of the summer of 1988. The new pastoral staff decided *not* to review the process of decision making, rather they decided to put it behind them and move ahead. Attempts made at public apology by some of the leaders did not seem to effect much healing. Emotions remained raw, with a notable decrease in Sunday Mass attendance—all this would portend the eventual complete separation of the West and East five years later.

The closing liturgies for the West Side churches were all scheduled on the same Sunday. For years afterward, many in the greater Englewood community noted the history of competition between the East Side and West Side Englewood churches and ongoing doubt about the appropriateness of the worship site. A new church on the East Side fed a sense of being second class. The associate pastor from the West Side attended all three closing Eucharists as preacher. He focused his homilies on giving hope, but he later noted they seemed a bit impotent against the lingering sense of betrayal: "They were simple Masses with regular Sunday resources and reception following. There were no other ritual components. We were making it up as we went along. We were not aware of any other resources. The focus was singing, praying, and preaching."[33]

After the formal announcement of consolidation by Cardinal Bernardin, the immediate focus of the East Englewood parishioners was on the construction of a new building. At the dedication (May 27, 1989) the Cardinal hailed a prominent, almost eye-level cornerstone with the inscribed names of the five closed parishes and the new church's grand immersion baptismal font as symbols of new life for the Englewood neighborhood.[34] The parish staff had carefully prepared a ritual for this dedication with a three-sided cornerstone at the front door of the new church building. They had asked parishioners to write out their dreams for their families and the new parish family of Benedict the African. These were to be placed within the stone like a time capsule. A former parishioner from Our Lady of Solace had lovingly placed a copy of its last bulletin with his dreams.

The singing of the hymn, "We've Come This Far by Faith" acknowledged that this new community stood on the collective history of the consolidated parishes. Another popular African American hymn, also etched on the cornerstone, was sung at the dedication ceremony: "There is a

[33] Fr. Bernard [pseudonym], interview by author, Chicago, Ill., March 16, 2001.
[34] Skerrett, *Catholicism, Chicago Style,* 166.

Sweet, Sweet Spirit in this Place." The words repeated each Sunday as the parish staff welcomes and introduces visitors at the end of Sunday Eucharist would continue to recall those days.[35] The details of this dedication ritual, even after more than ten years, were prominent enough that most of those interviewed for this study were still able to recall them.

Closure-consolidations in other parts the country, like those in Wheeling, West Virginia, separated the closure ceremonies from the leave taking of the buildings. This process allowed the newly amalgamated parish to use the former parish buildings for thirteen months before a final move to a completely renovated church. The focus of the parish closing rites in Wheeling was on the history and life of the community, not on the physical environment. "Hang time" to adjust to a new identity and larger community was important before taking leave of the buildings and worship environment. The general intercessions and the preparation of the gifts were used as thanksgiving for the history of the closing parish.[36] The most important detail was that as many parishioners as possible were involved with the *adequate remembering* of the former churches.

Consolidation Rituals:
Acknowledging Conflict and Disagreement

A community, like any blended family system, is never just merged. It is first closed. It dies, and then its parts, together or separately, move into another familial configuration. The calls for ritual honesty from both the Chicago and San Francisco case studies, were indicative that their rites overlooked or smoothed over conflict and disagreement. Most of the people interviewed at the St. Benedict the African East site felt they had access to all the information and at least gave consent to the reasons to close and realign the Englewood parishes. There was, however, suspicion in both sites that the criteria for consolidation were not applied consistently. Many in San Francisco went along with the decisions unconvinced the closure was warranted. Closure rites were almost entirely focused on a Sunday Eucharist without reference to the deep disagreement at the choice of worship sites.

[35] David Baldwin, "There Is a Sweet, Sweet Spirit in This Place," *Environment and Art* 3, no. 8 (October 1990) 58–61.

[36] Larry W. Dorsch, "The Rituals of Parish Consolidation," *Church* 17, no. 1 (Spring 2001) 30–35.

The consolidation of the three West Englewood parishes in 1989 attempted to briefly acknowledge the ongoing disharmony between them in
a familiar setting of the holidays. A candle ceremony used in the context
of the first midnight Christmas Mass attempted to perform a new sense of
unity. Representatives of the three consolidating parishes started the midnight Mass with a procession with candles from three corners of the new
worship site. Three representatives simply walked forward to put their
multicolored black, green, and red candles—traditional African American
colors—under the altar as the Mass began. Only the assistant pastor, however, made reference to details of this rite in subsequent interviews.

San Francisco's Immaculate Conception community held lingering ob-
jections to the conclusions that their parish was no longer viable and their
finances in need of greater collective resources. This disagreement was no
more apparent than in the ritual actions employed in the consolidation.
Without specific closure rituals, their ceremony was forced to perform a
sense of celebration up against a myriad of conflicting feelings to the
changes to their local communities. This was evident in the consolidation
rituals in two ways. Either, the details of the rite were sabotaged or the
people voted with their feet and did not show up at the event.

In a consolidation rite planned for the centenary at the San Francisco
receiving parish, leadership from both sites were asked by the staff to
bring a statue of their respective parishes in procession to a city park
halfway between the two churches. The morning of the ceremony, the
consolidating parish's Italian leadership asked to borrow a smaller replica
of their patron saint from the receiving parish's Nicaraguan society. They
further requested that members of the Hispanic youth group carry the
bier and statue for the two-block procession. The altered ceremony was
handicapped in its ability to perform and reflect the desired new unity.
The elderly group walked passively behind like bereaved family members
to a funeral.

The ritual was attached to the final Eucharist of the receiving parish's
year-long centenary. The local archbishop, celebrants, ministers, school
children with national flags, and group representatives with their standards gathered at a park between the two parish-school sites. After the procession with the statues arrived from the two parishes, the archbishop
greeted the representatives of both communities, thanked them for their
work on the consolidation, and invited them to prayer. Orations adapted
from the Rite of Laying the Foundation Stone or Beginning Work on the
Building of a Church were chosen by the parish staff to heighten the sense
of Jesus Christ as the foundation and cornerstone of local church. The

work of reconciliation would only be complete when all "arrive at last in your heavenly city."[37]

The archbishop then used holy water to bless in the directions of the two parish churches and prayed in Spanish that they become one body healed of all division.

A final proclamation by the archbishop was spoken in English, Spanish, and Latin, followed by a procession back to the receiving parish's school-yard for a festive multilingual Eucharist and reception. Displays for alumni and visiting dignitaries had been arranged to tell a now more inclusive history of the parish and school. The blessing of the two processions with their statues by the archbishop, however, seemed to leave the people angrier. The rite failed to convince most of the Catholic participants in the stability of the *domus domini fermiter aedificata*, the house of the Lord firmly built.

The rites inaugurating the consolidation in the park between the two parish plants attempted to speak a new foundation for the Catholic community in that neighborhood, but its ritual elements were premature for both communities. The receiving parish never wholly grasped that the fabric of its constituency would change with its inclusion of the Immaculate Conception community. Bitterness and resentment toward the archbishop and the planning process were spoken in conversation but not in the rite. A tremendous loss had not yet been grieved. The reasons had not been mused over, the stories repeatedly told as one does at the wake or funeral of a loved one. Lastly, the final proclamation left out the Italian language, failing to acknowledge the cultural root of the formerly Italian national parish. Some spoke of a sense of shame and having lost face. Another, more significant, percentage of the former community simply did not attend.

The rituals in all of these settings needed to be expansive enough to carry a host of human emotions: anger, thankfulness, grief, hope, depression and excitement. For some, the rituals were effective in accompanying their transition with its grief and loss. For most they were not. In Chicago, the people of St. Benedict the African East had moved quickly from the closure Masses to the formation of a building committee to complete a new parish church on the site of the former St. Bernard's Church. Much of the grief appeared to be projected into the excitement of a new building. Across the country, the construction of a new worship site or a major

---

[37] International Commission on English in the Liturgy, *The Rites of the Catholic Church*, vol. 2 (Collegeville, Minn.: Liturgical Press, 1991) 352.

renovation of the former one have been consistent qualities of even minimally successful consolidations. Attempts to locate a new parish in an old building, for the most part, have been extremely problematic. After the dedication of her new parish center, an Englewood parishioner noted in an interview with a local newspaper, "This church was built for us, in our time," a gift from an African American cultural experience of Catholicism to pass on to their children.[38]

Requiem: The Dead Must Be Remembered

One of the greatest losses for parishes closed during this time was the identity-shaping Catholic culture that built them. Liturgical scholar Nathan D. Mitchell has noted that in this culture, identity was the product of cult rather than doctrines: "Catholic identity arises from experience, from life lived by the seat of the pants, from image and icon, from story and ritual, from improvisation and ceremony, from poetry and art. To understand Catholic identity, you have to dance it, sing it, live in its skin and its stories."[39]

This loss of Catholic identity seemed to be validated as the people of Immaculate Conception in San Francisco spoke strong reactions to their closure: "No wonder the church is going to hell." "No one comes to Mass anymore or says the rosary . . . or goes to confession. And now this!" "We used to have hundreds of people at May devotions." This rage spoke multiple levels of loss. The decline of that popular devotion signed the end of that distinctive Catholic culture of ethnic San Francisco. The grief of this loss was mixed with strong feelings of helplessness at the consolidation processes used to decide the fate of their parish church and school. That Catholic neighborhood turf so dear to the enclaves of immigrants from the last era also died with the consolidations. These included language, social life, devotions, and roles of clerical authority and influence. The loss of the former pastor's paternal Italian leadership style and the "encultured" devotional life of their remaining Catholic sodalities were terrifying for many.

Another loss resulted from the changes to the structure of the local community—those who left in protest or fell away in the process of decision making. Staff from the amalgamated St. Anthony-Immaculate Con-

---

[38] Pick, "Resurrection," 27.

[39] Nathan D. Mitchell, "What's Next in the Catholic Liturgical Movement?" part 3, "The Loss of Catholic Culture," *Rite* 32, no. 4 (May–June 2001) 5.

ception parish school from the San Francisco setting approximated the loss of one hundred fifty families in the first three years of the consolidation. Staff from what became the parish of St. Benedict the African West in Chicago noted the loss of about one-third of those parishioners who had regularly attended Sunday Eucharist at one of the three consolidating parishes. Those who remained behind indicated deep feelings of grief at the permanent absence in the Sunday eucharistic assembly of friends, neighbors, and family members.

A conversation with the group of senior parishioners from Englewood's former St. Carthage parish revealed an additional nuance of loss overlooked in both the Chicago and San Francisco processes—the dead. Every parish keeps a written record of the funerals in a "Book of Interments" that is part of normal bookkeeping. Some use these ledgers in rituals around All Souls' Day or other annual celebrations of remembrance of those buried from the parish church. For a consolidated parish this is of even more importance. The list of ancestors increases significantly. One of the only men in the group spoke of a desire to see more names of parishioners remembered on the walls of the new church building. Others in the group mentioned that it had been done in the ritual of dedication with the large new cornerstone containing lists of names from the consolidated churches. But his struggle to articulate the remaining absence said that the ritual was somehow not adequate.

The closing of Chicago's St. Carthage attempted to integrate the history of the Catholic presence in that neighborhood. Their closing Eucharist included a procession with remembrances and artifacts selected to be taken to the new building at St. Benedict the African East. Their closing administrator had been a mother and former school parent after the withdrawal of the religious community who had oversight for the parish. She planned and assumed a very prominent place in the closing rites, despite the celebrant being a local auxiliary bishop who had likewise grown up in the parish. Some, however, expressed a feeling of violation and powerless as the diocesan officials pulled up in trucks the week after the closure to collect the pews, art, and other religious artifacts: "The building was to be used for a good purpose. The archdiocese took everything related to worship and stripped it to an empty shell. When I moved in, there was nothing . . . the Archdiocese moved so quickly after the final Eucharist and stripped everything from the building."[40]

---

[40] Maureen [pseudonym], interview by author, Chicago, Ill., December 14, 2000.

The preconciliar ritual for parish closure had made the process of dismantling a part of the rite. Most of those interviewed would have appreciated the opportunity. There is something healing to tasks like the cleaning and disposition of goods for a deceased family member. Both Chicago and San Francisco archdiocesan officials seemed to mistrust parishioners taking part in this for fear that things of value would disappear. Yet the disappearance of artifacts into the homes of former parishioners could have been the more effective way of making memorial.

The death of the parish as mentioned above likewise includes the dead buried from that worship site. The usual transfer of records to a neighboring parish does not acknowledge these records adequately. Those lives and families—memorialized in the windows, statuary and furnishings—become almost "disappeared," using a familiar term from the great human rights tragedies of the last decade. Their names are no longer memorialized. Closing ritual needs to call out these names once again and consign the parish itself to the care of these saints. This takes time. As the windows and statuary are dismantled or sold, some receptacle needed to be created for their benefactors. It would be impossible to ever completely remember those whose sacrifice crafted a church building. Still, there is a need to remember the people and stories of that generation passing away. Ritual needs to remember the narrative and say goodbye to the building that housed it.

The funeral model for the closing of a parish was suggested by many of those involved in the San Francisco and Chicago consolidation as the most appropriate way to bring closure to a parish history. More will be said about this in the coming chapter. But like a funeral, the final act of the life of a local church needs to be performed with the assistance of those who actually worshiped there. Creating the ritual for leave taking that makes effective memorial ensures the artifacts and memories anchored to them are bid a fond farewell and handled with the appropriate reverence.

A funeral usually concludes in the committal of a body to a place, and with the burial a need to make memorial. One parish staff crafted a "name signing ritual" for the floor of the receiving church to transfer the names of the dead from the former parish to the new worship site. After a festive parish potluck a few days before the inaugural liturgy of their newly consolidated parish the carpet was rolled back. The gathered parishioners were invited to write the names of all the families—and especially those not present—with magic markers on the cement floor of the church. After the ceremony, the staff recovered it with its carpet. In his opening homily at the inaugural Eucharist, the bishop referred to the ritual and reminded them that no one was a visitor to the space, they were part of the foundation on which the church was built as well as the kingdom of God.[41]

Annual cycles of remembrance have a particular comfort for consolidating communities. One staff included prayer for the dead at each meeting of the combined parish council for over a year after the completion of the process. Memorials of families whose names adorned the windows and statuary of the former worship site needed somehow to be included in the new structure. The rituals of the All Saints-All Souls cycle in November can be a further opportunity to attend to that ongoing need for transferring families to remember their heroes and dead. An Orthodox bishop closed a Pennsylvania parish of nearly a century of service with a series of rituals. After transferring its bells to another nearby parish, consuming the reserved sacrament, and taking formal possession of the relics and chrism, he celebrated a Requiem Mass for the dead of that place.

Pre-Vatican II liturgical texts for church closure suggested the option of fixing a permanent cross somewhere on the building to recall its once sacred character. This custom is worth revisiting. A permanent plaque on the entrance to a new worship site with the names and founding dates of the consolidated churches is a way of ensuring a place in the collective memory of future generations of Catholics. If the site is to be demolished, a nearby building might make room for a memorial plaque to be dedicated as part of the closure rites. One parish made panels from the stained glass windows for the homes of all registered parishioners as the church closed. The bell tower of St. John the Baptist in Cincinnati's "Over the Rhine" district was included in the new structure built over the former parish plant. Former parishioners noted that it made the translation of the parish to nearby St. Francis Seraph a little easier. Together with the closing Eucharist and sealing of the church doors, the story of St. John the Baptist came to an end, and their new story began.

Interviewees often made reference to the need for a place to gather, a shrine for ongoing remembrance, and a point of reference for anniversaries. Such a place could likewise serve as a locus of prayer for those, who, for whatever reason, were not able to participate in the rituals that closed a parish's history. Many of the people interviewed spoke of a need for some kind of permanent memorial to the closed building and its people. Several options for this emerged. The receiving parish can dedicate a new

---

[41] David G. Caron, "Information Packet on Parish Closings" (Miami, Fla., 1999) 4.

foundation stone and/or prominent plaque near its entrance to highlight the beginning of its new identity as a consolidated community.

The Rite of Reception and Memorial of the Closed Parish with a Blessing of the Foundation Stone in appendix 5.1, designed for a receiving parish consolidation, makes tribute to the former church and rededication of the foundation a focus of reception for the new reconfigured parish. One parish could not find a place near the closed site, so it placed a memorial in the local Catholic cemetery using some of the statuary from the former church. In Chicago, St. Benedict the African East designed a prominent cornerstone for its new parish church with the names of the five closed parishes near the church entrance. To walk into the parish church is to walk through the memories of the former parishes in that area.

The collective experience and the histories of the families and communities that established those original parishes, when spoken again and honored as sacred narrative, set its progeny free to start again. Commemorations from holy cards to fine art pieces of marble and bronze can redeem the struggles and turf battles, the rage and grief that often marked the process of decision making that closed these parishes. Chapels and meeting rooms dedicated to the closed parish structures amplify the sense of welcome. A synthesized parish calendar that includes pertinent dates from a predecessor's annual rhythm of remembrance continues to honor the legacy of its benefactors and saints. These symbols function best when they embrace as expansive a memory as possible of a local church's combined narratives.

Reconciliation of Dedicated Space: The Good of Souls

The area of *conflict turned to hate* evoked a particular brand of powerlessness in the processes of consolidation for this study. Participants from both the San Francisco and Englewood consolidations spoke of being shaken by conflicted situations between staff and leadership that became hateful. One interviewee made reference to the pastor—who facilitated her consolidation—subsequently becoming "the enemy." She felt compelled to organize others to unseat him by almost any means. Staff members, even members of religious communities, spoke of competitive feelings of envy and suspicion bordering on hatred for those who previously were friends or colleagues. In parish consolidations in this country, it has not been uncommon for the agents of these changes to receive threats of violence.[42]

> [I]t was creating a problem with people I had known since they were in diapers. People thought we had sold our souls to the devil because we were starting to see it Father [X's] way. There are some people who still kind of look at us with the evil eye, who think we betrayed them because we stuck it out.[43]

People in both locales mentioned this dynamic in the interactions of staff, clergy, religious, and lay leadership. When conflict turned to hate, people began to speak of the experience of powerlessness and scandal. Another staff member mentioned the sense of helplessness that overwhelmed even the attempts at professional conciliation:

> The rivalry and competition . . . had some deep roots in the community's history . . . It was a win/lose attitude for some time in the mentality of those in leadership and the clergy. There is a helplessness one feels in the face of this. Some of the staff called it evil. The story must be redeemed, but the question remained how to do it.[44]

This situation provokes another kind of ritual need: purification and deliverance. People experienced a need for cleansing from the attitudes and the cultural patterns of relating that fragment the sense of the common good.

Current church law gives an additional nuance of meaning to penance in the process of reconciliation. Canons 1211 and 1212 state that dedicated space that has been violated by some scandalous act is restored for worship by a penitential rite. As noted previously, there is some sense that

---

[42] Stanley Hauerwas connects the potential for violence, especially religiously motivated violence, to the need for order. When conflicts arise, the desire to reestablish order is never far behind. Since order is the force in human society that sets boundaries and norms for behavior, a challenge to church can profoundly disorder a community. Attention to order and naming the separating powers is the constant concern of conflict mediation. See Stanley Hauerwas, *The Peaceable Kingdom: Primer in Christian Ethics* (Notre Dame, Ind.: University of Notre Dame Press, 1983) 144, as quoted in Michael H. Crosby, *Do You Love Me?: Jesus Questions the Church* (Maryknoll, N.Y.: Orbis Books, 2000) 172–73.

[43] Frank A. [pseudonym], interview by Dinah P. Shaw, San Francisco, Calif., February 2, 2001.

[44] Eugene [pseudonym], interview by author, Chicago, Ill., February 2, 2001.

the intense conflict around changes to sacred space likewise requires reconciliation.

When church leadership is considered the perpetrator of this violation there is further complication. Perhaps someone else has to act as agent of reconciliation. Whom? Canon 1072 says it is "fitting that a bishop preside at a rite of reparation." This suggests that the ritual agent for reconciliation in the situation of changes to dedicated space is the agent of a parish's dedication in the first place, the local bishop. The San Francisco consolidation saw a great deal of anger laid at the feet of the local ordinary because he was not, in the view of the closing parishes, adequately present.

The staff of the consolidated St. Benedict the African were plagued by ongoing competition and resentment between the East and West Sides of the parish. Associate pastors and staff from each site found it increasingly difficult to work with the structure and with one another. A pastor shared between the two found himself increasingly isolated. One of the local auxiliary bishops was asked to assist, together with professional conciliation. In 1995 the consolidated parish was reduced to two autonomous parishes with the same name. No apparent ritual accompanied the announcement of the change. After more than five years, people from both sites continued to refer to that decision with some regret and confusion.

After the transfer of the consolidating pastor in San Francisco in 1999, those two sites also separated into autonomous communities. Structural and ecclesiological differences left the staff and leadership little energy for pastoral initiative or creativity. The new pastor returned sacramental financial records, although the parish remained canonically a single entity. There was no ritual or formalized announcement of this change. Many of those allied to the consolidation and most active in the years of pastoral planning meetings expressed confusion and anger. Intense conference table processes, and the rites that expressed them, seem to require a reciprocity as well in the processes and rites that un-do them. As with those places too abruptly closed or demolished, this imbalance seemed to leave a sense of violation in its wake.

Changes to sacred space require ongoing pastoral aftercare. Places that had served as a ritual focus of culture and family life continue to evoke ritual imagination. Without followup, the process is not completed, and people are left with wounds that often endure. Many of those interviewed suggested that if the ordinary ritual agent of reconciliation were not available, someone else should be assigned—another bishop, prominent clergy from another denomination, representatives of professional conciliation, or perhaps (gleaning from the early Church's experience) a survivor from another church's attempt at consolidation. By a compassionate sharing of experience and a remembering that God is God—and people are humanly fallible—a space can often be opened for healing memories.

Intense internal church conflict about the future of these places tended to linger in a unique way. The penitential rite for a desecrated building locates the disfigurement caused by any experience of scandal not in buildings but in the assembly, the true temple of God. Rituals need to be designed that address and bring to healing scars of broken trust and reputation: "Let this rite be for us an effective lesson that we must never disfigure the Church, God's dwelling place among us, by our sins. Let this rite be the occasion for our solemn affirmation that we will keep our own hearts as true temples of God."[45]

The healing of memory remains a vital agenda for the restructuring of local church. Often, the lingering memory around previously dedicated or consecrated space reduces the performance power of a bishop's letter of closure. Canon law and the 1977 rites for dedicating a church or an altar no longer use distinctions like "consecration" or "desecration" when it comes to buildings. As long as the memory of sacred rites persists—located in a particular place—that place is still dedicated in the human imagination and hence still vulnerable to scandal in the souls of the faithful.

"The good of souls," alluded to in Canon 1222 §2, offers a new operative criteria to the success of church consolidations and closures for the future. A participant from the San Francisco consolidation spoke of his frustration that those in authority could not embrace the strong feelings of those most affected by their planning decisions. He proposed several ritual structures associated with interpersonal and even sacramental reconciliation: venting, blessing, and laying on of hands:

> We didn't give people the opportunity to vent, be blessed, for a laying on of hands. Perhaps bringing someone in who has the expertise, who has been through this before and make them available to the people. Whoever made the decision, i.e., the Archbishop, should have made an appearance to say that he cared enough about these people and the parish to say "This is what occurred . . . Where were they in the caring of souls?"[46]

---

[45] Thomas G. Simons, *Holy People, Holy Place: Rites for the Church's House* (Chicago: Liturgy Training Publications, 1998) 89.

[46] William B. [pseudonym], interview by Dinah P. Shaw, San Francisco, Calif., January 25, 2001.

Attending to the soul of a parish has multiple levels of meaning in this context. An adequately credible pastoral leader acknowledges change and the initiatives of a community toward that project. He or she traces the boundary of the larger Catholic communion around "the vent" of intense emotions of anger, hurt, and fear. There is a sense of "blessing" when these reactions of a community at great loss are spoken within the context of the larger Christian mission. It helps to locate conflict itself as a sacred space, a place of social transformation. Honest non-manipulative ritual, composed of symbols ample enough to carry the ambiguity of conflictual interactions, is the principal vehicle of this task. It can focus the horizon of a larger purpose and translate even the most traumatic of events into new meanings and significance.

Chapter 5

Pastoral Solutions
Towards New Rituals of Reconciliation at the Closure of Sacred Space

When the [parish] school finally comes together there should be a celebration, perhaps a Mass, native music, festival, something that says: "After a year and a half of hard work, we are going to glorify what we did." The glorification would be a wonderful ritual, and the archbishop could come and say: "You died for us. We know you cried for us for two years. We know that your kids have struggled with this. God bless every one of you. I'm going to do communion and I want every one of you to come. I want to serve you communion as a way to say that we are in communion with one another and in communion with Christ." That never occurred. The work they did was never glorified.[1]

Reconciliation begins in a leap of imagination. This graced and hopeful initiative usually begins on the part of a victim, the one bearing the wound of a particular conflict. It requires people with the ability and willingness to catapult into these often uncharted waters, to dream what healing might look like in a particular wounded situation. The above participant in the San Francisco consolidation constructed a ritual in hindsight. His vision included a rite that was non-manipulative, that highlighted convergences

---

[1] William B. [pseudonym], interview by Dinah P. Shaw, San Francisco, Calif., January 25, 2001.

and digressions, that affirmed a whole Christian solidarity, and that sought to reestablish communion. It called for one of the most basic of human-kind's forgiveness rituals, the meal. Yet, a table with particularly expanded boundaries is imagined here. It permits conflicted parties to sit in safety with one another again. It attempts to draw links from their story to the greater narrative of the life, death, and resurrection of Jesus.

From the correlation of interviews, church tradition, and sociological data of the past decade of parish restructuring, some new patterns and focuses emerge for the U.S. church. Some ritual performances assisted people toward healing and reintegration into new worshiping communities and others did not.

Patricia Kelly has made reference to forgiveness and people's concept of church as integral to the successful revisioning of a local parish: "Lifting up the sense of church after the grief of change, making it more inclusive and universal was a very key element."[2] The interviewees for this study never specifically asked for examples or stories about forgiveness. Still, some beautiful ones emerged in the conversations. They indicated a grace that needs to be highlighted in the rites that serve the reorganization of local church.

Mid-level church leadership in these situations experienced what one of the first moderators of Chicago's Englewood consolidation called, "multiple levels of betrayal." The challenge was to acknowledge each level of a community's wound, to lay hands upon it, and to facilitate words of regret and acceptance. The task at times felt next to impossible:

> A suspicion grew among people that the priest who knows them and loves them might have another agenda. Most of the people are not close to you. Those on the margin can be the most vocal in a time of stress. You become the enemy especially to people on the fringe. The loudest voices are from those at the margins who never come to Mass

---

[2] Patricia Kelly, telephone interview by author, Chicago, Ill., October 16, 2000. Jay Barton of Cincinnati's Management Design Institute gives some further specifics to this ecclesial change. She calls it "an independent model of church." Rather than existing as separate entities, parishes in clustered relationships increasingly depend on one another as far as parish structures, priestly presence, ministerial formation, attitudes toward facilities, and parishioner affiliation. Ultimately this change of ecclesial model focuses on relationship and requires an accountability to others in new ways. The boundaries between parishes come down and are renegotiated in different configurations. See Joy Barton, "Parish Cluster Planning: Laying Deep Foundations" *Church* 10, no. 1 (Spring 1994) 35–37.

except after they hear about a closing. Or people who you thought were on your side blame you as being part of the problem . . . "downtown." There was a general sense of betrayal.[3]

These painful memories that sometimes shattered trust in church structures tended to linger. They often further eroded the privileged relationship between pastor and parishioner, between bishop and presbyter, between local lay and religious leadership. Often these mid-level leaders were mandated to carry out the consolidation of communities, themselves not convinced of the need for it. Memories of betrayal left unattended often get passed on in a popular narrative and are incorporated as a legacy in future storytelling. These stories, once grafted in the collective myth of a local community, are difficult to revise. Healing of memories becomes an ongoing and central pastoral issue of church reorganization.

The Christian ritual tradition is a pastoral repertoire that can be placed at the service of reconciliation in the fiery conflicts sometimes evoked by parochial consolidation and closures. After the conference table rituals of group process, the San Francisco pastoral plan attempted to put the consolidation of its parishes into a single formal ritual at each site. Most of the time it had limited effectiveness. Interviews in both Chicago and San Francisco seemed to highlight the need for a series of ritual moments, each addressing different pastoral needs. Included in these were (1) the consolidation processes themselves, (2) the experiences of parish closure, (3) leave taking of a parish building, (4) inauguration of a newly consolidated parish, and (5) anniversary and ongoing remembrance.[4]

The rites that developed over the centuries to dedicate Christian churches have roots in Eucharistic-, funerary-, exorcistic-, and initiatory-ritual traditions. Since there is no official rite of parish closure, it is noteworthy that most of the ceremonies created for the consolidation of the parishes studied here likewise borrowed from the above four sources. This ensemble of rites did not necessarily eliminate the sting and grief associated with the ending of a local parish community; rather they brought *a perspective of faith* to the experience. These rites served to facilitate the transition to new parish community, often using familiar church ritual in new ways.

---

[3] Fr. Donald G. [pseudonym], interview by author, Chicago, Ill., February 19, 2001.

[4] See Federation of Diocesan Liturgical Commissions, "Rituals for the Closing of a Parish Church," *FDLC Newsletter* 24, no. 5 (January 1998) 49–53.

The Eucharistic Celebration

The most common ritual used in both the San Francisco and Englewood consolidations was the celebration of the Eucharist. In Chicago it defined a place of safety and identity as African-American Catholics. People spoke with great fondness of the "unity Masses" employed in the early days of the Englewood consolidation. The quality of the monthly celebration and the eucharistic communion seemed to trace a boundary within which conflict could be contained.

> The unity Masses were different. We were coming together. Most of us felt good about it. We had unity Masses before we really heard the word merger. Some could see where it was going . . . We got to know one another before we started to fight! The music was important. A committee planned them (pastors, ministers, music coordinators, readers). The youth would often times do the entire Mass. The homily was very important. Sometimes youth would even preach.[5]

When the conversation in the Englewood cluster turned to reducing the number of parish churches, these unity Masses remained a foundation for relationship. They honored and pointed out what unity a fractured local church still had in common and could build upon. The parishes and their leadership knew one another and had a common history of nearly twenty years before considering the possibility of reorganizing their parish structures. This remains a unique feature of the Englewood consolidation.

From the most ancient days of the Church, the primary ritual for dedicating worship space was the Eucharist. The primary minister for dedication was the local bishop. Eucharist was a natural move for the Catholic analogical imagination to close the history of beloved worship spaces. In the settings of most intense conflict, the interviewees noted the call for the presence of the bishop to personally make the announcements of parochial reorganization, to accompany the affected communities through the conflict and grief, and to lead the ritual moments of closure and amalgamation.

The local pastor, moderator, or former pastor was often delegated to this role. In one instance, the presence of the diocesan bishop at the ritual of consolidation caused additional resentment and significantly reduced the efficacy of the consolidation ritual. The use of the media and closed circuit video for the official closure announcements and the delegation to

---

[5] Elizabeth [pseudonym], interview by author, Chicago, Ill., January 18, 2001.

other diocesan officials during the periods of most conflict, made his presiding at the closing Eucharist uncomfortable for many interviewed. The selection of some party to serve as a ritual agent of reconciliation in the situation of conflict around consolidation emerged as a crucial issue. Over and over the local bishop appeared to be the most logical choice. He is the one designated to dedicate a church; hence the one most appropriate to un-dedicate it and attend to the ensuing consequences generated by that event for its people.

The closing liturgies in Englewood were most often Sunday Masses with the best linen, gospel choirs, familiar music repertoire, and preaching. Their purpose, in the words of Fr. David Baldwin, the pastor of St. Benedict the African East, was threefold: "to celebrate what had been, to acknowledge what had happened, and to embrace a future we are going to do."[6] Still many noted the difficulty of sharing Eucharist or even a potluck with church leadership with whom they conflicted in the settings deciding the future of parishes and schools.

The penitential rite at the beginning of Mass took on added significance against the conflict implicit to the processes used for decision making in these locales. The familiar litany, "Lord have mercy," followed by an extended greeting of peace begins every Sunday Eucharist at Englewood's St. Benedict the African East. This ritual legacy of one of the consolidated parishes has continued for more than ten years. "We were an embracing parish," one participant said.[7] A number of those interviewed mentioned that this rite was particularly hospitable and soothing during the time when the five parishes were considering consolidation and the conflict most intense.

The penitential rite of the Eucharist lends itself to public apology. At the final Eucharist of my pastorate of the combined parish in San Francisco, I knelt and asked both communities for forgiveness of any hurts and injustices for which I was responsible. The rite was led, however, by another member of the staff who invited the people to extend their hands toward me and together to pronounce the absolution prayer, normally reserved to the ordained presider, "May Almighty God have mercy on us, forgive us our sins, and bring us to everlasting life." The pastoral agent who facilitates this kind of rite requires a particular credibility. As one well known and accepted among the various conflicting groups of the combined parish she could speak words normally reserved to the ordained. Public

---

[6] Fr. David Baldwin, interview by author, Chicago, Ill., August 27, 2001.

[7] Elizabeth [pseudonym], interview by author, Chicago, Ill., January 18, 2001.

apology in the familiar pattern of Sunday Eucharist took on a particular ritual effectiveness when the one expected to speak the words of absolution surrendered it to another. Many of us, the transitioning pastor, leadership and in the pews, parishioners, experienced a new sense of closure.

The presence of former parishioners, formerly assigned priests, and religious was an important detail in the memories of those who recounted the stories of that time. Intercessions that spoke honest feelings of loss, sadness, hope; gifts that honored the parish's history, brought forward in procession (during the preparation rites); and a festive reception with good food and drink after the liturgy, were details that stayed in memory. Some noted the need to reiterate the reasons for the parish's closure, clearly articulating why the parish was no longer viable on its own. Finally, others spoke of a desire for some kind of memento of the parish's history to take home and pass on to family members who could not attend the closing event.

Having a person or persons delegated to plan the closing ceremonies was another important detail to each setting of the five consolidated East Englewood communities. The planners needed to be local and on site. Some parishioners, for example at St. Carthage, felt the need to honor those who sacrificed to keep the facility open through the trying times of its final years, especially a parishioner who had stepped in as administrator. She planned the closing ceremonies there. Heroes needed to be thanked and benefactors honored, even the names of those inscribed on windows and church furnishings needed to be spoken. The solidarity of diocesan leadership and the presence of the receiving pastor and parish staff were important details to the closing Eucharist. Some mentioned that the presence of those from other neighboring parishes also experiencing closure was particularly supportive. Some sent flowers for the church and served the closing reception as a sign of their solidarity. In short, "doing Church," as one African-American priest called it, was no more crucial than in the midst of closure.

The Order of Christian Funerals

Changes to sacred space imply multiple levels of loss. Staff from the reformed St. Anthony-Immaculate Conception parish school from the San Francisco setting approximated the loss of 150 families in the first three years of the consolidation. Parish staff from what became St. Benedict the African West in Chicago noted the loss of about one-third of those parishioners who had regularly attended Sunday Eucharist at one of the three consolidating parishes. Those who remained behind indicated an additional level of grief because of the permanent absence in the Sunday eucharistic assembly of friends, neighbors, and family members.

Funeral rituals in the context of the truth commission work in South Africa and Central America emerged as one of the most notable resources for individuals, families, and whole church communities coping with the losses of human rights abuses. In the context of closures and consolidations, many of the interviewees mentioned the need to allow people to be sad, to grieve the loss of the sacred spaces, and to have the time to review the memories and histories anchored there. The pattern of the funeral ritual familiar even in its post-Vatican II format was particularly helpful. The connection in the Catholic imagination of building and assembly makes the funeral model an easily accessible resource for coping with the (often multiple) losses associated with a parish closure. Many of the clergy interviewed spoke of "funeral" as the most appropriate vehicle of pastoral care in that context.

The funerary roots of these rituals emerged from ancient Rome. By the early fifth century, cemetery churches were popularized at the tombs of local martyrs. Relics were buried under the altar including pieces of the "true cross," earth from the "Promised Land" (Holy Land) and relics of St. Peter and St. Paul. The cemetery churches became places of popular pilgrimage. The buildings erected to handle the crowds resembled the *mausolea* of Roman burial customs. The first dedication rituals developed to "translate" the relics of the martyrs to the new sites. These included fasting, vigils, procession, Eucharist and feasting.[8] The rituals used to dedicate the church buildings prior to Vatican II had devoted great attention to the translation of the relics of saints to the altar-table. They were solemnly "interred" in the mensa (top slab) of the altar-table, to be honored each time the priest kissed the altar. Postconciliar liturgical catechesis de-emphasized the altar stone with its relic and honored the whole table as symbol of the Lord.[9]

These funerary symbols appeared in the ritual innovations constructed to close local churches. Dominican David Caron's "Information Packet on Parish Closings" and Fr. Thomas Simons' *Holy People, Holy Place: Rites for the Church's House* collected rituals from diocesan and parish liturgy

[8] Ibid., 18.

[9] See the "General Instruction of the Roman Missal," §§295–307, the *Ceremonial of Bishops*, §48., and *Art and Environment in Catholic Worship*, §§71–73 in *The Liturgy Documents: A Parish Resource*, vol. 1 (Chicago: Liturgy Training Publications, 1991).

committees throughout the country. The rites tended to separate the closing of the parish and the leave taking from the building, as one separates the Mass of Christian burial from final committal.

Sr. Rita Fisher's 1996 article proposed ritual stations as a way of accompanying grief at parish closures. Her "Procession for Remembering" has multiple resonances of funeral ritual. She suggests a procession to the major stations of a church: the font, the reconciliation chapel, shrine areas, the ambo, and the altar to tell stories. The chanting of Psalm 90 accompanies the movement from place to place in the church. At the altar, the presider recalls the principal moments of the liturgical year and that the assembly of disciples is more than the buildings that house them:

> Let us remember the times we have gathered for the sacred banquet of the Triduum kept each year, the Sundays on which we worshiped faithfully, the first communion celebrations, the feast days of saints and martyrs, the weddings witnessed here, the funerals held here in hope. Let us pray. God our refuge, our home is in you. You are greater than any temple, church or cathedral that can be built by human hands, yet in this place we have met your divine majesty. This church building has been a place of blessing for us. Protect us on our way. Lead us to new friends in another faith community. We ask this through Christ our Lord.[10]

Participants, some chosen in advance of the service, were invited to share stories of the parish's history at each station. Fisher notes a fear that the stories could go on for long periods of time and make the ritual tedious. This fear of extended storytelling needs to be attended carefully. Grieving can not often be fitted into ritual time frames.

At the closure of St. Vitus' parish in Chicago, the Hispanic community suggested an all-night vigil the night before the final Eucharist. From this cultural context, vigil has two nuances of meaning: the waiting at the bedside of a dying loved one and the velorio or wake associated to a funeral. One liturgy could not provide adequate time to do this. Safe spaces are needed, abundant enough for the kind of repetitive storytelling that serves grief. As a final moment of leave taking, all present at St. Vitus were invited to a ritual gesture of kissing the altar. This familiar gesture, usually reserved to an ordained presider, has resonances to deep friendship and the respect reserved for elders. It is a way to honor the funerals, weddings, communions,

---

[10] Rita Fisher, I.H.M., "The Grace of This Place: Closing a Church," *Liturgy 90* 27, no. 2 (February–March 1996) 11.

and confirmations that have been located at the eucharistic table, in one tactile and tender ritual moment. This gesture at the end of a closing liturgy brings a particularly soothing and effective leave taking for a beloved worship space.[11] The parish then took their major icon, the Guadalupe, and marched as a group in a procession to St. Adalbert's for the inaugurating Sunday Eucharist.

Other parishes devised ceremonies of taking possession of the relics and processing with them to the receiving parish, to some place of honor, perhaps under the altar where the revised rite prescribes the interment or burial of a parish's relics. A sad, yet familiar image in church basements and storerooms is a stack of dust covered altar stones. The burial of these in the receiving building for a newly configured community could be a way of extending the "funeral rites" to the losses associated with that restructuring.

Numerous parish leaders made reference to the violence done to people by pastoral ministers trying to take the mood of a closing parish liturgy too quickly to thanksgiving. People need to grieve, weep, and say good-bye:

> The best ritual for closing is not a procession with the Eucharist from the closed parish to the receiving parish. This gives the impression that God has left the one building. The best way to ritualize is an Irish funeral. There is tremendous loss. Don't celebrate, "ain't this a wonderful thing?" Most of Englewood had been through four consolidations. Redoing it over and over had no point. Rather gather the people and grieve with tears, honest ritual, and acknowledgement. Powerlessness . . . so much of this is out of our hands. Not telling people they should feel good—rather the ritual needs to convey hope for the future. Then gradually, with lavish time, reform a community.[12]

Without an eventual movement from the emotions connected with grief to thanksgiving, the ritual process remains incomplete. The above pastor's observation that forcing a mood of celebration before the body and human spirit "gets there" is the greatest imposition, not to mention poor pastoral care. The translation of the Eucharist from the Mass of the Lord's

[11] Fr. Michael Bertram, O.F.M., Cap. of St. Mary Magdalen Parish in Hazel Park, Michigan, a suburb of Detroit, used this action as the final departure ritual from a space that was about to be renovated in the mid-nineties. The people kissed the altar with the priest then processed to the parish gymnasium where liturgies would be celebrated until the church's renovation was completed. The procession included the baptismal font, the reserved Eucharist and the vesture from the altar.

[12] Fr. Tom [pseudonym], interview by author, Chicago, Ill., February 21, 2001.

Supper in the Triduum was an adequately familiar rite to be brought to bear in the closure of a worship site. But it requires particular care so as not to suggest the abandonment of God's presence to a place, rather it is the accompaniment of God's presence to a people on pilgrimage.

The funeral pattern—with its vesture, tone, and stations from place of death to rites of vigil, funeral liturgy, and committal—was employed by various groups composing rituals for the waves of diocesan closures in the eighties and nineties. The Diocese of Harrisburg, Pennsylvania, for example, developed some rituals of transition in the face of a number of closures and consolidations in 1995. They employed a format that stretched through a final week of events before a church was closed. These included evenings of prayer around the paschal candle, with the formal storytelling such as would be done at a wake.

One night was given to the retelling of the parish history done with parish sacramental registers including those of baptism, confirmation and First Eucharist. One night's vigil would be particularly focused on the dead buried over the years of the parish's history with a focus on the interment register and more storytelling by the parish's elders. A final suggestion involved Benediction of the Blessed Sacrament and/or a celebration in honor of Mary or the parish's patron saint. Maintaining an open church building for the week before closing facilitated as much visitation as possible, time to savor the beauty, images, and atmosphere of a sacred place.[13]

After a tragic fire in 1991, Bishop Timothy Lyne presided over the closing Eucharist of St. Sebastian Church of the near North Side of Chicago. The rituals employed presented several other symbolic moments that have funeral nuances: the blessing at the doors, the procession behind the cross and intercession for the grieving family. After formally announcing, in the name of Cardinal Bernardin, the closure of the 78-year-old parish, the church doors were ritually closed and two parishioners sealed them with a purple ribbon.[14]

A procession formed from the burnt-out building to the nearby school auditorium for the final Eucharist. At the end of the procession the pastor carried a simple cross that had ornamented the church entrance. A crown

---

[13] Thomas G. Simons, *Holy People, Holy Place: Rites for the Church's House* (Chicago: Liturgy Training Publications, 1998) 102–3.

[14] William McManus, "A Funeral for a Parish," *Liturgy 90* 22, no. 2 (February–March 1991) 6–7. Simons notes that by the end of the fifth century the church doors became one of the principal symbols of the dedication rite. Church dedications from Spain and Gaul adapted the custom from Constantinople of anointing with chrism the tomb of the relics, and the altar, doors and walls of the building. *Holy People, Holy Place*, 18.

of thorns was its only ornamentation for this liturgy. In the penitential rite, special petitions were read that asked God's healing for the bitterness and frustration during the meetings, marches, and demonstrations held in the hopes of saving their parish. A festive *Gloria* followed "to shift its (the people's) mood from sorrow and regret to joy and hope."[15]

In the San Francisco consolidation, the parish's changed status was solemnly proclaimed by the local bishop at the beginning of the liturgy. But a single ritual gesture did not have the performative power to shift the people's mood at the decisions made by the diocesan pastoral planning process. A series of rituals would have better accompanied the people's gradual adaptation to the loss of their church's identity and autonomy.

The rite at St. Sebastian continued with the blessing of water in the baptismal font that had been saved from the fire. The pastor invited parishioners to dip their hands in it, to bless themselves, and to profess their continued faith in Jesus Christ and the Gospel. During the liturgy's concluding rites, the pastor led a litany of farewell that employed funeral metaphors and patterns with resonances of a funeral's final commendation:

> Leader: Whenever we eat this Eucharistic bread and wine, we proclaim the Lord's death until he comes.
>
> Pastor: Whatever table we gather around, may we be reminded of the love we have shared around this one.
>
> Leader: The grass withers, the flower fades, but the Word of our God will stand forever.
>
> Pastor: May we always be open to God's word; it challenges us to justice and comforts us with hope.
>
> Leader: [Holding the paschal candle] Jesus said, "I am the light of the world."
>
> Pastor: May we share the light of our faith with our new parishes. You are a chosen race, a royal priesthood, a holy nation, God's own people.

The bishop then repeated the official proclamation that began the liturgy; "With thanks to God for the good accomplished here, this parish of St. Sebastian is now closed."[16]

---

[15] Ibid., 105.

[16] McManus," A Funeral for a Parish," 7. Scriptural translation of John 8:12 and 1 Cor 11:26 taken from the parish's account of the day.

It is difficult to attain a sense of closure when conflict is still unresolved. The consolidation in Wheeling, West Virginia had attended in a different way to one parish that remained particularly defiant and conflicted during the processes of planning. Their transition team used a closing ceremony even more modeled on the funeral rite. The mourning tone was expressed in the black printing of the worship aid and in black drapes over some parts of the building—with some hints of green and white as signs of rebirth and hope. The celebrant wore old black funeral vestments. The funeral bell tolled at the moment of suppression, and symbols of the parish (icon of the parish's patron saint, keys, and sacramental registers) were transferred to the protection of St. Joseph, the patron of the new parish. The black vestments then were exchanged for white ones in honor of the new patron.[17]

Rituals taken from the funeral repertoire in no way reduce the pain or sense of loss at a consolidation. Their purpose is to confront and express it, to bring a perspective of faith to the experience of bereavement and provide pointers toward "a new state of healthy living" in the absence of what was lost.[18] These rituals help people move through grief rather than being mired in it. Once the buildings are really closed, the task of community building and memory building can proceed. Thanksgiving can often emerge when the loss is spoken and the stages of grieving are consigned to history.

Rage, Loss, and Lamentation

Another ritual resource to parochial closure is lamentation. It falls also within the funerary resources of dedication rites, but it has some elements particular to itself. Processions, the celebration of stations, and rituals modeled on the pattern of the lament psalms can be a valuable resource for the deep emotions stirred by changes to local church.

Fr. Steve Dunn from the Archdiocese of Milwaukee crafted "A Psalm for Healing When a Parish Changes or Closes" on the verses of Psalm 137 with its familiar

> By the rivers of Babylon
>   we sat down and there we wept
>   when we remembered Zion.
>   (v. 1; NRSV)

[17] Dorsch,"Rituals of Consolidation," 32.
[18] Margaret Smith, *Facing Death Together: Parish Funerals* (Chicago: Liturgy Training Publications, 1998) 24.

Psalm 137 exemplifies a second resonance in the lament literature that speaks to the deep feelings associated with changes to sacred space, the destruction of the Jerusalem Temple.[19] Dunn asks a series of questions articulating the losses, feelings at the time of church closure, together with opportunities and possibilities for a restored future worship. See appendix 6.1 for the complete text of his prayer service.

Simons, in his commentary on the rites of dedication, suggests Jerusalem's "Western Wall" (in the past, often called the "Wailing Wall") as another poignant monument connecting lamentation to the loss of sacred space.[20] The rebuilt Temple, destroyed finally in 70 C.E. at the hands of the Roman military, left behind this precious relic of a secure and even triumphant era of Hebrew history. Perhaps something analogous to the Wall—a designated place of lament—could be used in a faith-filled ritual that would facilitate, in a non-verbal forum, an expression of what is lost and remembered as parish churches close.

The closure of Catholic churches in urban neighborhoods marked the end of a triumphal era for American Catholicism. A unique and heroic expression of church that emerged from the combined cultural ethos of European Catholic immigrants passed as their descendants moved into the American mainstream. New expressions were only beginning to take shape. As these venerable institutions declined, additional senses of failure and loss were reflected in the struggle to craft other forms of Catholic neighborhood presence. Those who remained behind wrestled with how to speak a faith that God's presence had not abandoned its sanctuary among the people. New communities sought to articulate a vibrant expression of Catholicism from a different cultural ethos than the one reflected in the architecture that now housed them.

The celebration of the "Stations (or Way) of the Cross" was a familiar devotion of the Euro-American immigrant church. Schreiter proposes another nuance of meaning to "stations" as a ritual way of coming to terms with individual and collective memory. They are points of orientation, safe places where one is not drowned or overwhelmed by memories but carried and shaped by them. The Passion narratives of the Gospel function in this way. By naming and highlighting moments along the road of Jesus's suffering, the story takes on a new dimension of meaning. The arrangement and focus depends on the context of the remembering community: i.e., the Last Supper, the agony in the garden, the arrest and trial,

---

[19] Ibid.

[20] Simons, *Holy People, Holy Place*, 16–17.

the torture and humiliation, the death on the cross, etc.[21] The ritual movement from station to station, for the purpose of naming oppression and grieving loss, is a time-honored devotional use of the lament pattern. The funeral liturgy in its movement from station to station exemplifies this. The rite functions as a metaphor of the Christian pilgrimage naming stages of assent to the heavenly Jerusalem.[22]

Many of the Englewood interviewees referred to a funeral ritual that modeled this notion of lament in a powerful way. Fr. Ron Kondziolka, the former pastor of St. Brendan's, led his parishioners in a mock funeral after hearing about the proposed closure of his parish school. He illustrated another aspect of lament-protest. "It seemed fitting, because closing the school felt like a death," he said in an interview with *The Reader*, a local Chicago newspaper. A neighborhood funeral director donated a coffin, which was packed with mementos. The funeral service took place at the closing parish, and a procession of 76 cars conducted the coffin to a local cemetery, "no mean feat since it was tricky to secure a city permit to block traffic for a body-less cortege." At the cemetery, a trumpeter sounded taps, and someone laid a memorial to the school on the cemetery grounds.[23] Despite the almost cynical tone of the rite, it allowed people to express feelings about the closure no other official liturgy evoked. Many followed him the next day to walk in protest in front of the archbishop's residence.

The pattern of the lament psalm, as noted previously, has rich ritual potential for those beginning to cope with a loss or change like the consolidation of parish church. Arbuckle originally published a rite of group grieving, to assist religious communities who were at an impasse in the processes of chapter or strategic planning. Lament functions in what he

[21] Robert Schreiter makes reference to this notion of stations in *Working for Reconciliation: A Caritas Handbook* (Vatican City: Caritas Internationalis, 2003). Further reflection needs to follow the ritual development of this in Roman Catholic devotions and popular religiosity, especially as it might apply to those struggling with traumatic memories. Lewis Smedes refers to stations as "guideposts," a slightly different take on this notion. He lists them as estrangement, forgiveness, reconciliation, and hope. See Louis B. Smedes, "Stations on the Journey from Forgiveness to Hope," *Dimensions of Forgiveness: Psychological Research and Theological Perspectives*, ed. Everett L. Worthington, Jr. (Philadelphia: Templeton Foundation Press, 1998) 341–43.

[22] The general introduction to the 1989 *Order of Christian Funerals* speaks of procession as a way to strengthen the bond of community in the assembly. Settings of these psalms that are responsorial or litany in style allow the people to respond to the verses with an invariable refrain. National Conference of Catholic Bishops, *Order of Christian Funerals* (New York: Catholic Book Publishing, 1998) 11. See also J. Frank Henderson, *Liturgies of Lament* (Chicago: Liturgy Training Publications, 1994) 19–20.

[23] Grant Pick, "Resurrection," *The Reader* (Chicago), sec. 1, August 9, 1991.

calls a "loss/newness paradigm" and attempts to accompany a collective "letting go" to new insight and new configuration of relationship. It begins with the gathering of a community about a paschal candle in a darkened worship space. A proclamation of one of the lament psalms (especially one connected to the longing for the restored Temple) is followed by meditative silence and the naming of the loss or woe. At the conclusion, the leader invites participants to name a newness or joy that has entered the group's awareness or ministry with the relighting of the extinguished candles.[24] An adaptation of this more specifically to the situation of parish restructuring is found in appendix 1.1.

The articulation of deep anger and powerlessness in a ritual context can serve to cleanse strong negative emotions and facilitate healing for a local church.[25] Specific rituals of rage, like those of lamentation, underscore the need to integrate deep emotions in the context of prayer. There is an authenticity about ritual when it speaks the flesh and blood emotions of real people. It ultimately serves as an expression of deep faith, of a human spirit that can defy the odds and claim the possibility of new life from the ashes of lethal situations.[26] Finally, this ritual testifies that emoting is only half the story; the other half involves action to effect a shift in balance so that a new sense of justice can emerge.

---

[24] Gerald A. Arbuckle, S.M., *Refounding the Church: Dissent for Leadership* (Mary-knoll, N.Y.: Orbis Books, 1993) 197–98. See also Doris Donnelly, "Binding Up Wounds in a Healing Community," *Repentance and Reconciliation in the Church,* ed. Michael J. Henchal (Collegeville, Minn.: Liturgical Press, 1987) 11–31. She adds two other very creative liturgies in this same vein, a ritual of rage and a ritual of unbinding.

—A community gathers because of a common hurt—a citywide vote against providing shelter for the homeless or an injustice done to an individual.

—A representative of the group (the leader) articulates the focus of the rage. The assembly gives its assent.

—Readings from Scripture (Isaiah or Jeremiah, perhaps) or a more contemporary reading (from Martin Luther King, Jr., or Dorothy Day) are offered for focus and reflection.

—The words are juxtaposed with the particular rage expressed by the group in a carefully crafted homily.

—Prayers are offered that destructive energy be transformed into creative energy and that peace replace feelings of hostility.

—Petitions offered from the group should include prayers for wisdom, strength, forbearance, and yielding.

—A resolution to take action to correct the injustice and the cause of the rage concludes the ritual.

[25] Donnelly, 23.

[26] Ibid.

The challenge to name and ritualize the transition of worship space has confronted the Judeo-Christian community throughout its history. Articulating this in a ritual of parochial closure has a strength of solidarity about it. It testifies that liminal waiting in the loss, in honest lament, has transformative power. New identity and a renewed sense of power emerge with the acknowledgement of God's heavenly sanctuary that needs no space created for it. It occupies all space, most especially the reconciled space between human beings.[27]

Rites for Dedication of a Church and an Altar

In the absence of official closure rites for a parish church, parochial staffs, diocesan liturgical offices, and consultants over the last decade have crafted some very creative ritual processes. Some of these have been very helpful in walking people through the loss and hurt. Others appear a bit naive about their performance power. Criteria for effectiveness appears to be evolving through trial and error. *Environment and Art in Catholic Worship* (1978) defined liturgical appropriateness in relation to art as the ability (1) to bear the weight of mystery, awe, reverence and wonder—a transparency to that which is beyond it and (2) to clearly serve and not interrupt liturgical action which has its own structure, rhythm, and movement.[28]

A recent article in a diocesan newspaper related how a newly consolidating parish used the Easter candle as the focal point of their consolidation ritual. Neither of the consolidating parishes lit new paschal candles at their Easter vigil. They continued to use old ones from the previous year. During the closing service of the parish's first potluck, a new paschal

---

[27] Reflecting on the work of Catherine Pickstock, Nathan Mitchell develops the notion of the "preoccupation of sacred space," in a recent reflection on liturgical time. "[T]ime is God taking possession of the world as its freedom and future; time is God literally 'pre-occupying' our world and its history, filling them with divine presence and action even before we have a chance to contemplate or control the 'course of human events.'" Nathan D. Mitchell, "Year of Grace," *Assembly* 28, no. 1 (January 2002) 1. In other words, worship space is a location which worshipers occupy with a God who has pre-occupied it. Fr. Aiden Kavanagh notes that liturgical worship happens in space, "shaped into place by the meaning people discover within it." Religious people have shaped space with the discovery that the Creator abides throughout creation. Liturgical space belongs to the assembly only in the discovery that the space it occupies is God's first, and it is transformed for people by grace, faith, and sacrament. Aiden Kavanagh, O.S.B., *Elements of Rite* (Collegeville, Minn.: Liturgical Press, 1982) 14–15.

[28] *Environment and Art in Catholic Worship*, in *The Liturgy Documents*, vol. 1, 322.

candle was blessed. Parishioners lit small candles from its light until a darkened room was full of candlelight. The pastor sent out the people from the event with the charge, "Go, be a new church."[29]

One could question the choice of candle stubs to bear the weight of the resurrection mystery and whether an interruption of the initiation rites of the great Easter Vigil best serves to symbolize a new parish's history and identity. The consolidation of the two parishes, announced before those parish communities had shared a meal together, seems a bit out of sync. The decision to merge two communities is a tremendous one. If those involved had not participated in the decision, there would most likely be resistance. The injunction, "Go be a new church," would appear a bit dishonest if it had not first walked through any grief and resistance. The task of accompaniment demands additional ritual literacy, especially in the face of intense conflict. The above parish likewise included a fish fry and a talent comedy show in the rhythm of events marking the consolidation. Sometimes the rites outside of church have the ability to carry more of the weight of ambivalent emotions.

As mentioned previously, the rites to dedicate a church, developed over the centuries, have roots in funerary, exorcistic, and initiatory rituals. The 1977 revision of the rituals from the Rite of Dedication of a Church and an Altar significantly reduced the historical accretions to these rituals, leaned them more toward Christian initiation and "the full, conscious, and active" participation of the congregation at the core of Vatican II liturgical reform.[30] The rituals from this rite serve as additional resources to accompany the stages of grief to acceptance and finally, consent (or perhaps through the threshold phases of van Gennep's rites of passage-separation, liminality, and reaggregation). When they do, they serve reconciliation. They leave people with the freedom to reframe perspective and reengage with the local church. Finally if rejoining the newly configured parish is not possible, the rituals allow people to "move on," to join a parish experience in another location.

The rituals employed in the dedication of the majority of parish churches of more than a hundred years old (those of the past immigrant period) were intricate and solemn. Simons notes that according to an 1888 Roman Pontifical, the rites chanted or spoken in Latin from this era were so tedious and of such complexity that few understood them. People

---

[29] Scott A. McConinaha, "Parish Merger Event Features Comedy, Fried Fish," *Catholic Herald* (Milwaukee) June 7, 2001.

[30] Simons, *Holy People, Holy Place*, 20–21.

watched passively or were not even admitted until most of the rite was completed. This rite absorbed such a great amount of time, that after three or four hours, the presiding bishop often retired, exhausted. The rubrics even gave the bishop leave to delegate another priest to actually preside at the first solemn Eucharist in the new space.[31] This rigorous solemnity might still be required to take leave of a church building.

The current rite of dedication places its emphasis more on the members of the assembly than on the building. With their bishop, they incense, bless with holy water, anoint the church's walls and dress the altar, and finally, everything readied, they celebrate the Eucharist there for the first time. This ritual pattern (although not a familiar one to most) lends itself to the leave taking required when closing a worship space. None of those who closed a parish (an average of a century later), were present for the rites that dedicated them. Still, this ritual pattern provides an opportunity to highlight a liminal moment with rich post-Vatican II ecclesiology:

OUTLINE OF 1977 REVISED RITE OF
DEDICATION OF A CHURCH AND AN ALTAR
(and the 1978 English language translation)

- Preparing to celebrate the rite
- Entrance into the church
- Blessing and sprinkling with holy water
- Gloria / opening prayer
- Liturgy of the Word / dedication of the place for the word
- Litany of the saints
- Deposition of relics
- Prayer of dedication
- Anointing of the altar and walls
- Incensation of altar and church
- Illumination of altar and church
- Closing the altar / preparation of gifts
- Eucharist (special preface)
- Inauguration of the Blessed Sacrament chapel
- Concluding rite[32]

---

[31] Ibid., 22. See also Ignazio M. Calabuig, O.S.M., *The Dedication of a Church and an Altar: A Theological Commentary* (Washington, D.C.: United States Catholic Conference, 1980) 33.

[32] Ibid., 158. Additional commentary on the Rites of Dedication of a Church can be found in J. D. Crichton, *The Dedication of a Church: A Commentary* (Dublin: Veritas Publications, 1980).

Adaptations of this ritual pattern and its principal symbols have appeared in many of the rites designed by closing communities in recent years. The current rite is ample enough to hold ambivalent emotions and serve reconciliation as it has been defined above. This often means a movement "backwards" through the principal symbols of the building, recalling its founding narratives against the great story: the paschal mystery.

Orders of service collected from various closings employed in recent years seemed to highlight specific ritual stations for remembering a church's history—places in the building or around it where devotions and family legacies were anchored. Some were preconciliar, like small, unlighted confessionals or the communion rail. Others were items that evoked precious memories of marriages and funerals. Many expressed the need for ample time to attend to such things as the shrines of saints or the front doors— to even have separate rites for this kind of farewell and honoring, aside from a eucharistic celebration. Evening Liturgies of the Word or familiar devotions to Mary and other saints provided opportunities to linger at places of most tender memory. Their tone was often mellow and solemn, as would be the sharing of memories between grieving family members. What emerged was not a chronological series of steps, but moments of safety and focus. They were best attended with a *kairos* sense of time as they emerged from conversation and solitude in the weeks prior to leaving a cherished worship space. Liturgical catechesis could most likely enrich and heighten the symbols and patterns of the ritualizing. One parish setting experimented with short four-minute catechetical teachings at the end of the Sunday Eucharist to highlight elements of the liturgy as preparation for constructing a new church building.

The literature and interviews about other recent parish closures indicate that the following emerged as the principal stations or symbolic moments to be attended by the rituals and the pastoral care of leaders. These have resonances in both pre- and post-dedication liturgies and have not emerged in any order of preference.

(1) The Reserved Sacrament

The tabernacle, despite controversies over its place in contemporary ecclesial architecture, still holds a prominent place in defining the space of U.S. Catholic worship. The ritual of translation of the Eucharist from the Mass of the Lord's Supper in the Triduum was a familiar rite adapted by parish and diocesan liturgy teams for the rituals of church closure, most particularly for the rite of leave taking from a church building. A procession

—with the Eucharist and its sanctuary lamp, together with other prominent symbols of a worship space (processional cross, paschal candle, oils and even the font itself)—to the receiving church has served as a final act of leave taking for many closing parishes.[33]

(2) "The Relics" and the Patron Saint of the Parish

In the past, the relics enshrined in the Church were removed with a public and solemn ceremony if a church closed. The removal of relics with some ceremony still captures the imagination. The passing of the altar stone to diocesan officials for the use of a future new church of a diocese could be another way of symbolizing continuity of the legacy of a parish's worship. The "relics of a church" can be a larger category than just the relic(s) of a saint. In addition to the altar stone itself, gifts of furnishings, stained glass windows, vesture, bells, and even machinery like heating and sound systems often times have a story. Transition rituals need to give people an opportunity and adequate time to tell these stories. Objects of value need to be collected and perhaps boxed for storage. Some can be given away and others passed to new churches. The participation of as many parishioners as possible (those in transition) can be a healing and tender way for them to take leave of their past place of worship. The passing over of the keys, registry books and the principal icon of the patron saint to the receiving parish was often accompanied with traditional hymns, orations and storytelling.[34]

(3) Icons and Sacred Images

Devotional art and iconography in the church have great ties to the immigrant story of some American Catholic churches. Maximum involvement of parishioners in their future after a decision for closure is of great pastoral value. One parish used a ritualized inventory process to collect its sacred art. This gave as many parishioners as possible a chance to remember the devotions like May Crowning, Our Lady of Perpetual Help, St. Anthony

---

[33] Joseph Wuest's 1959 parochial handbook (also mentioned in chapter 2) suggested that the reduction of a church begins first with the discontinuance of eucharistic reservation, and the collection of the oils and sacred vessels. Rev. Joseph Wuest, C.SS.R., *Matters Liturgical: The Collectio Rerum Liturgicarum* (New York: Frederick Pustet, 1959) 71.

[34] Dorsch, "Rituals of Parish Consolidation," 33–34.

devotions, and the Stations of the Cross. Remembering those who gave the images and articulating gratitude for their value and history has a way of reducing the sense of violation and invasion articulated by some.

(4) The Main Altar

A stripping of the altar (familiar from the Triduum) together with ritual washing can provide a solemn leave-taking event that can involve many people. Ritual leaders of various kinds from the closing parish, such as Eucharistic ministers, could remove the altar linens and then wash the table and pour the water used into the sacrarium. The washing of the symbol of Christ's presence in the assembly has a cleansing, purifying sense about it. Every church has hurtful memories in its past, even skeletons in the closets. This rite could be another opportunity to sing another *Lord, have mercy* or *Kyrie eleison* with incense rising from a brazier on the altar much in the way that it was dedicated. A recalling of those who have received First Communion honors another significant memory connected to parochial life. A reverencing or kissing of the altar by the whole assembly (as does the presider at the beginning and end of every Eucharist) has been received as a powerful rite of leave taking from closed churches.

(5) The Word

A washing of the walls and ambo has been suggested as a way to extend the cleansing of a community's memories. If the church was consecrated, the twelve crosses on the inside walls and the two on the posts of the main entrance could be removed or washed and the water used poured into the sacrarium. A ritual washing of the ambo or podium by lectors or a Bible-study group could be a further opportunity to give thanks for the preached Word and to beg healing for the word that harmed, manipulated, or divided.

(6) The Place of Funerals

Remembering the deceased best takes place in the center front of the church where coffins were shrouded for Masses of Christian burial. Psalm 130, the *De profundis,* or one of the lament psalms have ample metaphor for any host of feelings. If the church is to be demolished, any of the remains of the deceased buried in the church itself or prominent memorial plaques need to be removed and transferred to another place. These kinds of acts need solemnity and proper ritual. A cemetery in the churchyard creates an additional challenge for the closure of a parish church. Some will need to retain limited functioning as public oratories. The registers of interments, vesture, funeral palls, incense pots, and vessels for holy water should also be employed in the rites. Other suggestions include: a series of Eucharists for those buried from the parish, and even perhaps memorial prayer cards or a stone marker in the nearby Catholic cemetery.

(7) Baptismal Waters

A closing blessing of the assembly from the baptismal font and a song of praise, most especially in a singing once again of the Litany of the Saints, attends to another level of a parish's identity. One parish sang a litany of the names of all those baptized from the parish's history. Word needs to be spoken also of the confessionals, the place of reconciliation. Locating this recognition near the font speaks of baptism and the renewal of baptismal promises.[35]

(8) Illumination

The church was blessed with a solemn illumination as part of its dedication. Taking leave with only the light of the paschal candle—the other candles in the church having been extinguished in a solemn way—speaks of a resurrection faith that is not located in any place, a light that accompanies God's people wherever they go. Prominent electric light fixtures and chandeliers with their benefactors may need to be recognized.

(9) The Doors

The closing and sealing of the church's principal doors offers a powerful sense of almost reverent finale. After the 1989 California earthquake, the closing of the Oakland cathedral was conducted on the steps outside

---

[35] Vocation and leadership is another level of a parish's life to be remembered. Those who pronounced marriage vows, religious vows, and oaths of office in the light of a community's faith need to be honored and remembered. For example, some have suggested that a prie-dieu with the registry of marriages be an additional station that honors this aspect of a parish's history. Calling out the names of pastors and others responsible for pastoral care through a parish's history could likewise be a key moment in saying goodbye.

the front doors. The declaration of closure by Bishop John Cummins in front of the sealed doors was a powerful ending to the rite. It is one of the principal steps of the rites of dedication. It is fitting that it be the final ritual moment in the closure of a worship site.[36]

(10) The Cross

Often one of the most prominent symbols in the last era of Catholic architecture, the crucifix can be a special focus of reverence during the final days of a parish's life. Removing the cross can be an important moment in saying goodbye. Many have carried such a cross with them to the receiving parish or to the newly consolidated buildings (or parish). The fixing of a permanent memorial was recommended in previous rites of closure, affixed at some suitable place on a closing building in memory of the once sacred character of the place.[37] The attempt to preserve some aspect of the church in the new building constructed on that site was soothing for some communities in transition. A permanent memorial or shrine, even at another locale, can serve as a locus for ongoing grief and the celebration of anniversaries.

The above stations can serve as the locus for rites of closure as mentioned at the beginning of this chapter. The discontinuance of eucharistic reservation and the stripping of the altars have peculiar resonances in the liturgies of Holy Week. The washings of walls and altars also have a purifying sense about them, offering perhaps even a cleansing of painful memories which might still exist in the narrative of a place of worship. The remembering (of heroes and leadership, of those married, ordained, and received into religious life, etc.), the attending to the dead, and the fixing of a permanent memorial do not necessarily function to bring closure. Rather, the church is present in prayer and faith as it raises to memory the closed community and includes it in the greater narrative, that of Jesus who made the journey from death to life.[38] The sense of trauma that overwhelms an individual's and group's ability to cope and find meaning in loss could perhaps occur less profoundly with leave taking that lingers adequately on a parish's most prominent stations. The movement recalls that in God's ritual time, no detail and no one is extraneous. Nothing is lost.

[36] Thomas G. Simons, "Requiem for a Church: Closing St. Francis de Sales Cathedral," *Environment and Art Newsletter* 70, no. 2 (April 1994) 16–19.
[37] Wuest, 72.
[38] Smith, *Facing Death Together*, 25.

Desecrated Churches: Exorcism, Deliverance, and Penance

The penitential service of reparation prescribed for a profaned worship space provides another ritual resource for reconciliation around parish closure. Participants in San Francisco and Englewood spoke of the intense conflict around the decision-making processes, as if the church buildings themselves had been desecrated. The blurred lines between church as edifice and assembly make this move a natural one. Assault to the building is assault to the community.

Medieval rituals prior to the Second Vatican Council prescribed elaborate ceremonies if a building was profaned. These included "lustrations"—blessings with baptismal water, later "Gregorian water" (water, salt, ashes, and wine), a circling of the building's exterior with lament psalmody, the washing of the place of defilement with blest water, and the singing of the Litany of the Saints.[39] The list of official acts of offense of sacred space have included: criminal homicide, the shedding of blood that causes an irreverence to the building, heretical or superstitious acts of worship, burial or entombment of an "infidel," any act of defilement committed in the church building itself, and desecration of the Reserved Sacrament.[40] Canon law and the concurrent liturgical documents have consistently used the word "reconciliation" for the process of restoring to worship a space that has been violated in some way. In this context, the scandal caused by the conflict around parish reorganization can be seen as a violation or an affront to the holiness of a place.[41]

Rites of exorcism, with their secrecy and resonances of superstition or magic, have always held an allure for the imagination. But against social processes and in the context of changes to worship space, strategies are called for that, rather than attempting to fix conflicted or traumatized relationships, perform a ritual assault on the reality of human evil. They can be called upon only when there is literally nothing else that can be

[39] Wuest, 63–69.

[40] Ibid.

[41] The 1917 Code of Canon Law focused a great deal of attention on the act that violated the holiness of a sacred place. The 1983 revision of the Code attends rather to the scandal caused to the faithful (CJC 1211) by such an act. The harm is repaired through a penitential rite before the place can be again used for worship. In the case of the conflict that turns to hate, worship lost its licitness until a breech of communion was attended by some act of penitential prayer. Simons, *Holy People, Holy Place*, 86–88. See also Harold Collins, *The Church Edifice and Its Appointments* (Westminster: The Newman Bookshop, 1935) 31–35. Reprinted 1946. Msgr. Collins defined reconciliations as "the purification of a desecrated church" (34).

done—when a community's resources of science, medicine, psychology, and group process have been exhausted, and when impasse has broken every option available to human ingenuity. Only then can a community take a stance of fear and awe at the reality of evil and the sovereignty of grace.

Charismatic renewal painted an image on the U.S. postconciliar imagination formerly reserved to evangelical Christianity, believers gathered around in "deliverance" prayer for one held bound by darkness or the addictions of sin. Since the early thirties, Alcoholics Anonymous has brought about a global revolution in recovery to those held by "demon rum," with its twelve steps against chemical and process addictions. The reading of the steps and the common admission of powerlessness and unmanageability make possible profound personal transformation.[42] In this context, social exorcism-ritual is a place to stand. It is a surrender in hope when all else fails, not of defeat, but "an exercise of deep wisdom . . . a deeper truth that we human beings dare not forget."[43] The forces of evil in all its manifestations have been conquered in the paschal mystery of the Christ. The naming of these forces against a bold proclamation of faith in that mystery reinforces a deeper sense of power in the face of powerlessness.

Lederach provides an example of this kind of exorcising ritual from contemporary conflict mediation. In situations of deadlock or impasse in highly political conflict negotiation, Lederach often suggests a role play employing the four virtues of Psalm 85:10 (truth, mercy, peace and justice). By asking participants from all the sides of an issue to address the conflict from those four perspectives, a simple exorcism takes place. As

---

[42] See Edward C. Sellner, "The Event of Self-Revelation in the Reconciliation Process: A Pastoral Theological Comparison of A.A.'s Fifth Step and the Sacrament of Penance" (doctoral dissertation, University of Notre Dame, 1980). Moral inventory, direct amendment, prayer, seeking forgiveness from God and (where possible) those wronged are essential steps to this perspective of reconciliation. See also the following article written from some of the dissertation's conclusions. Edward C. Sellner, "The Fifth Step and the Sacrament of Penance," *The Furrow* (April 1983) 214–39. Psychiatrist Gerald May's definitive work in this area addresses addiction recovery as deliverance. The program of Alcoholic's Anonymous can be an additional resource for churches if approached as a ritual of deliverance that enables change. Gerald May, *Addiction and Grace* (San Francisco: Harper and Row, 1988) 13, 152–55.

[43] Peter E. Fink, S.J., ed., *Alternative Futures for Worship*, vol. 4, *Reconciliation* (Collegeville, Minn.: Liturgical Press, 1987) 129. Fink's work suggests future ritual directions for the sacramental ritual of reconciliation in the face of social sin. Admitting that our ritual tradition focused primarily from the standpoint of the perpetrator, there is a need for a stretch of the ritual tradition into some new territory. He constructs some ritual forms of reconciliation addressed to a social rather than personal plane.

participants articulate the barriers to unity, the demons are named and a new definition of reconciliation appropriate to a very particular situation emerges.[44] Appendix 1.5 is a liturgy crafted along these lines using Lederach's role play of virtues in the context of a liturgy of the Word.

Rituals crafted for moments of "conflict turned to hate" in the processes of church restructuring often need to address purification. Fr. Peter Fink's work in social reconciliation suggested a liturgy modeled on the Jewish Day of Atonement. He employs symbols and ritual actions actually gleaned from the dedication ceremonies such as the incensation, sprinkling, and anointing of the altar. Fink suggests a purification rite that includes the ritual cleansing of an altar after the naming of the things that have contributed to the group's paralysis and deadlock. This same ritual would be a resource repeated in the rite of leave taking from a building, or even a prayer service connected to the dismantling of the sacred space. A final purification or washing ritual could even address intergenerational wounds, those still unhealed stories of hurt or scandal found in the walls of almost any building's legacy.

Interviewees from the various closed worship sites noted the need for ritual that addressed impasse and the wounds of heated, (often) even hateful exchanges of group process. Appendix 1.4 is a liturgy created for the experience of impasse adapted from the above-mentioned Rite of Reconciliation for a Day of Atonement. It directs ritual attention to those internal attitudes and motivations behind choices made in the processes of discernment around parish closure. Originally crafted for the last weekend of the liturgical year, this rite of fasting and prayer is particularly effective in the context of a parish renewal or mission. Orations borrowed from the Easter Vigil or "The Public Prayer after the Desecration of Church" express the preeminence of the Christ over all structures, powers, dominations, institutions, as well as creation itself. The preparation of the paschal candle at the beginning of the Easter vigil proclaims this—Christ "the beginning and the end," to whom even time belongs.[45]

Confession of Christ's sovereignty expresses the hope of Colossians 1:19-20 and Ephesians 1:9-10, that God is reconciling the fragmentation of the world to Godself, albeit in the *eschaton*. No human situation then

---

[44] John Paul Lederach, *The Journey Toward Reconciliation* (Scottsdale, Pa.: Herald Press, 1999) 51–61.

[45] From the Easter Vigil in *The Roman Missal*, International Commission on English in the Liturgy, Inc. All rights reserved. *The Sacramentary* (Collegeville, Minn.: Liturgical Press, 1985).

stands outside the realm of this vision of a human community at peace with itself and its world.

A ritual for the healing of memories is another adaptation of this ritual tradition; an example can be found in appendix 1.3. The Christian assembly can gather for a time of repentance and fasting, to pray for God's forgiveness and healing—particularly for memories holding intergenerational traumas and "unforgiven sins." Sometimes the bell towers across our urban skylines "sacrament" a selective memory. They have at times stood for ethnic competition, racism and classism, child abuse, and even violence. This kind of deliverance prayer articulates with some specificity the brokenness particular to the community itself, the sins of local church history that snap at the heels of any attempts to redesign itself. The Rite for the "Restoring of Things Profaned," from the Episcopal *Book of Occasional Services* exemplifies this.

> Almighty God, by the radiance of your Son's appearing you
> Have purified a world corrupted by sin: We humbly pray
> that you would continue to be our strong defense against the
> attacks of our enemies; and grant that [this _____,
> and] whatever in this church has been stained or defiled
> through the craft of Satan or by human malice, may be
> purified and cleansed by your abiding grace; that this place
> purged from all pollution, may be restored and sanctified, to
> the glory of your Name; through Jesus Christ our Lord, who
> lives and reigns with you and the Holy Spirit, one God, now
> and for ever. Amen.[46]

The power of the Church's ritual, in this context, is the expression given to feelings so painful and old that no other way can be found to bear them.[47]

Additional resources for the construction of these rituals could be found in the final stages of the Rites of Christian Initiation for Adults,[48] particularly the scrutinies, minor exorcisms, and the anointings with the

---

[46] Pp. 202–3 of *The Book of Occasional Services, 1979*, of the Episcopal Church, U.S.A., copyright 1980, © Church Pension Fund. All rights reserved. Used by permission of Church Publishing, Incorporated, New York, N.Y.

[47] Robert J. Schreiter, *Reconciliation: Mission and Ministry in a Changing Social Order*, Boston Theological Institute Series, vol. 3 (Maryknoll, N.Y.: Orbis Books, 1992) 75.

[48] For example, §94B, "Prayers of Exorcism," *Rite of Christian Initiation of Adults* (Chicago: Liturgy Training Publications, 1988) 42. This is also available in International Commission on English in the Liturgy, *The Rites of the Catholic Church*, vol. 1 (Collegeville, Minn: Liturgical Press, 1990).

oil of catechumens—as well as the eucharistic prayers for Masses of reconciliation. "The Prayer of Exorcism and Anointing" from the Infant Baptism ritual, the deliverance prayers from the "Commendation of the Dying" in the *Rite of Pastoral Care of the Sick*,[49] and the various penitential services in the appendix of the *Rite of Penance*[50] can also be modified to fit into the moments of this ritual pattern.

Much recent attention has been given in conflict negotiation to the "diabolical enemy image."[51] Often the first escalation in almost any social conflict occurs when the ideology of each side is based on the *demonization* of the other. Ritually naming those motives and systems behind a community's impasse or fragmentation releases a new freedom.[52] They can once again be lifted up into light of critique and into the consciousness of prayer. "History belongs to the intercessors," Walter Wink says, "who believe the future into being."[53] Ultimately, the most crucial resource for completing any restructuring of a local parish is a vision of an emerging church that is dynamic and transformative.

> We the Catholic Church (of San Francisco)
> in a communion of faith and charity
> with the successor of Peter
> reach out and receive with welcoming arms
> all of God's people:
>
> the saint and the sinner, the young and elderly;
> the poor and the rich; the immigrant and native;
> the lost sheep and the still searching.

[49] Other resources for this kind of deliverance prayer have powerful scriptural parallels like litany in option C of the 'Rite of Commendation of the Dying.' It repeats "Deliver your servant, Lord, as you delivered Noah from the flood, R. Lord, save you people." See "Pastoral Care of the Sick: Rites of Anointing and Viaticum," International Commission on English in the Liturgy, *The Rites of the Catholic Church*, vol. 1 (Collegeville, Minn.: Liturgical Press, 1990) 866–67.

[50] See appendix 2, "Sample Penitential Services," in "Rite of Penance," ibid., 592–624. For an excellent compendium of reflection and liturgical application of these options, see Daniel P. Grigassy, O.F.M., "Nonsacramental Rites of Reconciliation: Forsaken or Disguised?" *Liturgical Ministry* 4, no. 3 (Winter, 1995) 11–21.

[51] Michael H. Crosby, O.F.M., Cap., *Do You Love Me?: Jesus Questions the Church* (Maryknoll, N.Y.: Orbis Books, 2000) 60–61. See also Ralph K. White, *Nobody Wanted War: Misperception in Vietnam and Other Wars* (Garden City, N.Y.: Doubleday / Anchor Books, 1970).

[52] M. Scott Peck, *People of the Lie: The Hope for Healing Human Evil* (New York: Simon and Schuster, 1983) 68.

[53] Walter Wink, *The Powers that Be: Theology for a New Millennium* (New York: Doubleday, 1998) 185.

At this unique moment, as we stand at the crossroad
    (leading to the Third Millennium)
We recognize ourselves as a pilgrim people
Called by God and empowered by the Spirit
to be disciples of Jesus Christ.

We pledge ourselves to be a dynamic and collaborative community
    of faith
Known for its quality of leadership

its celebration of the Eucharist
its proclamation of the good news,
its service to all in need
and its promotion of justice, life and peace.

Rich in diversity of cultures and peoples
and united in faith hope and love
we dedicate ourselves to the glory of God.

In this our mission
we each day seek holiness
and one day heaven.[54]

Kairos *and the Conference Table:*
Honoring the Stages of Reconciliation of Groups

In the history of dedicating churches, as rituals became more complicated with funerary and exorcism accretions, other levels of ceremonies
were added with resonances to the rites of initiation. A litany of saints was
intoned over the space to be consecrated. The sprinklings of the floor and
the outside and inside of a church were a kind of baptism. Likewise, the
anointing of the door posts and walls were confirmation. The altar was
clothed in white and the rite of illumination lit the lamps with the Easter
fire like neophytes at the Paschal Vigil. "It was as if the building was being
baptized and confirmed and readied to receive the Body and Blood of the
Lord, the paschal sacraments."[55]

The rituals and processes of the conference table occupied major parts
of the San Francisco and Englewood consolidations. Most of the work

---

[54] "Our Mission" as quoted in "A Journey of Hope Toward the Third Millennium:
The Pastoral Plan of the Pilgrim Church of San Francisco" (promulgated December 15,
1995) 4. Used with permission.

[55] Ibid., 20.

happened not in churches but around the group dynamics of community organizing, butcher paper, and markers. One frailty of these rituals, as mentioned in the previous chapter, was the absence of a connection between the conference table to the table of Eucharist, and by extension, to the dinner tables in people's homes. Outside facilitators were engaged in both locations to assist the communities through group process, discernment, and especially the experiences of impasse. The works performed in these spaces needed a sense of sacredness, a way of integrating the emotional and spiritual energies released in this context. A spirituality of conflict needed to be articulated that could disarm the shame of conflict as the result of sin, and cultivate an openness to revelation and epiphany.

Any degree of movement toward reconciliation in a conflicted group process needed to be highlighted in a similar way as do the blessing and exorcism rites of adult Christian initiation. *Kairos* is ritual highlighting that arises from within the process of conciliation (1) to solidify and celebrate common ground and thereby raise it to the level of common myth and (2) to hold this common myth in remembrance as a context for ongoing deliberations. *Kairos* is not the seizing or manipulating of a moment for the possibility of some measure of conflict reduction or reconciliation. Rather it is an intuitive "latching onto" and celebration of whatever measure of communion or re-communion is achieved. It employs the influence of myth to claim allegiance, shape motivation, urge decision, and empower people toward the realization of full reconciliation.[56]

Kairos is also a ritual sense of time. Persons from both study sites spoke of the need to call time outs when conflict was heated in order to give people breathing space and allow the Spirit to reveal new options and possibilities. Breathing spaces of lag time were liminal moments, potentials of revelation, the space for dreams and visions. Members of both places likewise spoke of the need to address failure. Vocal spontaneous prayer, story, and the narrative resources of the Scriptures were important parts of this group process. Bible reading before and sometimes after meetings was employed to keep people on target. *Kairos* affirms grieving time to adjust to changes. Rites proposed in appendices 2.1 through 5.1 create ritual stations to acknowledge losses of autonomy and identity before proceeding with the tasks of restructuring the local expression of church.

Leaders in both case studies expressed fear that the uses of time outs and time limits were manipulative—that those in charge had the answers

---

[56] Fink, *Alternative Futures*, vol. 4, 150–51.

already at hand and that conference table rituals were just pretence. Facilitators of the process repeatedly sought to reassure people that their work had value and was integral to the decisions as to how the final solutions were constructed. When these decisions were "at loggerheads" with those finally chosen by the bishops and diocesan leadership, or not adequately explained, the roar of protest and rage was intense.

One of the essential components of the ministry of group reconciliation is to attend to the possible place or places where ritual action might generate solidarity. Taking care for inclusion of ritual acts within the processes of group conciliation and the construction of ritual acts to accompany those processes, is complex and delicate. Ritual can only be initiated within the context of the ministry to the people involved, making it difficult to create in advance. This presupposes a repertoire of ritual available at the fingertips of a skilled pastoral liturgist who accompanies the group process.

Honest rite attempts to localize reconciliation in the frank articulation of conflicted relationships and the barriers to it. Appendix 1.2 is a prayer experience built on this model. Its function is to highlight steps to restored communion—something many of those interviewed felt was difficult to grasp when parochial groups were locked in conflict. Rituals in the context of parish consolidation presume that a bishop be present at some point because of his prominence in the initiation and closure of parish community and its worship space. The first rite was constructed to celebrate and solidify the discovery of something a divided group has in common. Further, it focuses and acknowledges the commitment of each group to that common bond. Lastly, it inaugurates with prayer and blessing a new phase in the process of reconciliation that begins in the discovery and choice to pursue what has been found in common.

Symbols familiar and ample enough to bear ambiguous feelings serve reconciliation in this context. The prayer service uses a brazier of coals on the altar for incense that parallels the rite for the dedication of an altar. The paschal candle is placed in the midst of the assembly with smaller candles available for representatives of the conflicted groups. The rite is designed to be repeated as a group continues its work with one another toward the final common ground. The final version of this rite might specifically use the formulary of the sacrament of penance, including the absolution and proclamation of God's forgiveness.[57] When a group completes a process to full consensus, the rite needs to highlight the specific

[57] Fink, *Alternative Futures*, vol. 4, 153.

acknowledgement of sin overcome, responsibility spoken, and mutual forgiveness extended. Conflict among church people, negotiated well, uniquely testifies to God as the source and sustainer of any movement toward human reconciliation.

Ritual Honesty and the Elephant in the Dining Room

An article on parish-priest demographics from the Milwaukee *Catholic Herald* in February 2001 made reference to an overarching issue in the re-organization of U.S. parish life—declining clergy numbers. The shortage of the ordained is like an "elephant in a living room" according to a local lay parish administrator. In the context of church consolidation, perhaps "dining room" more fully enhances the metaphor. Some very creative solutions are being proposed in nearly every major diocese in the country.

Despite clustering parishes, extending the clergy retirement age, and even importing ordained ministers from other countries, the pool of those available to serve as pastors of local parish communities each year is further diminished. Like an elephant plopped in our most formal dining room, every attempt made to ignore it guarantees that people continue bumping into it. Many of those areas most impacted by parish closures are waiting for the ordination question to be raised, "and of course it is not being asked."[58] Official Vatican channels have closed the door on further dia-logue on the issue. Any attempt to extend the presbyterate beyond the ranks of celibate males is apparently deferred.[59]

From the questions asked at the beginning of this study, especially about the future of consolidation as a tool in the reorganization of the U.S. Catholic Church, strategies will need to be as complex as the local churches who plan them. The experience of the Catholic communities in San Francisco and Englewood demonstrates that among the staffing op-tions available as a result of the clergy shortage, merger-consolidation is one of the most expensive. People get hurt. People fall through the cracks

[58] Margaret Plevak, "Priests Busy, Getting Busier," *Catholic Herald* (Milwaukee), February 22, 2001.

[59] Fr. George Wilson, S.J., of Cincinnati's Management Design Institute posits that in the next five to seven years, the bumper crop of men ordained in the 1950s and early sixties will reach retirement age all at once. Some will continue working but the curve of clergy decline will not be a slow glide. It will go over a cliff. With this steep decline of clergy, the pressure on parishes and staff will increase as bishops look for alternatives for leadership by ordained ministers in established parishes. George Wilson, S.J., "Why Close St. Ben's," *America*, May 7, 2001, 20.

and drop away often without closure and healing, without forgiveness and a broader sense of church. A remark by Cleveland Bishop Anthony Pilla in his 2001 pastoral letter, "Vibrant Parish Life," speaks to a growing consensus among church leadership that consolidation is only one of a host of planning options for the local and diocesan churches of the future. The dynamism of the local church depends on local empowerment. The rituals employed to accompany this process will reveal the depth of local initiative and ownership:

> Our solutions cannot deal with the church's people and institutions by using impersonal or hurtful strategies. My resistance to formulating an aggressive and sweeping plan for parish consolidations or closings is that, rather than "fixing" a fundamental problem or strengthening the faith of the people, the actual result is that people experience tremendous pain and alienation. I do not believe that building vibrant parish life can be legislated. It must involve initiative at the local community level and be embraced willingly with the heart by those most affected.[60]

Management studies around business amalgamations parallel what we are learning in the churches: consolidation seldom increases the efficiency of an organization, "unless accompanied by post-merger management. Decisive splits often develop within the new management team as each manager retains loyalties to his former business."[61]

The experience in Englewood and San Francisco highlighted the need for ongoing pastoral care after the merger. Post-consolidation splitting caused immense frustration to both the people in middle-management (the pastoral teams and pastors) and those in the pews. Charles Handy cautions from the business amalgamation's perspective that organizations considering merger are "stuck with their pasts . . . their traditions. These things take years if not decades to change."[62] The criteria for viability and accompaniment of communities wrestling with the configuration of their future are key elements of pastoral care in this setting.

---

[60] Bishop Anthony Pilla, "Steps Toward Collaboration among Parishes," *Origins* 30, no. 39 (March 15, 2001) 626.

[61] Stuart Slatter, *Corporate Recovery* (London: Penguin Books, 1987) 245. As quoted in Gerald A. Arbuckle, S.M., "Merging Provinces," *Review for Religious* 53, no. 3 (May–June 1994) 353.

[62] Charles Handy, *Understanding Voluntary Organizations* (London: Penguin Books, 1988) 95. As quoted by Arbuckle, "Merging," 253.

It takes great courage for a parish to see that it is no longer viable and that for the good of the future parishioners, a merger with another parish or closing is needed.

I offer the people of any parish in difficulty my prayerful support and my guidance in coming to a wise decision about the steps that need to be taken. I understand that closing a parish without the consultation and support of its members can lead to lasting hurt and alienation from the church.[63]

Some of the early attempts at parish consolidation of formerly ethnic churches were responses to major demographic changes that had left small communities of Catholics "holding the bag." As with Englewood, these were often not the founding ethnic group. Larger, more dynamic communities with more resources were welcomed. But some of these planning processes attempted to include additional objectives such as the reduction of parishes in anticipation of diminished clergy numbers and new clustering strategies that could stretch the oversight of ordained ministers to multiple sites. These strategies reflected a significant change in job description from that of the immigrant pastor. The advocacy and ombudsman roles were assumed by professional and volunteer staff who, more often than not, conduct the day-to-day ministry of the parish.

The structural viability of single parish communities with multiple worship sites is still to be seen. In most instances, this solution needs to be time limited to when the new parish community can gather in a worship site that reflects its own culture and experience of church. The loss of priest availability in these scenarios often has added yet another level of grief. Those in parish leadership have often found themselves suspicious that with these innovations in parochial leadership, the vibrancy of the local church was being compromised.

Some in the San Francisco and Englewood consolidations articulated a reduced confidence in the stability of sacred space, "If they did it once they can do it again." Many in the West Englewood parish feared that the East would eventually subsume them. They feared that what had been salvaged would sooner or later be taken from them. If sacred space can so easily be undone by church authorities, what is to stop them from doing it again? Somehow the ground seems less holy if a simple written declaration of a bishop is all that is needed to un-dedicate it.

To dream what healing might look like in any wounded situation takes an ability and willingness to make an imaginative leap into uncharted

[63] Bishop Pilla, "Steps Toward Collaboration," 626.

waters. The task of reshaping local church is ultimately an imaginative one. The participant in the San Francisco consolidation quoted at the beginning of this chapter constructed an imaginary ritual. In it, he tried to re-anchor a sense of communion between those with very diverse understandings of church. His rite sought to specifically and publicly acknowledge the values of the Christian story and the struggle to discover them again, even with battle scars.

It's About Doing Church
Imaginings and Implications

At a parish renewal I recently conducted in a consolidating midwestern church, I noted to a mothers' prayer group that after walking around their nearly century-old parish churches that the culture which built them was dead. The shape of the stained glass windows and naves, the configuration of the pews and statuary pointed to an experience of church that no longer existed. A very animated, emotion-laden conversation ensued—some agreeing with my reflection and others vehemently disagreeing. Some left mad.

This book began with the personal struggle to understand the intense emotions around the consolidation and closure of parish churches. Resistance, both active and passive, to pastoral initiatives around the reshaping of ecclesial geographical and architectural boundaries seems to indicate that it stirs something deep in the Catholic imagination. "We U.S. Catholics are living with dangerous memories," noted Chicago's Sr. Patricia Foster. The changes in ecclesiology and identity sparked by documents of Vatican II have been slow to take root in large segments of parish populations in this country. Still others have taken the new vision of church and reshaped local parish life and ministry. We ritualize both at the same time. Many parishioners and their leadership had continued to function in a parochial bias—with primary concern for the geographical parish, rather than area or larger Church communions. Nothing shattered that sense of church like the closure of a local parochial institution.

To come to a new ecclesial understanding, new rituals are needed. Since there are no official rites for the closures of a parish church, those employed in the past few decades of Catholic history offer a window with a profound view of the Catholic cultures behind them, as well as of the attempts by leadership to shape this experience into some new meaning. The announcement by Detroit's Cardinal Szoka in the fall of 1988 of the imminent closure of forty-three urban parishes was a marker event between two experiences of church: the Euro-American immigrant Catholicism and the post-modern "globalizing" Church. The ritual of meeting with other parish leadership, forming a plan together, and implementing a configuration for local church is a sociological paradigm shift, a new way of doing the business of church. Habits which speak only to a geographical parish, rather than to larger boundaries of church, will require ongoing revision.[1]

The Sunday Eucharist was the ritual most utilized for this task in the case studies. As many of the San Francisco participants noted, the most efficacious ritual was first of all honest. It was expansive enough to highlight convergences and digressions. It sought to affirm (often) intense local work on the part of a whole Christian community, to highlight solidarity, and to reestablish communion. It permitted conflicted parties to begin to tell their stories and eat in safety with one another again. It ultimately sought to link their stories to the greater narrative of the life, death, and resurrection of Jesus. Catholic imagination often connects church assemblies and the buildings that house them.

The interviews in both Chicago and San Francisco seemed to highlight a series of ritual moments, each in need of its own attending pastoral care. These included: (1) the consolidation processes themselves with moments of acknowledgment of common ground and reconciliation, (2) the experience of closure for a parish, (3) the leave taking of a parish building, (4) the inauguration of a newly consolidated parish, and (5) the anniversary and ongoing remembrance. Rites that were developed over the centuries to dedicate Christian churches have roots in Eucharistic, funerary, exorcistic, and initiatory rituals. New rites and narrative processes to be applied to this ongoing task for the future can be mined from these same venues.[2]

----

[1] Patricia Forster, O.S.F, "The Chicago Story—and Boundaries to Parish Restructuring," in *Diocesan Efforts in Parish Reorganization: A Report* (Clearwater, Fla.: Conference of Pastoral Planning and Council Development, 1995) 76.

[2] Fr. Peter Fink noted that the imaginative work of reconciliation is to create new rituals for events that often fall between the cracks of our institutions. He calls for a

Rituals that dedicate churches need somehow to be mirrored in those that un-dedicate them. To "do church" from the beginning of a parish's life until its death emerged repeatedly as a priority for those involved in discernment processes across the country. Reconciliation is served when rites assist people through the stages of grief—at the losses of autonomy and identity—to the point that they can reengage church in a new way. Significant time and accompanying pastoral care is necessary for people to arrive at the place where they can wash the chrism from the altars of their church, incense and walk the Stations, seal the doors, sing a Litany of the Saints, and fix a final memorial on the walls. Once there, the chances of forming what Fr. Robert Schrieter calls a new community of memory and hope are heightened.

Faces of Forgiveness and Church

A few summers back I had the marvelous opportunity to attend a retreat with the bishop who initiated our pastoral planning process in San Francisco. A few days into the retreat, I asked for some private time with him. More than five years had passed and both of us admitted that our feelings remained still somewhat raw from the experience. We spoke of fears, loss, and the personal cost of attempting to reshape the perimeters of local church. It was a very tender and honest moment for both of us. I found something of my perspective made a subtle and nearly immediate change.

The human face of forgiveness has been a central preoccupation of this study. If trauma means wound or injury, this conversation brought some of the painful memories of the San Francisco consolidation to healing. I asked the archbishop for his forgiveness for any ways I may have injured him during that time, and he asked me for mine. The work of Robert Enright, Suzanne Freedman, and Julio Rique mentioned in this study, seeks to articulate the stages of interpersonal forgiveness. One of the key stages of

---

service of reconciliation for alienation between a group and an individual. In the situation of parish restructuring, a group will sometimes wound an individual in the heat of conflict about a parish's future, especially leadership in middle management. There is a need to create a way for the group to acknowledge such responsibility and seek the forgiveness of the individual. Social reconciliation is often served when the one wounded leads the group in the creation of a forgiveness rite and acceptance of the apology. See Peter E. Fink, S.J., ed., *Alternative Futures for Worship*, vol. 4, Reconciliation (Collegeville, Minn.: Liturgical Press, 1987) 163–66.

their paradigm is "reframing." The decision to include in one's perspective the context of the offender (or the one perceived as perpetrator of a traumatic wound) anchors reconciliation individually and collectively. Even though we were at odds during much of the process of parish strategic planning in San Francisco, I felt a new sense of solidarity with the bishop as another minister attempting to bring his skills to a difficult situation.

The purpose of this work has not been to criticize or judge the work of leadership or other participants in either the San Francisco or Englewood consolidations. The interviews were moving exchanges for me and I commend the courage and creativity of the people in both locales. As a former staff member has said, "Most of us were making this up as we went along." Their stories contained more than a few models of how to successfully negotiate the terrain of this kind of church and educational reorganization.

The examination of the experience of parish consolidations and closures—from the window of ritual and through the lens of reconciliation— has been a challenging task. Preserving and restoring communion is highlighted from these perspectives. It was my hope simply to look at these tumultuous experiences through ritual, from its descriptive and prescriptive functions, to see what could be seen. What was performed? What shape did the rituals give to the experiences? Finally I sought to look at what new pastoral care could be proposed from the experiences of these two communities that might be put to the service of other dioceses in the midst of parish restructuring.

The religious landscape of the U.S. has been altered by the movement of Catholic populations and the consolidation or closure of their religious institutions. The two communities for this work are representative of this reality. Though separated by thousands of miles, one in Chicago's Englewood and the other in San Francisco's Bernal Heights, the issues raised by their experience were common to many other communities throughout the country. Their rituals fell into three categories: rituals of the conference table, rituals of the Eucharistic table, and funeral rituals of protest and lament.

Church folks tend to feel ashamed about internal conflict. Yet throughout Christian history conflict has brought about the greatest breakthroughs of Christian thought and experience. Forgiveness and reconciliation from numerous sources of Christian tradition, most especially the Scriptures, is a powerful lens to examine the changes of local church in recent decades. Reconciliation includes personal forgiveness but is about the broader task of restoration of human communion. Communion in the wake of restructuring parishes is a central issue. In the context of parochial consolidation and closure, this experience is affiliated with the expansion of the parish's geographical boundaries. The reframing of perspective, so crucial to forgiveness, is coupled with the reframing of the boundaries of church, making it more inclusive and dynamic.

The reconciliation of any social rift begins in imagination and the confluence of church as assembly and as building. Five ritual moments were proposed to parish consolidation. These included: the rituals of the conference table, closure of a parish community, leave taking of a building, inauguration of a newly configured parish, and the fixing of a permanent memorial. Some ritual "stations" were proposed to this task including, the Reserved Sacrament, the relics, sacred images, the altar, podium, the place of the dead, baptismal font, illumination, the doors, and the cross—the fixing of permanent memorial. This ritual pattern is the collected work of several liturgists and pastoral leaders like Sr. Rita Fisher, Fr. Tom Simmons, and Fr. Larry Dorsch. What gives this ritual pattern a different shape is the honest acknowledgement of conflict and the context of social reconciliation. It is hoped that the series of model rites proposed in the appendices will be a ritual resource of some value to parochial communities just beginning this process.

Two kinds of consolidations were attended to in this study. The first was a consolidation of several parishes into a new configuration. The second was the receiving parish model: a parish is closed and blended into an existing parish in the area. A new parish is best ritualized by a new worship space. The most applicable consolidation rituals for those configuring several parishes into one would be the Rite of Dedication of a Church and an Altar.

If a new church cannot be built for the consolidated community, recent experience suggests that at least a substantial renovation of the space with a new ritual dedication helps to support a new identity. Secondary worship sites in nearly all the parishes surveyed were problematic. When a parish is consolidated, a new worshipping community is effectively created.

Imagining a Vital Catholicism

The final question for those interviewed for this study was what kind of recommendations would they make to other parishes and schools facing closures and reconfigurations in the future. Many participants in the churches of South Chicago and San Francisco noted that a vision of church, a sense of where we might be going, was integral to completing local restructuring. One had to imagine what kind of local community would be connected to a place before structures and buildings could be designed for it.

The desire for "honest ritual" was the most common recommendation of the thirty-five interviewees of this study. Elaine Ramshaw has defined rite that lacks honesty as rite at variance with real life situations, imputing feelings to a congregation's state of mind or forcing people to ritual statements they are not inclined or ready to make.[3] The losses to local church communities described here have been multiple and far reaching. Recent studies of sacramental reconciliation underscored that its future must be "multi-strategic." No one ritual size fits all.[4] The same can be said of the ritual needs for recently consolidated and closed parochial communities (or ones about to be closed or consolitdated) in the U.S. A whole repertoire of ritual is needed.

Pastoral care and ritual need space and time for lamentation, dissent, and grief. The manipulation of these resources in order to take a community to some predetermined place seemed to further wound something deep in the Catholic imagination. Adequate time to grieve the loss of autonomy and identity, and to begin the creation of a new sense of community was also mentioned with some regularity by those interviewed. Effective uses of ritual time included "time outs" called when conflict was intense; deadlines were extended to attempt consensus, and lavish time was given to share memories, even repeat narratives until people were sated and ready to move on. Ritual that accompanied and even provoked these interludes honestly motivated people to move through the liminal darkness of interpersonal conflict—even impasse—toward new community.

A realistic criterion for parish viability was also noted repeatedly in interviews. Many felt this was another critical area for the success of new parish configurations. People needed to participate in the discussions that determine what would constitute a vibrant parish, especially in the cultural reality of those most affected. The more empowered a community felt in establishing this criteria and participated in the decision-making processes that implements it, the less was the sense of trauma.

The agent of reconciliation in settings of ecclesial conflict was a critical area in the reflections of those surveyed. The question was often asked in both locations, "Where's the bishop?" The ritual role of the local bishop in

---

[3] Elaine Ramshaw, *Ritual and Pastoral Care* (Philadelphia: Fortress Press, 1987) 26–27.

[4] James Dallen and Joseph Favazza, *Removing the Barriers: The Practice of Reconciliation* (Chicago: Liturgy Training Publications, 1991) 30–31.

the establishing of a parish and worship site is primary. Yet local bishops were generally absent from the processes closing parishes throughout the country. Many delegated the onsite work to local pastors or chancery office administrators. The conflict appeared to frighten many away to the protection of ritual roles and corporate structures. Often the local pastors, who themselves sided with the people, were the focal point of people's rage and sense of betrayal. The corporation sole, the one with the most power over a parish's viability and future, who initiates and ritually calls a parish into being, is the local ordinary. The most ritually dense liturgy of the Church's repertoire after the Great Vigil of Easter, is the Rite of Dedication of a Church and an Altar. Since the early days of Christianity, the ritual agent of reconciliation has been the bishop. The agent of parish closure and consolidation is likewise the ordinary. Of all of the bishop's many roles, this one should perhaps not be delegated.

Many of those interviewed spoke of the need for ongoing accompaniment in the years immediately after consolidation. If a diocese provided "aftercare," it normally ended with the consolidation ceremony. How do people reconcile in this context? When asked, a former pastor from the Englewood consolidation noted a sobering fact. "They don't. Most just go away."[5] Why some individuals and groups complete a process of reconciliation after the closure or consolidation of a church and others stay locked into a sense of ongoing trauma, remains a mystery. As with any death, the most intense grieving for loved ones frequently took place after the funeral rituals. Closing neighborhood churches marked the death of the Catholic immigrant culture of the last century. Still, conflict and the closing of sacred space have other nuances of meaning to the ethnic communities that now live in those neighborhoods and worship in those churches.

Attending to the voices left out of this conversation has also been an ongoing preoccupation of this work. Both locations saw people decline to be interviewed noting still conflicted and strong emotions. The withdrawal of the San Francisco Hispanic leadership from the interview process, and the ongoing sense of violation from "downtown" spoken of by African American leadership in Englewood, highlights cultural nuances of meaning in conflict and criticism. Several noted a fear of appearing over critical of their pastors or former leadership. It is impossible to attend to all the voices in a situation as complex as this, I was frequently reminded. Those "in the pews" who didn't participate in the planning processes or those

[5] Fr. Donald [pseudonym], interview by author, Chicago, Ill., February 19, 2001.

who withdrew before these decisions were complete, tended to carry strong feelings the longest. Searching out these voices and attending to their stories will be the ongoing task of pastors. The rites and pastoral care appropriate for them are in need of further study. Yet having a place for memorial and celebrating rites on anniversaries may both be excellent resources for inviting the hurting and alienated back into the conversation.

Conclusions from the interviews and research on parish restructuring cannot be drawn in the traditional sense of the word. The parallel experiences of the two sites chosen as case studies simply open up further questions and lay the groundwork for further critical reflection. Statistics and research are just beginning to appear on this issue. They will shed new light on these events, and this information will be among the tools used for constructive local restructuring. But the collected experience of people whose lives have been impacted by the closing and consolidations of parish churches in recent years, remains the richest resource for future pastoral care. It must continue to be mined and placed at the service of those just beginning this journey.

The vitality of Catholicism in the United States has depended on the health of the local church. The parish has been that fundamental institution around which Catholics gathered during the last century of the Euro-American immigrant church. Its future shape and character depend on visionary, courageous leadership and the willingness of communities to try on new faces of local church. With the decline of clergy numbers, the changes to U.S. Catholic demographics, and the landscape of its ministry, the future may require an even greater variety of expressions than the past.

One of the participants of the Englewood consolidation recently passed to me a prayer card used in the later months of their process. It synthesized two recurrent themes of the conversations about parish closure: the restoration of trust and the call to new expressions of church. An immensity of forgiveness is required. Ultimately, only God can pull that off.

Our prayer then, is not just for ourselves,
   but for the five communities of
      East Englewood: St Bernard, St. Brendan, St. Carthage, St. Martin
         and Our Lady of Solace.
We hope these months of preparation will find us open
   to new possibilities of being church
      so that we may pray, worship and serve one another in your name.

We know that you have already given us all we need
      to make our hopes for ourselves and for this church a reality.
Our prayer is that we trust in and rely on your goodness.
When the day comes for us to worship in our new house,
      we will sing your praises as a church marked by its unity,
      and strong in the knowledge that you are with us.

Author's Note

I want to thank the parishes, diocesan liturgy and planning offices that permitted interviews and submitted liturgical resources used from their various locales, most especially the Archdioceses of Milwaukee, Dubuque, San Francisco and Chicago. Without a universally approved rite, most took their transition and closure ritual materials from other places or "made them up." Every effort has been made to trace the rituals used by the various communities resourced for this study to their primary source. It has been painstaking and sometimes frustrating work. My apology, in advance, for any resources that I may have unwittingly overlooked as I made my way through secondary or tertiary sources.

The following appendices contain some model rites based on the experience of the communities interviewed for this study and my own. They are not approved liturgies of the church and every attempt has been made to keep this distinction clear. Rather, they are simply offered as a gift to pastoral leadership beginning this journey of parish restructuring in other locales. The United States Conference of Catholic Bishops has not officially approved these rites. With the recent announcement of sixty-five new closures in the Boston Archdiocese, it is my hope that these resources could assist in the crafting of such rites that will someday receive official consideration.

I want to particularly acknowledge the help of ICEL, the International Commission on English in the Liturgy and BCL, the Secretariat for the Bishops Committee on the Liturgy. When copies of these appendices were initially submitted for permission to reprint, they hesitated to grant permission. "They have the marks of a liturgy of the Church, without approval and confirmation by the respective ecclesiastical authorities." Secondly, as noted by their correspondence with me, "liturgical texts approved and confirmed for a particular use (e.g., Rite for the Dedication of a Church) may not be used for other occasions without a canonical vote of the Bishop members of the USCCB and confirmation of the Holy See."

Yet without official rites adequate for parish restructuring, particularly for the conflict generated by these pastoral initiatives at closure or consolidation, local leadership gleaned them from other ritual locations. Notable among these were "official" funerary, reconciliation, rites of Dedication of a Church, and even marriage rites. Often the celebrants of these rites were local bishops themselves. Beyond common domain, direct citing of ICEL copywrited texts has been avoided as according to the instructions received, and I am extremely grateful for their attention to the draft texts of this study.

A Ritual of Group Grieving

The following ritual has been developed specifically to assist religious communities in the processes of grieving. It can be used with large or small groups; its simplicity, the use of the loss-newness paradigm, and periods of meditative silence invariably evoke in communities a freeing experience of letting go to allow the new to enter.

Preliminary instructions

As participants enter in silence into the darkened room they are given a lighted candle and move into groups of eight (or fewer) in circles; the paschal candle is alight in the center of the room; meditative background music can be played. It is advisable not to extend the ritual beyond approximately one hour. If the ritual is to be a community experience, then ideally the ritual presider should be the community leader or someone elected by the community as its representative.[1]

Rite of Lament

1. Presider: Reads Isaiah 45:7. Invites all to enter into the darkness of the tomb so that they may discover the newness of the resurrection.

---

[1] Adapted from: Gerald Arbuckle, S.M., *Refounding the Church* (Maryknoll, N.Y.: Orbis Books, 1993) 198.

2. Reader: Reads Psalm 79 or 84, lament specifically connected to the Jerusalem Temple. A sung version like the simple Gelineau version in GIA *Gather Comprehensive* (#78) will help to focus this prayer.[2]

3. Presider: Invites all to ponder the question, What significant thing do I feel I have lost personally or communally? **Silence:** pause for a few moments perhaps with some gentle instrumental music.

4. Participants are invited to name some loss or grief that they have experienced, advising them to keep their naming to one word or a phrase. There is no discussion on what is named. (If it is not possible to sit in small groups, participants may be invited to write their loss on large sheets of paper fixed to walls or tables.)

   After each participant names a loss, the personal candle is extinguished; the paschal candle and lights are extinguished by the presider.

5. Silence is suggested for another short period.

6. Reader: Once all have extinguished their candles, Psalm 88 is read. A time of lengthy silence is suggested.

7. Presider: The paschal candle is lit. The presider invites participants to identify some newness or joy that has entered the group or their ministry. After a short time the presider invites the group to name the newness (or write it on sheets around the room). Each participant, having named a newness, then lights his or her candle from the paschal candle.

8. Presider: After all candles have been lit, there is a short period of silence, followed by the presider reading Revelation 21:1-7.

   Closing Prayer

   Most merciful God, whose wisdom is beyond our understanding, surround our family of _____ with your love, so that we may not be overwhelmed by our loss. Let us find comfort in our sadness, certainty in our doubt, courage to live through this hour, and strength to meet the days to come. (We ask this through Christ our Lord, Amen.)[3]

---

[2] For other options see Frank J. Henderson, *Liturgies of Lament* (Chicago: Liturgy Training Publications, 1994) 54–56. Despite clear consensus among scholars about the lament classification, the author assembles a comprehensive list of psalmody that falls under the general lament pattern helpful to ritual planners.

[3] A prayer of Bishop John Cummins at the closure of St. Francis de Sales Cathedral, Oakland, California, October 24, 1993. As quoted in Thomas G. Simons, "Requiem for

9. A resurrection hymn follows. All are then invited to give the sign of peace.

Summary

Participants are invited by the ritual leader to make some brief statements about general directions the group has prayed and perhaps what has been learned.

Kairos
A Ritual Honoring Common Ground

This rite is suggested to celebrate and solidify the discovery of something which divided groups might discover in common, to celebrate and solidify a commitment on the part of each to that common bond, and to inaugurate new foundations for ongoing dialogue with prayer and blessing.

The outline of this ritual makes it simple to repeat in the process of deliberations of a conflicted group. The rite is designed for church, for heated times of deliberations around closure and consolidation. The choice of the ritual presider is an important one. This person could perhaps be a local clergyperson, a retired pastoral leader, a leader in another diocese or denomination, or even a professional facilitator. This person also needs to be included in planning the ritual.

It begins in a darkened church. A vessel with burning coals should be prepared in the altar with incense available nearby. A paschal candle should be placed in the midst of the assembly with two smaller candles available for representatives of the two groups. Any other questions about environment and the particular setting for the ritual, as well as any embellishments in terms of music and gesture, will need to be determined by the groups with their own particular circumstances.[1]

---

[1] Adapted from Peter E. Fink, S.J. and Denis J. Woods, "Liturgy for the Reconciliation of Groups," in *Alternative Futures of Worship*, ed. Peter E. Fink, S.J., vol. 4, *Reconciliation* (Collegeville, Minn.: Liturgical Press, 1987) 153–59.

Introductory Rites

Gathering

Presider: Sisters and brothers in Christ, We come together to embrace and rejoice in God's new gift to us.

Our time together continues to yield insight and wisdom, hope and understanding, and an ever more firm grasp on that which unites us in the face of all that still divides. Representative of the respective groups together light the Paschal Candle and sit quietly in its light for a moment. The presider continues:

Revitalized church is marked by a willingness to approach with fresh eyes, open minds and changed hearts what conflicts us. The presence of our God makes it possible to go directly to these issues in a respectful sense of dialogue, in a space created by praise and worship.

Penitential Litany[2]

Presider: For the times we have attributed to ourselves a sense of complete monopoly on the truth, Lord have mercy.

All: Lord have mercy.

Presider: For the times we have envisioned ourselves as the church's saving remnant, Lord have mercy.

All: Lord have mercy.

Presider: For the times we have failed to test all proposals for pastoral realism for the most common good, Lord have mercy.

All: Lord have mercy.

Presider: For the times we have presumed that those we differ with are not acting in good faith, worthy of civility, charity, and understanding, Lord have mercy.

All: Lord have mercy.

Presider: For the times we have failed to appreciate the strength of our opponents' proposals, Lord, have mercy.

All: Lord have mercy.

---

[2] Adapted from literature of the Catholic Common Ground Initiative. Philip J. Murnion, "Called To Be Catholic," a statement from the National Pastoral Life Center, 18 Bleecker Street, New York, N.Y. 10012. Used with permission.

Presider: For the times we have demonized or ascribed motives of disloyalty to those with whom we have differing viewpoints, Lord have mercy.

   All: Lord have mercy.

Presider: For the times we have failed to look at our own culture critically and at another's with adequate respect, Lord have mercy.

   All: Lord have mercy.

Members of the conflicting groups are invited to come forward in groups of two to kiss the altar accompanied by some soft instrumental music.

Presider: Reconciliation is both a journey and a place. Today we rejoice in a new bond of common ground that has been given to us. In the journey of conflict we disciples have often been given the opportunity to see the face of the God who accompanies us in the faces of our opponents.

Someone with adequate credibility of all parties tells the story of their conflict, to state (to date) where they have come from to this impasse.

Opening Prayer

Presider: Let us pray. God of mercy, source of all wisdom and insight, gift of forgiveness and promise of peace, look with kindness upon us and on the work we continue in your name. Though the walls that divide us remain strong, you have given us a glimpse through those walls.

Grant us a renewed hope that they can be toppled. In gratitude and hope we ask that you stay with us on our journey till we find, with your help, the full reconciliation which you hold out to us. We ask this together through Christ, our Lord.

   All: Amen

Liturgy of the Word

Readings appropriate may arise from the needs and desires of the groups involved. The following are suggestions.

First Reading   2 Corinthians 5:16-20

"We implore you . . . be reconciled to God" (v. 20).

Responsorial Psalm   Psalm 84:2-6

Cantor/Reader: How lovely your dwelling, / O Lord of hosts!

        All: How lovely your dwelling, / O Lord of hosts!

Cantor/Reader: My soul yearns and pines
        for the courts of the LORD.
  My heart and my flesh cry out
        for the living God. *Resp.*

Cantor/Reader: As the sparrow finds a home,
        and the swallow a nest to settle her young,
  My home is by your altars,
        LORD of hosts, my king and my God! *Resp.*

Cantor/Reader: Happy are those who dwell in your house!
        They never cease to praise you.
  Happy are those who find refuge in you,
        whose hearts are set on pilgrim roads. *Resp.*

Gospel   John 17:6-19 "[T]hat they may be one just as we are. . . . Consecrate them in the truth" (vv. 11 and 17).

Homily

Rite of Recommitment to Common Ground

Introduction

Presider: You have come together before God and in the midst of this
      assembly to claim and to affirm once again the common bond
      which you share. You come to acknowledge with heartfelt
      thanks that you are closer now to reconciliation than when
      you first began. God indeed has been good in your midst, and
      you have been open to God's work among you. May I invite
      someone from each group to come forward to name and to
      claim this new common ground that has been given to us to
      share together.

Response

Representatives of each group come forward with written copies of the work the group has done, naming the common ground as they understood it or the new level of reconciliation that has been achieved. This could be as simple as a new insight about identity or a shared consensus. For example, "We ten parishes are the Catholic community of Englewood. We have common heritage; we are Hispanic American Catholics. We want so see our children grow up in a place of safety and Christian principles, etc." The written documents are left on the altar.

Presider: *(After each representative speaks)* May God who has begun this good work in our midst, graciously bring it to completion.

All: Amen.

Instruction

Any instruction needs to be done in light of the specific dispute in question. It must be crafted and performed in light of the common ground that is decided upon and claimed, and in light of the actual level of reconciliation that has been achieved by the group.

The action and commitment of both sides in the dispute should be named here in terms of their significance in God's work of reconciliation. The common ground and the reconciliation achieved should be located squarely in Christ's work of reconciliation, and should affirm or reaffirm the part each group will play in that work.

Prayer

Presider: Let us pray now in silence for the continued blessings of God upon our common endeavors, that all divisions may in God's time be healed and that God may be blessed and praised.

As the assembly prays silently, representatives from each group come forward and place incense on the burning coals. It may be an even more expressive symbol if the representative of each side gives the incense to the representative of the other side before the incense is placed on the coals.

The presider's hands are extended above the representatives.

Presider: Tender and gracious God, there is no power to love or forgive unless you yourself place that power within our hearts. We have no power to understand, to respect, and to rejoice in the differences that are ours unless your Spirit within us calls us to a deeper and more abiding reconciliation. Send this Spirit upon us once again to lead us more firmly to that hope for which your own Son prayed, that we be one in you. We make this prayer through Christ, our Lord.

   All: Amen.

Concluding Rites

Let us entrust this common ground to _____ until we gather again.

(A trusted member of the group or professional facilitator takes formal possession of the written documents from the altar to be brought to the subsequent gathering.)

In the meantime, let us maintain the energy and focus of this night's work so that the peace among us can grow into a more effective sign of the Kingdom of God in the prayer often attributed to Francis of Assisi.

Peace Prayer of St. Francis

   All: Lord, make me (us) an instrument of Your peace.
           Where there is hatred, let me sow love;
           where there is injury, pardon;
           where there is doubt, faith;
           where there is despair, hope;
           where there is darkness, light;
           and where there is sadness, joy.

   Presider: O Divine Master,
           Grant that I (we) may not so much seek
           to be consoled as to console;
           to be understood as to understand;
           to be loved, as to love;
           for it is in giving that we receive,
           it is in pardoning that we are pardoned,
           and it is in dying that we are born to eternal life.[3]

   [3] Recent research traces this most popular of the works attributed to St. Francis to a popular magazine in Normandy, France the early twentieth century. See Lawrence S. Cunningham, *Francis of Assisi: Performing the Gospel Life* (Grand Rapids, Michigan and Cambridge, U.K.: William B. Eerdmans Publishing Company, 2004) 146–49.

Note: It is important that the formal Greeting of Peace not be used until enough healing and common ground have been achieved that the gesture is honest to the participants and their process. It is best to honestly recognize the need for peace and the right relations it implies and pray for it than to use it too soon in the group's deliberations. As part of the ongoing process toward reconciliation, at the beginning of each deliberation session, some part of the above ritual may be repeated, for example, the prayer, the instruction, or the passage from Scripture.

A Service of the Word for
Healing of Memories[1]

Introductory Rites

Opening Song

There is a hymn followed by instrumental music.

The presider needs to be carefully chosen for this prayer. He or she needs to be a person with a credibility honored by the whole community. A senior clergy, a retired or "acknowledged" grandparent (or elder) of the community, or perhaps a religious leader outside the denomination of the wounded community.

Presider: We gather together in the presence of the healing love of God, for we have come to ask for God's guidance and blessing, and to rededicate ourselves to the service of one another. We ask God to help us to know where to pray and to make us attentive to all the memories.

There is an extended time of silence.

---

[1] Adapted from Mari West Zimmerman, "Service of Healing for a Congregation" in *Take and Make Holy: Honoring the Sacred in the Healing of Abuse Survivors* (Chicago: Liturgy Training Publications, 1995) 82–91; © 1995, Archdiocese of Chicago, Liturgy Training Publications, 1800 North Hermitage Ave., Chicago, Ill. 60622-1101, 1-800-933-1800, fax 1-800-933-7094, email: orders@ltp.org. All rights reserved.

Opening Prayer

Presider: Let us pray. God, you are goodness, supreme and complete goodness. In the story of creation you proclaimed that all your creatures were good and you gave them their name. Be with us as we seek to follow the lead of your spirit through our community's story. Guide your church through the darkness when the way is not clear. Lead us to gratitude through the stories of peace and intimate fellowship. Heal the divisions in our hearts, in our congregation, and families so that we may glorify you with one voice, united by our love for you. Amen.

Liturgy of the Word

First Reading   Isaiah 58:1-10

This lovely reading employs images of food and water to describe the restored humanity of those who attend to the poor. Compassionate generosity restores the foundations of a community and repairs the breach of relationship between peoples.

Responsorial Psalm   Psalm 90:1-2, 16-17

A sung version is preferred (Gather #84, Psalm 90, "Fill Us with Your Love O Lord," Roy James Stewart, GIA, 1993).

Cantor/Reader: Lord, you have been our refuge
through all generations.

All: Lord, you have been our refuge
through all generations.

Cantor/Reader: Before the mountains were born,
the earth and the world brought forth,
from eternity to eternity you are God. *Resp.*

Cantor/Reader: Show your deeds to your servants,
your glory to their children. *Resp.*

Cantor/Reader: May the favor of the Lord our God be ours.
Prosper the work of our hands!
Prosper the work of our hands! *Resp.*

Second Reading 1 Corinthians 3:3-9

Quarreling allegiances to religious leaders like Apollos or Paul are the context of this exhortation to the Corinthian church. As servants and field hands, each adds a unique gift to God's building and everyone will receive a more than just wage according to the contribution made.

Gospel John 4:19-24

A conversation with the Samaritan focuses on the location of authentic worship. Jesus takes the locus of prayer from a location to an encounter with God's anointed. A time approaches to worship in spirit and truth.

Homily

Intercessory Prayer

A Litany of Penance and Healing[2]

Incense is placed in a stationery bowel near the cross. The first petitions are spoken with background instrumental music.

Presider: O God the Father, Creator of Heaven and Earth, have mercy upon us.

　　All: Have mercy on us. *The response is the same for the following invocations.*

Presider: O God the Son, Redeemer of the World,
　　have mercy on us. *Resp.*

　　O God the Holy Ghost, Sanctifier of the Baptized,
　　have mercy on us. *Resp.*

　　O Holy, Blessed, and Glorious Trinity, one God,
　　have mercy on us. *Resp.*

Presider: Remember not, Lord Jesus, our offenses, nor the offenses of our forebears; do not punish our sins. Spare us, good God, spare your people whom you have redeemed by the wounds of the cross and your most Precious Blood, and by your mercy hold us in the great communion of the saints forever.

　　All: Amen.

---

[2] Adapted from The Great Litany in The Book of Common Prayer (1979) of the Episcopal Church, U.S.A.

A Gesture of Penitence

With a gesture of humility (the crossing of one's hands over one's heart and a bowing of the head as the litany begins), the Jesus prayer is repeated after the cantor several times in plain chant.

Cantor: Lord Jesus Christ, Son of the living God, have mercy on us.

All: Lord Jesus Christ, Son of the living God, have mercy on us.

Deliverance Invocations

Cantor: From all evil and wickedness; from sin; from the crafts and assaults of the prince of lies; and from everlasting damnation, deliver us, O Lord.

All: Deliver us, O Lord. *The response is the same for the following invocations.*

Cantor: From all blindness of heart; from pride, vainglory, and hypocrisy; from envy, hatred, and malice; and from all want of charity, deliver us, O Lord. *Resp.*

From all inordinate and sinful affections; and from all the deceits of the world, the flesh, and the devil, deliver us, O Lord. *Resp.*

From all false doctrine, heresy, and schism; from hardness of heart, and contempt of your Word and commandment, deliver us, O Lord. *Resp.*

From lightning and tempest; from earthquake, fire, and flood; from plague, pestilence, and famine, deliver us, O Lord. *Resp.*

From all oppression, conspiracy, and rebellion; from violence, battle, and murder; and from dying suddenly and unprepared, deliver us, O Lord. *Resp.*

By the mystery of your holy incarnation; by your holy nativity and submission to the Law; by your baptism, fasting, and temptation, deliver us, O Lord. *Resp.*

By the sweat and blood of your agony in the garden; by your cross and passion; by your precious death and burial; by your glorious resurrection and ascension; and by the coming of the Holy Spirit, deliver us, O Lord. *Resp.*

In all time of tribulation; in all time of prosperity; in the hour of our death and in the day of judgment, deliver us, O Lord. *Resp.*

Presider: We sinners beg you to hear us, O Source of life and font of all love; that you might guide and govern your holy Church Universal in the way of justice and holiness.

Using a simple Gregorian format the cantor (or several alternating cantors) continues.

Cantor: That it may please you to illumine all church leadership, bishops, priests, and deacons, with true knowledge and understanding of your Word; that both by their preaching and living, they may set it forth, and proclaim it effectively, we pray to you, Lord.

All: Lord, hear our prayer. *The response is the same for the following petitions.*

Cantor: That it may please you to bless and keep all your people, we pray to you, Lord. *Resp.*

That it may please you to send forth laborers into your harvest, and to draw all humankind into the fullness of your eternal kingdom, we pray to you, Lord. *Resp.*

That it may please you to give all people increase of grace to receive and honor human dignity and to bring forth the freedom of your children, we pray to you, Lord. *Resp.*

That it may please you to bring into your truth all who have lost their way in error, and have been deceived by seductions of pleasure, power, and reputation, we pray to you, Lord. *Resp.*

That it may please you to give us a heart to love and fear you, and to diligently live your commandments to love you and our neighbor, we pray to you, Lord. *Resp.*

That it may please you to rule the hearts of the leadership of this nation, the President of the United States, legislators and all others in authority, that they may do justice, and love mercy, and walk in the ways of truth, we pray to you, Lord. *Resp.*

That it may please you to make all warfare and violence cease in our world; to give to all nations unity, peace, and concord; and to bestow freedom upon all peoples, we pray to you, Lord. *Resp.*

That it may please you to show your mercy upon all prisoners and captives, the homeless and the hungry, and all who are desolate and oppressed, we pray to you, Lord. *Resp.*

That it may please you to give and preserve the ecology and health of our mother the earth, so that all peoples may enjoy its produce in justice and dignity we pray to you, Lord. *Resp.*

That it may please you to inspire us, in our many callings and states of life, to do the work which you gave us to do with singleness of heart as your servants, and for the common good, we pray to you, Lord. *Resp.*

That it may please you to preserve all who are in danger by reason of their labor, professions, or their travel, we pray to you, Lord. *Resp.*

That it may please you to preserve, and provide for, all women in childbirth, young children and orphans, the widowed, and all whose homes are broken or torn by violence, we pray to you, Lord. *Resp.*

That it may please you to accompany the lonely; to strengthen all who suffer in mind, body, and spirit; and to comfort with your presence those who are failing and infirm, we pray to you, Lord. *Resp.*

That it may please you to support, help, and comfort all who are in danger, need, and tribulation, we pray to you, Lord. *Resp.*

That it may please you to show your mercy on all nations, cultures, and races of the human family and to draw us together into new configurations of cooperation and loyalty, we pray to you, Lord. *Resp.*

That it may please you to give us true repentance; to forgive us all our sins, especially those based on negligence and ignorance; and to bestow upon us the graces of your Holy Spirit to amend our lives according to your holy Word, we pray to you, Lord. *Resp.*

That it may please you to forgive our enemies; to help us to sincerely pray for those who have persecuted and slandered us; and to turn our hearts to new forms of compassion, inclusion, and tolerance, we pray to you, Lord. *Resp.*

That it may please you to forgive our ancestors, to help us with your grace to forgive ourselves, and even to forgive you for any unresolved painful or bitter events of our past lives, we pray to you, Lord. *Resp.*

For the healing of hurtful family memories and unspoken family secrets, for the healing of the stories whispered in gossip or told again and again which have provoked a sense of victimization and a desire for revenge, we pray to you, Lord. *Resp.*

For the healing of those wounds caused by bishops, religious, clergy and other church leadership who have wounded instead of cared and guided us, we pray to you, Lord. *Resp.*

For those traumas of the past we can't remember, those written on our bodies and skins, that your grace will bring them to memory and healing, we pray to you, Lord. *Resp.*

For all competition between churches, for memories of inter-Christian injustice and prejudice, especially the violence and fear caused by *(name the organization or specific event)* and other organizations that have so distorted the Christian proclamation of peace, we pray to you, Lord. *Resp.*

For the traumatic wounds of the past contained in the buildings and architecture of this place, for the healing of ethnic competition and violence, for the resolution in Christ's peace of anything that impedes us from building here a community of memory and hope, we pray to you, Lord. *Resp.*

For wounds caused by educators and school systems, for the rifts between Catholic and public systems of education, for the healing of strife caused by sports and overzealous school affiliations, for the healing of hurtful competitions between the various Catholic schools and the religious communities of those who sponsor them, we pray to you, Lord. *Resp.*

For a weaving together of the many communities of this place, especially _____ *(for example, the north and south, or east and west sides of a town or a neighborhood)* that you might strengthen, comfort, and help those broken by life's failures and cruelties; that you might raise up those who have fallen; and that you finally break those powers of darkness that continue to fragment and polarize your people, we pray to you, Lord. *Resp.*

That it may please you to grant to all the faithful departed of this place, to all the dead the details of whose lives are known to you alone, eternal life and eternal peace, we pray to you, Lord. *Resp.*

That it may please you to grant us, in the fellowship of _____ *(patron saints of the closing parish churches)* and all the saints, that we be a faithful sacrament of your kingdom in this part of the Great State of _____, we pray to you, Lord. *Resp.*

Trisagion*

All: (in unison)

Holy God, Holy Mighty One,
Holy Immortal One,
Have mercy on us.

Holy God, Holy Mighty One,
Holy Immortal One,
Have mercy on us.

Holy God, Holy Mighty One,
Holy Immortal One,
Have mercy on us.

Presider: God of our ancestors, you have walked with us from generation to generation, bring us together in the presence of your compassion. You have made us aware of wounds left in this community's memory of its past. Fill in those places of animosity, lingering hurt, rage, violation, or oppression with your truth, justice, peace, and mercy. Reconstruct now the boundaries of this community in the most inclusive way, that we may be a more authentic sacrament of the fellowship at the table where you live and reign forever and ever.

All: Amen.

---

*Trisagion translation taken from Peter E. Fink, S.J., "Liturgy for a Christian Day of Atonement," in *Alternative Futures for Worship,* ed. Peter E. Fink, S.J., vol. 4, *Reconciliation* (Collegeville, Minn.: Liturgical Press, 1987) 137.

Meditations on the Cross

First Cantor: As you are moved to do so, all are invited to come up to the cross. Kneel, bow, or touch the cross for a moment, especially the wounds of the Christ. In the presence of the risen Lord, know that you are in solidarity with all those who suffer wounds to their souls throughout our history in this community and in our world.

Second Cantor: Once you have reverenced the cross, you are invited in the silence of this moment to trace the pattern of the cross on the forehead of one another, the place where the cross was onced placed at baptism. We especially invite you to stretch and expand your normal circle of relationship to those you do not know, to those with whom you have some breach of relationship, or to those who may have some breach in your families. Be attentive to your own heart, to your own history and to those people around you as you enter this ritual prayer.

Presider: Let us stand here in this place before the power of God's mercy and compassion.

All: For that mercy endures forever.

Taizé-style antiphonal music, Dan Shutte's "Behold the Wood," or other antiphonal and instrumental music is used here (Daniel L. Schutte and New Dawn Music, 1976, in Gather Comprehensive *[Chicago: G.I.A.] 420).*

The veneration of the cross takes place in silence. Leave abundant time for people to go near the cross and to exchange blessings.

Concluding Rites

Closing Prayer

The presider speaks a spontaneous prayer that can note the mood that settles on the community through the Great Litany, as well as honor any immediate indications of healing or changed relationship.

Greeting of Peace (If the group has not begun to exchange a Greeting of Peace spontaneously.)

Closing Song

A sung antiphonal response or familiar hymn is used so that no program is needed as the peace is exchanged.

Rite of Reconciliation
A Vigil for a Christian "Day of Atonement"

When ecclesial conflict turns to hate, there is a need to address in the context of worship the powerlessness and the accompanying sense of scandal, as experience has shown. This ritual of Christian atonement would seem to fit where a deep sense of the evil with its accompanying helplessness has pervaded a community's group process and paralyzed its ability to discern. A faith and hope-filled act of entrustment to God can be seen as a positive action at the point of powerlessness and impasse. It is not without precedent in Christian ritual history to suggest fasting and prayer in the face of evils too large to cast aside just by one's own volition. Nor is it an irresponsible excuse for inaction to change things.

The ritual uses some of the symbols associated with the dedication of a church building, in a reverse order from the originial rite. Its focus is toward a renewal of the values associated with a parish's foundation, even perhaps as it closes. It likewise employs symbols associated with Christian initiation—the oil of catechumens, and orations associated with the baptism ritual for infants and the Lenten scrutinies of the RCIA. This ritual could be used in the case of conflict that is deadlocked in hurt and rage in order to "turn directly" in faith toward the evil that paralyzes and scandalizes the Body of Christ.

Whereas the Jewish Day of Atonement called for the sprinkling of blood to effect the purification, this ritual calls on the waters of Christian baptism. Incense is burned as a prayer of rededication recalling the original anointing of an altar. The actions speak humanity's deepest longings and at the same time God's own deepest yearnings for us, as specifically as possible in the context of the current conflict.

The ritual is offered in three parts as a "vigil" for the solemnity of Christ the King. The texts of the celebration which bring the liturgical year to its conclusion combine the longing for purification and acknowledgement of the sovereignty of Christ over all the powers. It begins in a solemn opening of the weekend Day of Atonement on Friday evening, to take place in the assembly of the local parish church. The second part offers a collection of table prayers to be used at home on both Friday and Saturday evenings. The third is the Mass liturgy of Christ the King honoring the sovereignty of Christ's kingship over all human powers and bringing the Day of Atonement to a conclusion.

The table prayers both give structure to the day of fast and bring the Church's ritual prayer into the home. They offer some new avenues for linking the public prayer at the altar table, the conference table, and dinner table in the home.

The Mass preface for Christ the King constructs a litany of the qualities needed to mark a Christian community: "truth and life," "holiness and grace," "justice, love, and peace." The eucharistic prayers for Masses of reconciliation could bring the feast to a new significance. The lordship of Christ is about forgiveness as well as eschatological reign and universal sovereignty over the powers that be. One parish in San Francisco created a drama of the Year A, "great judgment" scene of Matthew's Gospel (25:31-46) with its separation of sheep and goats. They presented it in a neighborhood park, attracting the attention of neighbors, adjoining parishes, and even the art community of that city.[1]

PART I:
SOLEMN OPENING OF A DAY OF ATONEMENT

Rite of Reconciliation

The ritual takes place in darkened church. The altar is bare except for a cross and a thurible with coals burning.

---

[1] Adapted from Peter E. Fink, S.J., "Liturgy for a Christian Day of Atonement," in *Alternative Futures for Worship*, ed. Peter E. Fink, S.J., vol. 4, *Reconciliation* (Collegeville, Minn.: Liturgical Press, 1987) 132–45.

Gathering

The assembly gathers on Friday evening. The presider and ministers take their places in silence.

Opening Chant

At the appointed time the cantor or choir chants the Lord, have mercy or Kyrie eleison slowly and prayerfully, using a tone appropriate to the occasion.

Reading   Matthew 23:37-39

Responsorial Psalm   Psalm 130

The Gelineau version of the "de Profundis" is recommended. Gather #128, "Psalm 130: I Place All My Trust In You," (GIA, 1962).

All kneel and sing the psalm.

> *All:* I place all my trust in you, my God; all my hope is in your mercy.

Opening Prayer

The presider stands for the prayer; all others remain kneeling.

Presider: God of mercy and compassion, look graciously upon the world which you have made, and on the people who are won for you by the blood of your Son, Jesus Christ. Our sins are many: make them white as snow. Bathe us once more in the blood of the Lamb, that, by your power, all the wounds we inflict on each other may be healed, and all the scars we mark upon the earth may be taken away. We ask this through Jesus Christ, our Lord, who lives and rules with you and the Holy Spirit, one God, forever and ever.

> *All:* Amen.

All are seated.

Liturgy of the Word

First Reading   Hosea 6:1-6

Responsorial Psalm   Psalm 95

> *All:* If today you hear his voice, harden not your hearts (cf. vv. 8-9).

Second Reading 2 Corinthians 5:16-21

Gospel Acclamation

Cantor: Alleluia . . .

  All: Alleluia . . .

Cantor: Let us glory in the cross of our Lord Jesus Christ. He saves us and sets us free; through him we find salvation, life, and resurrection.

  All: Alleluia . . .

Gospel John 13:1-10

Homily

Solemn Rite of Atonement

Blessing of Water

Several basins of water to be used in the ceremony of cleansing are brought before the presider for blessing as the atonement prayer begins. During the rite of washing, several ministers will be needed with towels to assist the people.

Presider: Sisters and brothers, in solemn prayer we open this weekend Day of Atonement. Our eyes are turned to the Crucified One whose death has broken the bonds of sin and death. Before the power of our own sin and the sin of others, we stand helpless. We have no place to turn but to him who is mercy itself. This night we pray to the Lord of all to blot out and pardon our own sin and all the sins upon the earth. We place ourselves at the mercy of our God who alone can reconcile the world to the Godhead. Let us ask God's blessing on this water that it may bring to us, to our Church, and to our world, the cleansing grace of our Lord Jesus Christ.

Pause for silent prayer.

Presider: Gracious and loving God, on this night of holy atonement, we ask you to breathe your mercy on this water that it be for us the forgiveness of our sin, the healing of all division, and the dawn of your life within us. Send your Spirit upon us and upon the water of this font. May all of us who are washed with your water of life find in your mercy pardon and peace. We ask this through Christ, our Lord.

  All: Amen.

Prayer for the Local Community

Presider: Let us pray now, my brothers and sisters, that our own sins may be taken away. Let us entrust our life together as a community of believers in Christ to the tender mercy of our God.

All kneel. A member of the community, or one of the ministers, comes to the altar and places some incense on the coals in the thurible. The presider begins the Confiteor and all join in.

Presider: Please come forward, and with hearts contrite, bathe your hands in the forgiveness of our God.

All in the assembly come forward, wash their hands in the water that has been blessed, and return to their places. During this ritual washing, an appropriate song or psalm, such as Psalm 51, may be sung. When all have returned to their places, they kneel.

When the assembly has finished, after a pause, the presider stands with hands extended over the assembly.

Presider: Merciful God, we place our sins and all their harmful effects into the offering of your Son, Jesus Christ. We ask you to heal and transform them with the same power with which you raised Jesus from the dead. As once you formed us to be your people, we ask you now to heal the wounds that divide us and pardon all our sins. Bind us more deeply in faith, hope, and love so that we may be signs of your healing grace to all upon the earth. We ask this through Christ, our Lord.

All: Amen.

All are seated.

Prayer for the Church

Presider: And now, my sisters and brothers, let us ask the mercy and forgiveness of God upon our Church. We are broken and divided, though the Lord asks us to be one. We are touched by spots of blindness, though the Lord has opened our eyes. We are not without our own moments of darkness, though the Lord has called us light for the world. Mixed with the wheat of God's gracious work among us remain the weeds of our own sin. For our Church, weak and divided, let us ask the atonement of Christ.

In silence, a member of the assembly goes forward to place, for a second time, some incense in the thurible.

All stand.

Reader: For the Church throughout the world, let us pray to the Lord.

All: Lord, have mercy. The response is the same for the following petitions.

Reader: That divisions may cease among us, let us pray to the Lord. *Resp.*

That we may learn the unity for which Christ prayed, let us pray to the Lord. *Resp.*

That our hearts may be opened to the fullness of Christ's word, let us pray to the Lord. *Resp.*

That the grip of our pride may be loosened by the power of the humble Christ, let us pray to the Lord. *Resp.*

That our selfishness may be transformed into generous love and service, let us pray to the Lord. *Resp.*

That we may never use power to abuse or oppress, let us pray to the Lord. *Resp.*

That we may be purified of our sins: those we see and those to which we are blind, let us pray to the Lord. *Resp.*

Presider: O tender and compassionate God, we ask that you be merciful to your Church throughout the world. Brighten our darkness, and make us your radiant bride. Heal our divisions, and weave us into your seamless robe. Cast from us all signs of unwelcome, and make us your holy temple where you, our God, will be pleased to dwell. We ask this through Christ, our Lord.

All: Amen.

All are seated. As a symbol of the Church being cleansed, the four faces of the altar and its mensa are now washed by members of the assembly. Meanwhile, the assembly or choir sings the Trisagion which may be chanted in the vernacular alone or in addition to Greek and Latin (or other languages of the parish: Spanish, Italian, Polish, etc.) as well.

All: Hagios o Theos, hagios ischyros, hagios
athanatos eleison imas.

Sanctus Deus, sanctus fortis, sanctus immortalis,
   miserere nobis.

Holy God, holy mighty One, holy immortal One,
   have mercy on us.

Dios Santissimo y dios todopodoroso
Señor inmortal
   Ten piedad de nosotros . . .*

The chant continues until the washing of the altar is completed.

Prayer for the World

Presider: Brothers and sisters, we are one with the people of the earth.
In this final prayer of atonement, we raise our voices for God's
gracious mercy upon north and south, and east and west, upon
all nations, all peoples, and all creation itself.

*For a third time, a member of the assembly approaches the altar and places
incense on the coals.*

All stand.

All: God of all the nations, God of the heavens and the earth, we lift
up to you the voices of all creation as they yearn for deliverance.
Loosen the bonds that entrap us. Release us from every power
of evil that sets nation against nation, sister against brother,
parent against child. We scatter your healing waters to the four
corners of the earth and raise our voice in humble prayer. Hear
the deep sighs and groans from within your creation itself,
and speedily bring to all people the redemption your Son has
gained for us. We ask this through Christ, our Lord. Amen.

*The presider sprinkles water to the north, south, east, and west and pro-
claims in a loud voice:*

Presider: Holy God, holy mighty One, holy immortal One, have mercy
on us.[2]

---

*Trisagion translation taken from Peter E. Fink, S.J., "Liturgy for a Christian Day of
Atonement," in *Alternative Futures*, 137. Spanish translation is author's.
[2] From the Easter Vigil.

At the conclusion of the sprinkling and proclamation, the assembly joins in a suitable song of praise and dedication.

Concluding Rites

Presider: Let us now join together in the prayer which Jesus taught us

    All: Our Father . . . But deliver us from evil, for the kingdom . . . now and forever. Amen.

Presider: Our weekend Day of Atonement has begun. Let us go forth to keep the fast and to pray with united voice for the healing mercy of our God. May Almighty God bless you, the Father, and the Son, + and the Holy Spirit.

    All: Amen.

Since this service opens out on the day of fasting, no concluding song is necessary. However, if a song is sung, it should be in a tone proper to the beginning of a day of fast and prayer.

PART II:

TABLE PRAYERS FOR THE HOME

The following prayers are adapted from the previous service in order to show the continuity between the liturgical service and prayer in the home during this solemn Day of Atonement.

The table prayers constitute a short prayer service to be offered at the beginning of the evening meal on both Friday and Saturday nights. In place of the incense and water used in the church service, three candles are set on the table. They will be lighted in turn as each of the petitions is prayed.

Call to Prayer

Leader: Compassionate Creator, as we approach the tables of our lives, tables where we gather to dream and to dialogue, tables where we gather to break open your Word and break bread, tables where we pass around a cup of wine, which holds both our hopes and our hurts, give us the grace to face whatever anger, resentment, or disgrace we hold in the fragile chalices of our hearts.

In our prayerful meditation before we come to the table, may we sip holy silence and taste the flavor of your forgiving love. Before bringing the many gifts of our lives to the table, enable us to see how your mercy will free us from our fears.

O Gracious God, help us to meditate on your mercy, to remember your mercy and to radiate your mercy and your love +.[3] (We ask this the name of Holy and immortal one, Jesus the Christ.)

All: Amen.

Prayer for the Local Community

Leader: Let us pray, first of all, for our family gathered here, [or, "for our table gathering"] that God will heal us from the harm we bring to each other.

A first candle is lit in silence.

Leader: Merciful God, we place our sins as a family, the sins as friends and neighbors, into the offering of your Son, Jesus Christ. We ask you to heal the wounds we inflict on each other, and give us your pardon and your peace. In your mercy forgive us all our sins.

All: Have mercy on us, O Lord! Teach us your ways of love and life. Have mercy on us, O Lord.

Prayer for the Church

Leader: Let us pray too for the Church throughout the world, that all divisions may cease and that the salvation won by Jesus Christ may come to all people.

A second candle is lighted in silence.

[3] Excerpted from Joseph Nassal, C.PP.S., *Premeditated Mercy: A Spirituality of Reconciliation* © 2000. Used with the permission of the publisher, Forest of Peace, an imprint of Ave Maria Press, Notre Dame, Ind. 46556; www.avemariapress.com.

Leader: O tender and compassionate God, be merciful to us, your
Church. Heal our divisions. Brighten our darkness. Make us a
holy temple where you, our God, will be pleased to dwell.
In your mercy forgive us all our sins.

All: Have mercy on us, O Lord! Teach us your ways of love and life.
Have mercy on us, O Lord.

Prayer for the World

Leader: Let us now ask God's mercy and love for all peoples upon the
earth.

A third candle is lighted in silence.

Leader: God of all the nations; God of heaven and of earth! Hear the
voice of your creation as it yearns for deliverance. Release us
from every force that sets nation against nation, sister against
brother, parent against child; and give to all peoples of the earth
your own lasting peace. In your mercy forgive us all our sins:

All: Have mercy on us, O Lord! Teach us your ways of love and life.
Have mercy on us, O Lord!

Blessing before the Meal

Leader: Bless us, Lord, and this food we share, and grant your mercy to
us all through Christ, our Lord.

All: Amen.

The meal is shared.

Thanksgiving after the Meal

*Prepare towels and bowls of warm soapy water. Read together John 13:1-15
and tenderly wash one another's feet.*

PART III:
THE MASS OF THE SOLEMNITY OF CHRIST THE KING

Common musical settings can anchor the Penitential Rite, the Responsorial Psalm and General Intercessions from the Mass of Christ the King to those of the previous days of the vigil.

After the homily, the Renewal of Baptism promises and the Sprinkling of the people with Blessed Water would be especially appropriate. The preacher (chosen carefully for his/her credibility to the group process) sets the stage for this.

Solemn Blessing chosen from Dedication of a Church.[4] Closing Proclamation from the Weekend "Day of Atonement."

Presider or deacon:
> Sisters and brothers,
> We bring our Atonement vigil to its conclusion
> at the throne of Christ
> who is Lord and King of all.
> We lift up to him the future of our church and community
> who is God's mercy on the earth.
>
> Let us go in peace to love and serve the Lord.

[4] Rite of Dedication of a Church and Altar," International Commission on English in the Liturgy, The Rites of the Catholic Church, vol. 2 (Collegeville, Minn.: Liturgical Press, 1991) 388.

Reconciliation Rite for Impasse

This prayer service is constructed to be used only once in a process that is conflicted, at a point in deliberations that reconciliation and consensus do not look probable. It uses some pertinent Scripture readings, intercession and role play. The facilitator or facilitating team needs to play an important part in this prayer service. They will need to follow up on it in their next session around the conference table. But having a night (or longer) to sleep on it will be an important time for rest after this ritual. It is hoped that by confronting the personalities of peace, truth, mercy, and justice in an environment of prayer, a perspective of reconciliation emerges unique to that circumstance.[1]

A Rite for Impasse

A hymn may be sung, or instrumental music may be played.

Presider: We gather together in the presence of the healing love of God, to ask for God's guidance and blessing and to rededicate

---

[1] Adapted from Mari West Zimmerman, "Service of Healing for a Congregation" in *Take and Make Holy: Honoring the Sacred in the Healing of Abuse Survivors* (Chicago: Liturgy Training Publications, 1995) 82–91 (Reprinted from *Take and Make Holy,* © 1995, Archdiocese of Chicago, Liturgy Training Publications, 1800 North Hermitage Ave., Chicago, Ill. 60622-1101, 1-800-933-1800, fax 1-800-933-7094, email: amcclure@ltp.org. All rights reserved.) and John Paul Lederach, *The Journey Toward Reconciliation* (Scottsdale, Pa.: Herald Press, 1999) 51–61.

ourselves to the foundations of human community. We are stuck. Our deliberations have reached a place where we feel powerless to make further movement. Let us turn then to a source of wisdom and power to lead us to the next steps on the road to conciliation and communion.

One or several participants are asked to summarize the progress of the deliberations to this point, particularly noting common ground.

Presider: Let us pray,

Holy Spirit, you are the Spirit of unity. We invite you into our lives this day. Keep us singular in mind and purpose as we work to bring God's Kingdom upon earth.

Bless our Church—all its leaders, its members, its young people. Help all of us to overcome trials, separations, mistakes, and ignorance. Ward off any extremes or superstitions. Ignite us with your fire of zeal and courage.

May your truth be our beacon and our shelter. May nothing separate us, or those we love, from our Lord and Savior, Jesus Christ. Amen.[2]

First Reading   Isaiah 58:10-12

Reader: A reading from the book of the prophet Isaiah.

The reading follows. This lovely reading employs images of food and water to describe the restored humanity of those who attend to the poor. Compassionate generosity restores the foundations of a community and repairs the breach of relationship between peoples.

Reader: The Word of the Lord.

All: Thanks be to God.

  [2] Adapted from Joan M. Bernier, S.N.D., Summer Reflections, '97 Archdiocese of Hartford (Conn.). Reprinted with permission from *Grieving, Healings and New Beginnings: Resources for Parish Leaders and Parishioners.* Archdiocese of Dubuque, Iowa, (February 2003), see also §94B, "Prayers of Exorcism," *Rite of Christian Initiation of Adults* (Chicago: Liturgy Training Publications, 1988) 42.

Silence

Responsorial Psalm   Psalm 90:1-2, 16-17

Sung version preferred, for example, Gather #84, *"Fill Us with Your Love, O Lord," Roy James Stewart, GIA, 1993.*

Cantor/Reader: Lord, you have been our refuge / through all generations.

    All: Lord, you have been our refuge / through all generations.

Cantor/Reader: Before the mountains were born,
            the earth and the world brought forth,
            from eternity to eternity you are God. *Resp.*

Cantor/Reader: Show your deeds to your servants,
            your glory to their children.
            May the favor of the Lord our God be ours.
            Prosper the work of our hands!
            Prosper the work of our hands! *Resp.*

Second Reading   1 Corinthians 3:3-9

Reader: A reading from the First Letter of Paul to the Corinthians.

Quarreling allegiances to religious leaders like Apollos or Paul are the context of this exhortation to the Corinthian church. As servants and field hands, each adds a unique gift to God's building and everyone will receive a more than just wage according to the contribution made.

Reader: The Word of the Lord.

    All: Thanks be to God.

Gospel Reading   Luke 10:25-37

Presider: A reading from the Gospel in the tradition of Luke.

A question to Jesus about the requirements for eternal life, prompts the response familiar to any Jew to God: "with heart, soul and strength" to which Jesus adds "neighbor as self." He illustrates this with the parable of the Good Samaritan. Jesus expands the notion of neighbor to anyone in need, going beyond contemporary sensibilities. Compassionate and generous self giving guarantees long life in the land.

Presider: The Gospel of the Lord.

   All: Praise to you, Lord Jesus Christ.

A generous time of meditation music and silence follows.

Homily or Reflection

This is given by one of those acting as facilitator.

Role Play and Intercessory Prayer

Presider: Psalm 85 [verses 10-11] proclaims a dance of four important
   figures in the transformation of any human conflict: Near
   indeed is [God's] salvation for the loyal; / prosperity will fill our
   land. / Love (mercy) and truth will meet; / justice and peace
   will kiss.

   Let us pray to know those principles working among us, to hear
   their voices. *Pause.*

   We pray for an awareness of your presence as we build this
   community on the foundation of justice; strengthen us when we
   are tempted to do what is expedient rather than what is just.

   We pray, be with us, God of justice.

   All: Be with us, God of justice.

*At this point a participant, who has been chosen to speak to the situation
from the perspective of justice, presents to the assembly. What does he or
she see? What is required to meet the demands of justice?*

*A clearly limited time should be agreed upon for this and each of the
following presentations.*

Presider: We pray for courage to speak of what we have learned from
   our own integrity and that of our people and cultures. The
   truth of the Gospel brings in its wake freedom. We pray that
   our church family may flourish in the light of an honest and
   listening environment.

   We pray, be with us, God of truth.

   All: Be with us, God of truth.

A participant, who has been chosen to speak to the conflicted situation from the perspective of truth presents to the assembly. What does he or she see? What is required to meet the demands of truth?

Presider: Spirit of the living God, look with mercy on the communities gathered here. Give us the grace to seek you in adversity and to reach out to each other in tolerance and mutual respect, to give and to receive your tender mercies.

We pray, be with us, God of mercy.

All: Be with us, God of mercy.

A participant, who has been chosen to speak to the conflicted situation from the perspective of mercy presents to the assembly. What does he or she see? What is required to meet the demands of mercy?

Presider: As members of the body of Christ, may we continue searching for consensus in our deliberations. May we find some way to name the walls that divide us and break through our impasse. May God give us the gifts of the Spirit to impel us forward with new service to the Christian community of this place. Let us be for one another a sign of your presence that we may know you have not abandoned us.

We pray, be with us, God of Peace.

All: Be with us, God of Peace.

A participant, who has been chosen to speak to the conflicted situation from the perspective of peace presents to the assembly. What does he or she see? What is required to meet the demands of peace?

Justice, peace, truth and mercy are asked to have a conversation with each other. What does each bring to the table, both positive and negative? What do the participants appreciate about each perspective? What do each fear about the other?

Leader: We pray silently now for any needs that remain unspoken in our hearts.

Pause for silent prayer.

Leader: For all the needs known only to our selves and to God, we pray. God of Jesus the Christ, bring us together in the presence of your love that we may be a source of support for one another.

We pray in the name of Jesus, the truth, the justice, the peace, and the mercy of God, now and forever.

All: Amen.

Blessing

Presider: May God who has begun this good work in our midst graciously bring it to completion.

All: Thanks be to God.

Meditation on the Cross

This ritual ends with a Taizé-like meditation on the cross. There is a large painted cross with vigil candles about it, upright in the sanctuary. (This has been prepared beforehand.) Two participants approach the cross and lay it on the floor of the front of the sanctuary. The vigil candles are arranged on it. After several minutes of music, the leader invites the members of the assembly to go to the cross individually.

Leader: As you are moved to do so, all are invited to come up to the cross. Kneel, bow, or touch the cross for a moment. In the presence of the risen Christ, know that we are united with all those who are searching for God's will in the midst of confusing and conflicted times.

The leader goes to the cross first. When all who wish to do so have prayed at the cross, the music is concluded. Before the participants leave the building, a follow-up session needs to be announced to build on what emerges from this prayer. Often at least a night is required to "sleep on" the ritual experience and allow new alternatives to surface to address the group's impasse.

Rituals of Transition
A Week of Farewell for Parish Closure

Since parish closures evoke such strong feelings of grief and anger, these liturgies need to acknowledge the many emotions in honest ritual and give people a chance to work through them. They presume the processes of decision making and discernment are concluded. They further presume that outstanding appeals to higher ecclesiastical and civil courts are likewise concluded.

This type of celebration requires careful preparation but would be a way of telling the parish story and allowing good memories to accompany the parishioners during this time of closure, transition, and consolidation. This rite is predicated on a situation where there has been significant conflict. Before the planning of these rites, it is necessary to assess the emotional habitus of the community, how far have they come toward resignation and consent with the closure. Enright, Freedman and Rique's four-phase pattern of interpersonal forgiveness, referred to in chapter 3, can give pastoral ministers some key indicators for this assessment. Their work considers "the psychological variables involved when we forgive."

A Week of Prayer and Memory

Sunday Inauguration Liturgy

This rite, inaugurating the final week of prayer for a closing parish, is a blessing and dismissal to close a Eucharist or evening prayer. After the closing prayer, the assembly comes forward with tapers or candles and receives light from the paschal candle, held by the presider. It would be an appropriate time to read the official document closing the parish from the local bishop. This decree is best accompanied by a letter expressing support to the parish during the transition and the solidarity of the whole diocesan community in the task of restructuring their parish. A Litany of the Saints, including the name of the parish patron, is sung by the assembly as all process out of the building led by the presider with the paschal candle. The final prayer over the people and the blessing are proclaimed from the doors of the church, and a warm invitation to return for the week's events is given from the same place.

Vigil Week

During the week between the inauguration liturgy and the closing liturgy in the new parish, a series of vigil celebrations takes place. These may either take the form of evening prayer from the Liturgy of the Hours or a liturgy of the Word. During the singing of the Gospel Canticle of evening prayer, the altar, paschal candle and people are incensed. Before the final blessing, a member or members of the community may be invited to offer remembrances about the parish. The paschal candle remains in its place throughout the week and is lighted during other liturgies that take place. The sung Litany of the Saints accompanies the recession at each service. Leadership, particularly former pastors and staff, can be particularly welcomed to preside at these prayer events. The themes of these days can be alternated or used interchangeably.

Day 1: Foundation Stories and Baptism

It is suggested that the first evening gathering be dedicated to telling the parish's history. After a liturgy of the Word, names of members of the parish could be read from the baptismal register. Particular attention could be paid to those who were baptized during the first year of the parish's existence and those who were baptized during the final year. Some anecdotes by the pastor or senior parishioners would be appreciated. After a group of names is recited, an acclamation (such as the Taizé, "Jesus, Remember Me" [*Gather* #404, Jacques Berthier, Les Presses de Taizé, GIA, 1981]) could be sung. Slide shows of parish history are nearly always welcome additions to celebrations like these. A reflection on the sacrament of baptism could be given, perhaps by a parishioner who helps with baptismal preparation.

Day 2: Eucharist and Religious Education

Celebrations during the second day might include the Exposition and Benediction of the Blessed Sacrament. It is recommended that the church be made available to parishioners for visitation as much as possible during the week of closing. They should be afforded the opportunity to savor its beauty, images, and atmosphere.

Children could be involved in the vigils throughout the week. One suggestion is in a service honoring those who have made First Communion over the years of a parish's history. Photos and memorabilia from First Communions over the years could permit the mystery of the Eucharist to be honored from a child's perspective.

Memories of cooking, potlucks, and cookbooks, of food collected for and prepared for the poor need to be highlighted. A food collection would be a marvelous way of continuing to "do church" in the midst of closure. St. Vincent de Paul Societies (or similar charitable providers) need to be thanked and the stories told.

Christian education needs to be highlighted both in and out of the Catholic school tradition. The stories need to be told of the religious women and men, and lay teachers that cared for the flame of faith in the young.

If there has been a parish school phased out or consolidated, those involved may want to celebrate some of their own specific activities during the week. It is crucial that Catholic education not be divorced from the parish's celebration of its history. These activities could be perhaps located in the former school, convent, or other special building. Ongoing Catholic education in the area will depend on careful planning, perhaps using these events for gathering new patrons and the transfer of resources, including in some cases, buildings into new configurations.

Day 3: Relics and Devotions

This day is dedicated to celebrations in honor of the Blessed Virgin Mary and/or of the patron saint of the closing parish. Devotions that were popular through the years can be organized and prayed for a final time before the transition. Groups of the parish connected to those devotions or others could plan and oversee these devotions. Rosaries and Mother of Perpetual Help Novenas, May Crowning and Sorrowful Mother devotions were the landscape of U.S. Catholicism.

Statuary, reliquaries, and gifts from the various sodalities need to be prominent and the stories told by senior members and invited guests.

Day 4: Vocations: Marriage, Religious Life and Ordination

Evening prayer on this day could invite clergy and professional staff who have served the parish in the past to preach. Vowed religious, or couples who serve in marriage preparation could also be excellent presiders for this night and its reflections.

There are several formularies for the renewal of marriage vows and the renewal of religious vows. These renewals would add life and warmth to this part of the parish's remembering. How couples met and why vows in religious life were spoken are stories that never lose their tenderness.

Day 5: Healing and Reconciliation

The liturgies in appendices 1.1–1.4 were suggested for the decision-making time of parish consolidation. Some of these may be helpful to repeat on this day of the vigil. The washing of hands, the altar, the walls of the church, and where the crosses of the building's original dedication were anointed could accompany ongoing adjustment to the parish's closure. Appendix 1.4, the weekend "Day of Atonement," contains the details of this.

Stories about the confessionals of the parish, confessors and times of personal and/or communal reconciliation might draw out the theme of healing in some new directions. Giving prominence to the three oils blest each year at the chrism Mass (chrism, the oil of catechumens, and the oil of the sick) by honoring them with incense and giving reflections about healing could make for a grace-filled day.

The availability of confessors after the liturgy for extended individual reconciliation would be a gift to those who might still be conflicted about the final outcomes of the process and closure-consolidation decisions.

Day 6: The Dead

The liturgy of this day would begin as all those of the vigil week, with the gathering around the paschal candle and the singing of a Litany of Saints. The book of parish interments and/or a "book of the dead" would be the focus of the prayer. Reading out the names of those buried over the years followed by stories and song could take most of the day. The Office of the Dead would add a form to the day with different people joining the prayer at different times given work and family schedules. Some musical settings of lament psalmody would allow people to grieve or perhaps extend the healing of grief into other unhealed relationships.

A potluck supper would give parishioners adequate time to deal with the feelings of sadness and grief while still in this familiar setting. This evening would be an intimate and private time, like a funeral wake, to swap stories and sit quietly.

Some may want to keep vigil through the night. This kind of prayer may be particularly comforting and healing to prepare for a changed tone of worship on the following day.

Rite on the Occasion of a Parish Closing[1]

This liturgy focuses more on the history and life of the community than on its physical environment. Its tone is one of thanksgiving and tenderness of memory. A separate rite of leave taking of the building should be arranged some time later, possibly at a separate evening prayer at the end of the day or another time when people can gather to say good-bye more specifically to the building.

On the day of the formal closing rites for the parish, all gather outside the parish church to be closed, if circumstances permit. The liturgy may begin outside the worship space with a gathering hymn. Representatives from the receiving and closing parishes should be involved in the opening procession and ministries of the liturgy. Nametags should be made available and worn by all, and hospitality for alums and guests should be carefully planned. The paschal candle is again used in place of the processional cross.

Introductory Rites

Opening Comment

After the greeting, the presider speaks to the assembly in these or similar words.

Presider: As the Lord's temple, God's holy people, let us give thanks today for the ____ years St. _____ Parish has served the (neighborhood) community. At the table of God's Word and

---

[1] Adapted from "Liturgy on the Occasion of Closing a Parish," in David G. Caron, "Information Packet on Parish Closing," Miami, Fla.: privately published, 1999.

the table of the Eucharist our communion with Christ and one another will be strengthened for our ongoing journey of faith. Especially aware of any unresolved conflict or broken relationship because of the consolidation discernment, let us prepare our minds and hearts for these holy mysteries, by acknowledging the need for the mercy of God in all of our lives.

Penitential Rite

A sung version of the Taizé Kyrie chant, with its extended litany, would be a healing form of the familiar Lord, have mercy, *speaking to those areas still unhealed or painful. The presider can create some space in the rite for public apology (should it be necessary) especially for words spoken in the heat of attempts to save the parish during the processes of decision making.*

Gloria

This needs to be festive and accompanied by the ringing of the bells, where possible.

Liturgy of the Word

The Lectionary readings for the "Dedication of a Church" would allow this liturgy to celebrate church with as rich and inclusive an ecclesiology as possible.

Prayers of the Faithful

In addition to intercessions for the general needs of the Church and the world, some of the following may be of particular use for the closing of a parish.

The response to each petition is: Lord, hear our prayer.

1. For the Pope and local bishop, that God may bless them with wisdom and insight as they continue to shepherd the Church of the twenty-first century, we pray to the Lord.

2. We remember with particular tenderness the pastors and local leadership who have served in this parish throughout its history. In gratitude we pray to the Lord.

3. For other parishes, schools, and institutions throughout the country facing significant changes and transitions, that the love and solidarity of all Catholics may overcome all fear and sadness, we pray to the Lord.

4. For the founders, benefactors, and all past parishioners of this parish; for all those whose faith, vision, and generosity has been the cornerstone of our parish's history, we pray to the Lord.

5. For the priests and vowed religious who have faithfully served this parish through preaching and teaching, prayer and pastoral care, we pray to the Lord.

6. For the ability to rejoice in the blessings we have received through this parish and for the courage to move onward with hope, we pray to the Lord.

7. For those who are still conflicted after the decision to close St. _____ Parish, for the healing and reconciliation of any words spoke in anger or frustration during this time of discernment for this community's future, and for any relationships that remain broken or strained, we pray to the Lord.

8. For the unsung heroes of St. _____ Parish who have contributed so much of themselves for the success of the parish, we pray to the Lord.

9. For the dead, especially those buried from this church over its ____-year history, we pray to the Lord.

The concluding prayer may be said by all.

Presider
or all: Lord God, in Christ you made us your people, a chosen race, a royal priesthood. Throughout these past years your Church has been realized in the life of this parish. Although the service of this parish has now come to an end, we pray that you keep us ever mindful that wherever two or three are gathered in your name your holy presence will be known. Wherever you lead us we will continue to be your holy people, your imperishable temple. Hear us as we raise our minds and hearts to you through Christ our Lord.

All: Amen.

Liturgy of the Eucharist

Preparation Rite

As the collection is taken the presider calls to remembrance the generous stewardship of the parishioners over the years of its history.

Presider: We bring to the Lord not only today's contribution to the work of our parish, but all the hard earned dollars and cents of ____ years.

A trustee or chair of the parish council speaks the following.

Speaker: Lord, Sunday after Sunday we have offered to you a share of our work and our resources. We have offered not only our money, but also our work, our time, and our talent. With our own hands and money we built a rectory, a school, and this place of worship; we have supported the work of your Church. Thank you for working with us and through us.

Mass proceeds as usual with the eucharistic prayer and the communion rite. For the eucharistic prayer, a preface for the "Dedication of a Church" is suggested.

Suggestion: Use Preface 52 or 53 for the Dedication of a Church.

At the end of the Liturgy of Eucharist, while all are still in their places, ministers remove the altar cloth during a communion song. These ministers continue to stand in the sanctuary area with altar cloth and lighted altar candles. A brazier is set in the center of the altar with hot charcoal.

A Final Commendation[2]

Presider: Before we take leave of (St. Sebastian Parish), let us pause to once more express our deep affection for this place and the history of Christian community life that has taken place here.

Farewell Song

Gather #649, *"You Are Mine," David Haas, GIA, 1991.*

---

[2] Adapted from the closure rites of Chicago's Saint Sebastian Parish in 1990, in William McManus, "A Funeral for a Parish," *Liturgy 90* 22, no. 2 (February–March 1991) 6–7, © 1991 Archdiocese of Chicago: Liturgy Training Publications, 1800 North Hermitage Avenue, Chicago, Ill. 60622-1101; 1-800-933-1800, fax 1-800-933-7094, email: orders@ltp.org. All rights reserved. Used with permission.

(The presider could incense the altar a final time or add incense to a brassier that has been placed on the altar reminiscent of the Dedication rites.)

Presider: Whenever we eat this eucharistic bread and wine we proclaim the Lord's death until he comes.

    All: Whatever table we gather around may we be reminded of the love we have shared around this one.

Presider: The grass withers, the flower fades, but the word of our God will stand forever.

    All: May we always be open to God's word: it challenges us to justice and comforts us with hope.

Presider: (holding the paschal candle) Jesus said: "I am the light of the world."

    All: May we share the light of our faith with our new parishes. We are a chosen race, a royal priesthood, a holy nation, God's own people.

> (During, the closing rites for Chicago's St. Sebastian, the presider, Chicago Auxiliary Bishop Timothy Lyne, once again thanked the parishioners for their cooperation during the previous months' life-and-death struggle in the parish. Another request could be spoken for forgiveness for any of the hurts brought about during the life of the parish prior to a final official proclamation of closure.)

"With thanks to God for the good accomplished here, this parish of (St. Sebastian) is now closed."

A Gesture of Farewell

During the singing of the final hymn, all are invited to come forward and kiss the altar (or offer a profound bow) as a gesture of leave taking.

Procession

If there is a parish banner, this can be carried out of the assembly with cross, candles, altar clothes, ministers, and presider. The procession leaves in the normal way. Most transfer of other religious items will take place during the rite of leave taking.

Liturgy Notes

All can then proceed to the hall for a reception. If there are church bells, they should be rung during this movement. Where possible, this formal reception should be hosted by the receiving parish. More story-telling, blessing, and remembering needs to be initiated and welcomed. Displays of parish history and scrapbooks should be abundant.

A prayer card with important dates (for example, of the parish's history) would be a lovely gift to send home with every guest.

Additional speeches and addresses might be given at the reception. Honored guests need to be recognized. Experience says that a great deal of attention needs to be given to the details of this reception.

A final note: The presence of the receiving pastor and staff, encouraging and welcoming people individually to the combined parish, is a kindness people remember for years afterward.

Rite of Leave Taking of a Church

This rite is predicated on a situation of conflict, although it could be adapted to one where there is more resignation to the closure and consolidation into another parish location. It repeats ritual stations, albeit briefly, like those employed in the "Rituals of Transition: A Week of Farewell for Parish Closure" (appendix 2.1) because repetition of narrative is so common to situations of individual and collective grief.[1]

Prelude

During the prelude, the deacon (or a server) incenses the entire assembly by walking throughout the room, using all the aisles.

Then the church is darkened. Only the candles near the altar are lit, those to be carried in procession. The altar is stripped except for a corporal on which to place the ciborium that will be carried in procession to the new church. The following will be used in the process: the processional cross, paschal candle, Book of the Gospels, incense, and a large clear container to carry water from the baptismal font. Other items of value can also be chosen to take in the translation to the new parish church.

Introductory Rite

Greeting

The greeting is in the presider's own words, then the following words are added.

[1] Adapted from Rita Fisher, I.H.M., "The Grace of this Place: Closing a Church," *Liturgy 90* (February–March 1996) 9–10; © 1991 Archdiocese of Chicago: Liturgy Training Publications, 1800 North Hermitage Avenue, Chicago, Ill. 60622-1101; 1-800-933-1800, fax 1-800-933-7094, email: orders@ltp.org. All rights reserved. Used with permission. And adapted from Larry W. Dorsch, "The Rituals of Parish Consolidation," *Church* 17, no. 1 (Spring 2001) 33–34. Used with permission.

Presider: We gather to remember a community and a history and to say a
final good-bye to this place where that community lived. May
our farewell express our affection for this people and place.
May it ease our sadness and strengthen our hope that one day
we will be gathered again when the love of Christ, which
conquers all things, even death itself. Let us enter with full
hearts into thanksgiving for the gifts of God and the graces of
this place.[2]

A Night Prayer with extended Liturgy of the Word

The format is from the Liturgy of the Hours. The rubrics for Night Prayer
offer the option of a brief examination of conscience. In a communal celebration, a Penitential rite using one of the formulas of the Mass is suggested. The presider might direct this with specific reflections on any
breaches of relationship caused by the decision to leave the parish worship
space with the familiar "Lord have mercy," at the end of each reflection.
The rite concludes with the absolution, "May almighty God have mercy
on us, forgive us our sins, and bring us to everlasting life. Amen."

The hymn chosen for the prayer needs to speak reconciliation and hope.
Suggestion: *Gather* #882, "Healer of Our Every Ill," Marty Haugen, GIA
Publications, 1987.

Psalmody Psalm 91

An alternative could be Psalm 85 or the Canticle of Daniel 3:26.

Reading Revelation 21:1-5, 6-7

An alternative could be Revelation 22:4-5.

Homily

*A brief homily could focus on God's dwelling place among people, the God
who comforts and makes all things new, God who is the beginning and end
of all things.*

---

[2] This includes words from the prayer of commendation from the *Order of Christian Funerals.*

Responsory

A sung version of Responsory entrusting the day into the hands of God is preferred.

Gospel Canticle   Luke 2:29-32 and antiphon

The altar, the Book of the Gospels, and the Reserved Sacrament are incensed. The first few words of the canticle may be intoned by a cantor or recited by the presider.

In place of the final prayer, some instrumental music continues as ministers prepare for a procession through some important stations and out of the building. The ciboria with the Reserved Sacrament is placed on the altar, much in the way as for the translation of the Eucharist on Holy Thursday.

Presider: Blessed are you, loving God. In this place we have known your love. We trust our future to your care. We thank you and we praise you O God.

All sing: We praise you, O Lord, for all your works are wonderful. We praise you, O Lord, forever is your love.

(Gather #541, "We Praise You," Darryl Ducote and Gary Daigle, Damean Music, GIA Publications, 1978).

Particular care should be taken with some of the wedding verses connected to this lovely hymn. A more traditional hymn or series of hymns could be substituted depend on the needs of the particular community.

Procession

Presider: As we leave this place of worship, we give thanks to God for all the blessings we have found here.

If possible, for remembering, the whole assembly is to join in the procession through some significant ritual stations of the church: the font, confessional-reconciliation chapel, the twelfth Station of the Cross, the shrine of Mary and/or the patron saint, the ambo, and finally the altar. A route should be adapted according to the layout of the building, but the procession should culminate at the altar.

Those who cannot process are invited to turn in the direction of the procession and stations, and sing between each thanksgiving. Candle bearers lead the procession to the various areas.

At the Font

Presider: Let us pause to remember the baptisms celebrated over the years here at this font.

Pause for a time of silence.

Presider: We thank you and we praise you for the life of faith given to all who have passed through the waters of new life at this font. We thank you and we praise you O God!

    All: We Praise You, O Lord . . .

At the Confessional or Reconciliation Chapel

Presider: Let us remember the times when we have been forgiven, comforted, consoled in the sacrament of penance.

Pause for a time of silence.

Presider: We thank you and we praise you for the healing and reconciling love that has been given through the sacrament of penance in this church. We thank you and we praise you O God!

    All: We Praise You, O Lord . . .

At the Twelfth Station of the Cross

Presider: Let us remember those who walked these stations of prayer and devotion over the years. For the Lenten Fridays and Good Fridays of people's lives, we remember.

Pause for a time of silence.

Presider: The twelfth station of Christ's Way of the Cross, "Jesus Dies on the Cross." We adore you O Christ, and we bless you, because by your holy cross, you have redeemed the world. We thank you and we praise you O God!

    All: We Praise You, O Lord . . .

At the Shrine of Our Lady

Presider: Let us remember the generations of prayer and devotion that this sacred image has inspired.

Pause for a time of silence.

Presider: We thank you and we praise you for the consolation of our ancestors and we have found in prayer to Mary, the Mother of God. For the prayers whispered here by our mothers, for the solace found, for the wisdom and miracles that took place here. . . . (All are invited to join in the familiar words of the prayer to Our Lady.) Hail Mary, full of grace, the Lord is with you. We thank you and we praise you O God!

    All: We Praise You, O Lord . . .

At the Image or Statue of the Parish's Patron Saint

Presider: We thank you and we praise you for the inspiration and identity our ancestors passed on to us in devotion to _____. For the prayers whispered here, for the solace found, for the wisdom and miracles that took place here (all are invited to join in the familiar doxology "Glory be to the Father, and to the Son and to the Holy Spirit, as it was in the beginning, is now and ever shall be world without end. Amen."). . . . We thank you and we praise you O God!

Pause for a time of silence.

    All: We Praise You, O Lord . . .

At the Ambo

Presider: Let us remember the power of God's Word proclaimed here in Scripture and in preaching.

Pause for a time of silence.

Presider: We thank you and we praise you for your holy Word proclaimed here in faith and preached here in sincerity. May it always echo in our hearts. We thank you and we praise you O God!

    All: We Praise You, O Lord . . .

At the Altar

Presider: Let us remember the times we have gathered for the sacred banquet of the Triduum kept each year, the Sundays on which we worshiped faithfully, the First Communion celebrations, the feast days of saints and martyrs, the weddings witnessed here, the funerals held here in hope. Let us pray.

Pause for a longer time of silence.

Presider: God our refuge, our home is in you. You are greater than any temple, church or cathedral that can be built by human hands, yet in this place we have met your divine majesty. This church building has been a place of blessing for us. Protect us on our way. Lead us to new friends in another faith community. We ask this through Christ our Lord.

All: We Praise You, O Lord . . .

Immediate Preparation for Departure

After the prayer, the following or similar words are spoken by a representative of the parish.

Speaker: As we mark the closing of St. _____ Parish, there are many memories we hold close to our hearts. To keep the memory of St. _____ Parish alive we will take with us today some of our sacred symbols and the parish records which record the history of our parish. These in turn will be received [next Sunday] at St. _____ Parish which so many of us will soon call our own.

We take with us the sacramental registers of baptism, Eucharist, confirmation, marriage and interment; a container of water; the oils and paschal candle from their place at the baptismal font; the Reserved Sacrament and tabernacle light; the relic[s] of _____ [a significant relic such as the altar stone or crosses on the walls that marked the consecration of this church]; a time capsule prepared with mementos for the new cornerstone [or a commemorative plaque for the receiving parish church]; a parish banner [or significant devotional icon like the Our Lady of Guadalupe]; our processional cross [if it has some roots in the history of the parish] and two altar candles.

Especially if the entire community is being transferred to another church, members of the parish can be delegated to carry objects that will be transferred to the new place. These delegates are presented with the objects. Suggested members for this delegation include: the parish council president, the council itself, the eldest member of the parish, the youngest member of the parish, etc. This delegation could simply be one person with one object.

Presider: The life of this community will continue in another place. N._____ receive this _____ [name of item] that will be used at _____ [name of the new church]. Take it (directly) from this place to _____ [name of the new pastor/pastoral administrator] as a sign that our journey of faith will continue there.

This is repeated when there are multiple delegates.

The blessing is omitted.[3]

A Final Hymn to Our Lady

The choice of this hymn may be an important moment in this farewell. "Hail Holy Queen," "Immaculate Mary" or the Salve Regina will most likely have deep resonances for those leaving behind churches founded in the U.S. in the late nineteenth and early twentieth centuries.

During the hymn, all process to the principle entrance of the church.

Closing of the Church Doors

Presider: Here we—and those who have gone before us—have celebrated our joys and sorrows. In this church we have encountered Jesus Christ in Word, sacrament, and one another. But now, after ____ years of faith, with thanks to God for the good accomplished here, I declare this Church of St. _____ closed.

The Presider closes and locks the doors. Several representatives of the parish, especially senior members, seal the church doors with purple ribbon.

Sending Prayer

Presider: The history of this parish has been a privileged period of grace given us by God. We who have come in trust to this holy place are moved with a new resolve to be renewed in heart.

---

[3] Thus the pattern of the final commendation in the *Order of Christian Funerals*.

Let us pray,

Lord God,
in Christ you made us your people,
a chosen race, a royal priesthood.
Throughout these past years
your Church has been realized in the life of this parish.
Although the service of this parish has now come to an end,
we pray that you keep us ever mindful
that wherever two or three are gathered in your name
your holy presence will be known.
Wherever you lead us
we will continue to be your holy people,
your imperishable temple.[4]

Accompany us as we move from here to new sacred places
and new gatherings of your holy people,
we pray through Christ our Lord.

All: Amen.

Presider: Let us go in peace.

All: Thanks be to God.

Procession to the Receiving Church

If the parish where the majority of the parishioners will now worship is prepared, there might be a procession to the new church. The community proceeds to the new or receiving parish church for a short welcome, reception of the articles to be transferred, and a blessing of a new cornerstone or memorial plaque. The entire congregation is asked to join in the procession (walking, or in automobiles and buses) led by the cross bearer, acolytes, and those persons with items being taken from the church.

[4] Adapted from "Liturgy on the Occasion of Closing a Parish," in David G. Caron, "Information Packet on Parish Closing," Miami, Fla.: privately published, 1999. Another option for this sending prayer can be found in "Order of Blessing of Pilgrims before or after their return," *Book of Blessings* prepared by the International Commission on English in the Liturgy (Collegeville, Minn.: Liturgical Press, 1989) 214.

Rite of Reception and Memorial of the Closed Parish with a Blessing of the Foundation Stone

This rite presumes a receiving-model consolidation. An already formed parish with a previously dedicated worship space is receiving the closed parish into its community. Much changes for the receiving parish with the addition of new members and another foundation myth. It is presumed that the receiving parish has spent some time in preparation. Hospitality must be at its peak with name cards, a reception for the closing community (or communities) and a very prominent presence of the pastor and parish staff of the receiving parish. Groups and ministries need to be ready to reconfigure their membership, structure, and leadership to include those moving into the community, even though the parish and its name will not change.

Stories and traditions are inherited and both communities will sense the extent of these changes in the months that follow. The closing parish and the receiving community need to have prepared a sealed capsule to be included in the new stone. The capsule will contain mementos and papers —memories and hopes of their respective parish's history, as well as new hopes and dreams for the consolidated parish. The sign of this enlarged identity is the foundation of the building and its "foundation stone."

Rituals of transition will have been celebrated at the closing site. The community will arrive by procession immediately after the conclusion of their service (if the site is within walking distance) or in a procession of automobiles like a funeral procession. It is possible to adjust the rite and do this the next day, as is frequently the case with the interment after a funeral. But this ritual is arranged as if the members of the closed parish come immediately after their leave taking of their building. Local funeral directors could be a resource for arranging police escorts and limousines for the main elements of the procession: Paschal candle, processional cross, parish banners, sacramental registers (initiation, marriage, and burials), oils and water from the baptismal font. Some prominent member of the closing community should carry the capsule containing mementos, note cards with memories, and dreams for the new parish—all to be placed in the foundation stone of the receiving church. It should be carried in a decorated, colorful container, perhaps one made by the children of the closing parish community.

The bishop is the main celebrant of this simple ritual adapted from the Rite of Laying the Foundation Stone or Beginning Work on the Building of a Church.[1] The ritual here likewise has funerary elements, particularly those of committal. The procession makes its way to the receiving church. The bishop, receiving pastor, ministers and group representatives with their standards gather at front of the newly designated parish church.

The cornerstone or a new dedication stone at the entrance of the church is open with room inside to place and seal the time capsules. The name, foundation dates, and closing dates of the closed parish and perhaps other words of dedication are written on the outside of the stone. A stonemason with mortar is on hand to immediately close and seal the stone after its brief dedication.

Reception and Greeting

When the procession arrives, the bishop greets the representatives of both communities at the door of the church. Led by the new banner of the consolidated parish and the banners of the former parishes, he accompanies the reserved Sacrament to the empty tabernacle.

After the sacrament has been placed in the tabernacle and the light of the former parishes' sanctuary lamps arranged in front, a hymn begins.

Gather #541, "We Praise You," Darryl Ducote and Gary Daigle, Damean Music, GIA Publications, 1978. All of the verses are recommended. The nuptial imagery may be particularly appropriate to this station of the consolidation process.

---

[1] International Commission on English in the Liturgy, *The Rites of the Catholic Church*, vol. 2 (Collegeville, Minn.: Liturgical Press, 1991) 348–57.

Opening Prayer[2]

> *Bishop:* Almighty God, hear our prayers for the communities of _____
> and _____ who have come here today to be united as one
> faith community. Increase their faith in you and in each other,
> and through them, bless your Church. We ask this through our
> Lord Jesus Christ, your Son, who lives and reigns with you and
> the Holy Spirit, one God, forever and ever.

> *All:* Amen.

Liturgy of the Word

Reading of the Word of God

A brief passage of Sacred Scripture (proclaimed well) follows. The following selections specifically focus on the image of a foundation stone.

1. 1 Kings 5:2-18. At the king's orders they quarried huge, special stones for the laying of the temple foundations.

2. Isaiah 28:16-17. See, in Zion God lays a stone of witness, a precious cornerstone, a foundation stone.

3. Luke 6:46-49. A strong foundation can withstand the winds and torrents.

4. Ephesians 2:19-22. We are "built upon the foundation of the apostles and prophets, with Christ Jesus himself as the capstone" (v. 20).

Homily

After a brief homily, the document consolidating the parishes may be read and a copy perhaps enclosed in the foundation stone.

Rededication of the Foundation

The bishop accompanies a procession to the place where the two time capsules will be placed and the new corner stone blessed. While pouring water

---

[2] Adapted from "A Rite for the Merging of Parishes" Diocese of Altoona-Johnstown (Pa.), as quoted in the *FDLC Newsletter* 24, no. 5, Federation of Diocesan Liturgical Commissions (December 1997–January 1998) 52–53. Used with permission.

into a single basin from the fonts of the two formerly independent parishes,
he encourages the community by reminding them that no one should be a
visitor to this place. The stories and sacrifices of those who built the original
church structures must now be a part of the foundation upon which the com-
bined parish is built. Ultimately Christ himself is that foundation. It is the
space for making new stories that make present the reign of God.

Bishop: Let us pray.

> O Lord, we are filled with faith, energized by the power of
> your love, and united by the mission you have entrusted to us
> as we pray for the (new parish's name). Guide the efforts of all
> involved in this process to bring renewal to our local Church.
> May the richness, diversity and gifts of our people be treasured
> and used in the service of your name. Let us view this moment
> of change and renewal, not as a threat to what has been, but as
> an invitation to build up the foundation which has been given
> to us, a new and shining community of faith, one in purpose
> and dedicated ever more fruitfully to the building up of your
> Kingdom. We ask this through you who live and reign forever
> and ever. Amen.[3]

The bishop sprinkles the foundation of the building with holy water. To do this
he may stand at the site of the new cornerstone or go in procession around
the building with the assembly and its ministers while a traditional hymn
such as "The Church's One Foundation" (Gather, #661) is sung.

Sealing of the Time Capsule and Blessing of a New Cornerstone

The two pastors (from both the closing and receiving parishes) place the two
capsules with mementos of the memories and dreams of the two communi-
ties in the cornerstone.

The Bishop takes holy water to bless it from the same container as used to
rededicate the foundation. The ICEL text for the Laying of a Foundation
Stone (§§27–28) makes reference to the "cornerstone" imagery of Ephe-
sians 2:20. It notes that the work of building church continues until "they

---

[3] "Prayer for the Pastoral Planning Process," Archdiocese of San Francisco, as quoted
in, "A Journey of Hope toward the Third Millennium: A Pastoral Plan for the Archdiocese of San Francisco," First Phase Recommendations (November 19, 1993). Used
with permission.

arrive at last in your heavenly city." The Episcopalian text for Laying of a Cornerstone recommends the collect for the Patron or Title of the Church be prayed.[4]

A stone mason then seals in the time capsules and fixes the stone with whatever additional mortar is needed. Meanwhile, if the occasion demands, the following antiphon is proclaimed or sung in the languages of the combined community.

[Latin]   Haec est domus domini fermiter aedificata. (Alleluia).
[English]   This is the House of the Lord firmly built. (Alleluia).
[Spanish] Esta es la casa del Señor edificada muy fuerte. (Alleluia).[5]

Other languages appropriate to the consolidating communities may be used for this proclamation.

Another appropriate song may be sung.

General Intercessions

Bishop: United in Christ, we lift our prayers to the Lord. Confident of God's love, we voice our petitions.

Response: We praise and thank you, Lord!

For the Church throughout the world and for our local Church of _____, we proclaim:

For the people of this newly established faith community within the Diocese, we proclaim:

For the poor, the sick, the lost and homeless, that Christians meet the needs of God's people, we proclaim:

---

[4] *The Book of Occasional Services, 1979*, Episcopal Church, U.S.A. (New York: Church Hymnal Corporation, 1980) 199.

[5] From the consolidation rites of St. Anthony and Immaculate Conception San Francisco, California, September 17, 1994. Fr. David G. Caron, as noted earlier, suggests an alternative to this with a "Name Signing Ritual." At the first potluck of the combined parish, the carpet in the church is rolled back and the newly consolidated community is given magic markers. They are invited to write their own names, and the names of everyone who is not present and the dead from their families and extended communities once connected to the former communities. The carpet is then recovered. This later alternative makes the point that with consolidation, the parish's identity changes. See Caron's "Information Packet on Parish Closings" (Miami, Fla., 1999) 4.

That the celebration of Word and Sacrament be the binding force to our new community, we proclaim:

For the gift of this merger and the celebration of our unity as one parish, we proclaim:

Bishop: Gracious God, unite us in peace and harmony. May your Son's farewell gift of peace be with the people of _____. We ask this through Christ our Lord.

All: Amen.

Exchange of Peace

The Bishop prays for peace and then exchanges a formal greeting of peace with pastor and presidents of former parish councils. He then invites the Sign of Peace is to be exchanged throughout the assembly.

Concluding Prayer

Bishop: Let us pray.

Lord, hear the prayers of your people and bring the hearts of believers together in praise. May all peoples rejoice in the perfect unity of your Church, and move together as one to eternal life in your kingdom. Make us able and willing to do what you ask. May Christ's peace be our sign of unity and bond of charity. We ask this through Christ our Lord.

All: Amen.[6]

Blessing and Dismissal

Taken from the "Dedication of a Church in Which Mass Is Already Being Celebrated Regularly," §39.[7]

---

[6] Adapted from "A Rite for the Merging of Parishes," Diocese of Altoona-Johnstown (Pa.), from the *FDLC Newsletter* 24, no. 5, Federation of Diocesan Liturgical Commissions (December 1997–January 1998) 52–53. Used with permission.

[7] International Committee In English in the Liturgy, *The Rites*, vol. 2 (Collegeville, Minn.: Liturgical Press, 1991) 403–4.

Rites for the Inauguration of a Newly Consolidated Parish

New Worship Space

It is presumed that if a new parish is formed from several consolidating ones, it will be inaugurated with a new or significantly renovated worship space. The rite for inaugurating the new church would be the Rite for the Dedication of a Church and an Altar. If two parishes formally consolidate in the space of one of the former parishes, the new worship space serves best if it is renamed with a new patron. A shrine or memorial in a prominent place could honor the former patrons. A major renovation or new structure clearly designates the reconfigured parish as new. When this happens, it is important that the space be rededicated with the full liturgy for the dedication of a church and an altar. It has been the experience of parishes surveyed for this study that the rite of inauguration be celebrated as soon as possible after the leave taking of a closed parish building.

Receiving Parish Consolidation

In this rite for a "receiving-parish consolidation," baptismal symbols predominate. The last of a series of rituals that have accompanied the re-framing of the boundaries around a local church, its focus is hospitality and commitment. In a "receiving-parish consolidation," it is presumed the receiving parish is already dedicated. There is no need to repeat it. If there is a new altar or podium, built for the occasion, a part of the dedication ritual would be appropriate. Allowing the space and parish programs to be claimed by the arriving community is important. In many places this has been a source of ongoing conflict. "We have always done it this way" is a mantra to be avoided. Ongoing pastoral care, and support from the bishop and diocesan administration are also very important. The rededication of other worship spaces in the new parish complex, using the name of the closed parish is important for a sense of home. The dedicating of space (such as the daily Mass chapel, parish hall, or another space) in the name of the patron saint of the closing parish has been a well-received gesture of inclusion.

The presider for this liturgy should be the new pastor. If a bishop is present, it might be pastorally judicious to allow local leadership to perform the major liturgical functions. This liturgy is about "re-forming" communion at the level of the local parish.

Liturgical Notes

The altar. The altar should be bare at the beginning of the rite, because it will be clothed, incensed and given light at the preparation of gifts. The following will be needed: a new altar cloth, fresh candles, a sufficient amount of bread and wine for a now larger congregation, ciboria and cups for Communion under both species. Some of these could be items carried from the closed church.

Liturgical Environment. The articles from the now closed parish need to be arranged in a prominent place: the processional, cross, oils and sanctuary light. The celebration will need: a large container of blessed water from the fonts of the now combined parishes, the three registers of marriage, Christian initiation and burials and the paschal candles.

Orations and Preface. Orations from the Common of the Dedication of a Church are suggested for this liturgy. There are a number of prefaces in the Sacramentary appropriate for a dedication or the anniversary of dedication. One of them can be chosen for this celebration. It is important to heighten the broadest possible sense of Church.

Just representation. Even though the people of the closed parish are being welcomed into an already formed parish, the more flexibility the structures, the less newly arriving parishioners will feel second class. The involvement of an equal number of ministers from the closing parish in distributing Holy Communion and in reading the Scriptures is an important detail. This presumes some practice with the ministers will take place before the liturgy so that everyone is comfortable with the flow of this special liturgy.

Hospitality. Provide greeters, even outside of church if possible, to welcome newcomers to the parish and have the people gather in front of the church or else in the vestibule. Provide tables with nametags to facilitate people meeting the new parishioners. It is presumed that they have met each other for a significant period of time before the consolidating eucharistic liturgy.[1]

Rite of Inauguration

Introductory Rites

A welcome is extended to the newly consolidated parish community. The focus of the liturgy is unity, the treasure brought from the closed parishes: "one Lord, one faith, one baptism; one God and Father of all, who is over all and through all and in all" (Eph 4:5). The liturgy begins by gathering outdoors (or in the vestibule), in order to see itself as a new worshiping community and to walk together to prayer and Eucharist. Representatives carry two large containers of water and the three registry books from each of the original combined parishes. The lit Paschal candles are arranged by the font. They can be used interchangeably in the months ahead before the next Triduum.

The new pastor accompanied by liturgical ministers, parish council leaders, parish staff, and concelebrants (hopefully including the former pastor) extends a warm welcome to the assembly in front of the church building. The foundation stone is recognized (filled with memories and dreams and dedicated the previous night). It signs a changed foundation to the parish. New stories and families have been added. The closed parish brought water from their baptismal font and the registry books that recorded its initiation sacraments (baptism, confirmation and first communion), marriages, and deaths over its history. This day members of this receiving parish add water from their font and present the books that record its history.

The congregation proceeds into church, to the font, while singing the first verses of the processional hymn. The ringing of the church bells is a festive way to accompany the procession as it moves into the body of the church.

[1] Adapted from David G. Caron, "Opening Liturgy for a Consolidated Parish" in his unpublished "Information Packet on Parish Closings" from the Diocese of Harrisburg (Pa.). Used with permission. And adapted from the 1995 "Rituals of Transition" in Thomas Simons, *Holy Place, Holy People: Rites for the Church's House,* 102–4; © 1998 Archdiocese of Chicago: Liturgy Training Publications, 1800 North Hermitage Avenue, Chicago, Ill. 60622-1101; 1-800-933-1800, fax 1-800-933-7094, email: orders@ltp.org. All rights reserved. Used with permission.

When most people have found a seat, the presider reverences the altar and moves to the blessing of the water and the font.

Invocation over the Baptismal Water

The large glass containers of baptismal waters from the fonts of each of the former parish communities are poured slowly into the empty font with some accompanying instrumental music behind the prayer.

Presider: My dear brothers and sisters, as we come to this Baptismal font, let us rededicate our lives to the gospel as newly configured parish community.

Facing the font as the representatives of the consolidated parishes continue to pour the blessed water, the presider rededicates the font using words from a dedication of baptismal water already blessed from the Easter season (§224 from the Rite of Baptism for Children).[2] The Blessing employs images of Baptismal adoption and new life. It invokes the Spirit as the source of new unity and the bond of charity.

Presider: Let us pray, God our Creator, we gather today as a new parish community. We come with memories and great hopes for our future. We come in need of God's grace, with confidence that Jesus is our Good Shepherd, who knows and loves us all. May this assembly be a place where new friendships are born and old friendships strengthened. May it be a source of grace and blessing to our neighbors and community. May all of us here today, and all those in days to come, be united in a spirit of peace, goodwill and love. We ask this through Christ our Lord.

All: Amen.

The Gloria is intoned as the presider moves to the chair for the Opening Prayer.

Opening Prayer

§52 from the Rite of Dedication of a Church and an Altar.

---

[2] "Blessing and Invocation of God Over Baptismal Water" in The Rite of Baptism for Children, from *The Rites of the Catholic Church*, vol. 1 (Collegeville, Minn.: Liturgical Press, 1990) 452.

Liturgy of the Word

The Sunday Readings or the Lectionary readings for the dedication of a Church and an Altar are recommended. Alternatively, for a first reading, 1 Kings 8:22-23, 27-30 links dedication and forgiveness.

Homily

Renewal of Baptismal Commitment

Presider: Dear friends,
since we have been called to be a new parish community,
let us renew the promises we made in baptism,
when we rejected Satan and his works,
and promised to serve God faithfully
as his holy Church.

The renunciations and profession of faith taken from the Rite of Christian Initiation of Adults, §§581–82.

Sprinkling with Baptismal Water

The choir sings a Litany of the Saints as the presider and concelebrants sprinkle the people and the walls of the church.

Concluding prayer §583 from The Rite of Christian Initiation of Adults.

(Option A)
A Proclamation of the Consent of the People: The Presidents of each parish pastoral council lead their respective communities in the following proclamation.

Presider: What do you ask of God and this Diocesan Church?

All: We, the people of (Parish) come here freely and publicly state our desire to become one faith community. We promise to work tirelessly for that unity of faith celebrated in the Church and in the sacraments. Scripture proclaims that the dying and rising of Christ has won our salvation. We will live this mystery of love as one faith community.[3]

Presider: May God who began this good work bring it to completion.

---

[3] Adapted from "A Rite for the Merging of Parishes," Diocese of Altoona-Johnstown (Pa.), from the *FDLC Newsletter* 24, no. 5, Federation of Diocesan Liturgical Commissions (December 1997–January 1998) 53. Used with permission.

(Option B)

Appointment of Pastor: An Official Proclamation of the local bishop's appointment letter of pastor to the newly consolidated parish. A fitting response could be a simplified version of the "Renewal of Commitment to Priestly Service" from the text of the Chrism Mass. (See the Sacramentary (pp. 131–132). This could also be an opportunity to introduce the new parish staff and pastoral council with a prayer of dedication from the "Order for the Blessing of Those Who Exercise Pastoral Service (§§1808–12) in The Rites, *vol. 2, or the "Order for the Blessing of a Parish Council" from (§1204) from the* Book of Blessings.

Prayer of the Faithful

The following suggestions need to be personalized for the concrete situation of the newly consolidated parish.

Presider: Let us now place our petitions before God, confidant that God will bless our efforts to become the new parish family of St. _____ Church.

Reader: In gratitude for our leadership and pastors, our Pope, our bishop and pastors, may they be given continued wisdom and discernment to lead our Christian community through the coming years, we pray.

All: Lord, hear our prayer.

Reader: For continued progress in resolving the differences that affect God's family here and throughout the world [name specific places of particular tension and discord], we pray. *Resp.*

Reader: For patience and perseverance as we begin the process of working and worshiping together as one parish family, we pray. *Resp.*

Reader: In thanksgiving for the friendships, the benefactors, and the traditions we treasure from the _____ parishes that formed St. _____ Parish, we pray. *Resp.*

Reader: For all the deceased members of all our parish members and families, especially (names of any of the recently deceased), that they find their peace with God, we pray. *Resp.*

The reader may invite additional petitions or a time of silent prayer of the heart. If the latter, after a pause the reader continues. If the former, the presider concludes without a further invitation from the reader.

[*Reader:* We pray to the Lord. *Resp.*]

Presider: Gracious God, we thank you for the grace that sustains and supports our lives. Be especially close to us. Help us to discover your presence among us each time we gather. Renew our trust and build us into a powerful sacrament of your presence for this community. We ask this through Christ our Lord.

All: Amen.

Liturgy of the Eucharist

Preparation Rite

The music may need to be instrumental to permit the presentation of the registry books and the clothing of the altar. Perhaps verses of the song can be begun during the preparation of the altar, and the presentation of the bread and wine.

Presentation of the Registry Books

The procession of gifts moves in several units to the sanctuary after the collection. The presider receives the symbols, perhaps with the parish secretaries or other office staff at his side.

As symbols of the new members and their former parish, the presider will be presented with the registry books of Christian initiation, marriage, and interments from the former parish. At the same time he will receive the same books from the receiving parish. All of these books are placed on a table near the font perhaps by parish staff who are the caretakers of these documents.

A commentator can read the following words as the three registry books are brought forward.

Commentator: Today, the people of St. _____ Parish entrust to us the precious books, which contain the names of the people who have been baptized, married, and buried from St. _____ Parish. The memory of these good people will live on in our new parish, and we will pray for them in all our future Masses.

The procession now comes to the altar to clothe it with a new altar cloth, fresh candles and candle holders, flowers near the altar, and finally the usual gifts of bread and wine. The altar and registry books are then incensed.

The Mass proceeds as usual until after Communion.

Communion Rite

The presider returns to the chair to say the Prayer after Communion and possibly announces a rededication of the daily Mass chapel or other part of the parish worship space to the patron of the closed church. Devotional items brought from the closing parish can be pointed out and details of their story told there. Gratitude needs to be expressed to the former pastors and the main leadership of the consolidation processes. The former pastor needs to be very tenderly recognized and affirmed.

Concluding Rites

(A further option: A Dedication Prayer for Icons and Devotional Art) Before leaving the church, the presider may point out shrines and other places designed for devotional prayer, e.g. the statues, the stations of the cross, the stained glass windows, etc. This will be important if there has been a major renovation of the space concurrent with the consolidation. Before the people leave, the presider may lead a thanksgiving prayer for any especially noteworthy icons and other devotional art within sight of the assembly, especially those brought from the closed parish church.

Prayer for Icons and Devotional Art

> Dear brothers and sisters in Christ,
> we have genuine reason to rejoice,
> because we have so many beautiful objects of devotion
> that decorate our church.

(Here mention a few objects, especially any new pieces brought from parishes that have been closed.)

> These images honor, above all, the truth
> that Jesus is Head of his Body, the Church.
> He is the beginning, the firstborn from the dead,
> in him all fullness was pleased to dwell.
> We see his face in these saints whose images grace our church.

We hear his voice in the acts of courage and love
exemplified in the lives of these saints.
We desire to follow in their steps
and live as God's saints on earth.
May all who pray before these shrines and icons
be led to a deeper union with God and his people.
We ask this through Christ our Lord. Amen.[4]

Prayer After Communion §38 from the Dedication of a Church

Blessing and Dismissal

§84 from The Dedication of a Church emphasizes the assembly as temple and dwelling place of the Holy Spirit.[5] *One of the solemn blessings from the* Sacramentary *could also be most appropriate.*

---

[4] Adapted from "Opening Liturgy for a Consolidated Parish: Stational Approach" in David G. Caron, D. Min., in his unpublished "Information Packet on Parish Closings" (Miami, Fla., March 1999). A further option would be taken from §874 in the *Book of Blessings*, "Order of Blessing Religious Articles."

[5] From the Rite of Dedication of a Church and an Altar in International Commission on English in the Liturgy, *The Rites of the Catholic Church*, vol. 2 (Collegeville, Minn.: Liturgical Press, 1991) 388.

Lament and Parish Closure

A Psalm for Healing when a Parish Changes or Closes:
Remembering and Lamenting the Loss of the Temple

Fr. Steve Dunn, *Archdiocese of Milwaukee*

Psalm 137

¹By the rivers of Babylon—
    there we sat down and there we wept
    when we remembered Zion.
²On the willows there
    we hung up our harps.
³For there our captors
    asked us for songs,
and our tormentors asked for mirth, saying,
    "Sing us one of the songs of Zion!"

⁴How could we sing the LORD'S song
    in a foreign land?
⁵If I forget you, O Jerusalem,
    let my right hand wither!
⁶Let my tongue cling to the roof of my mouth,
    if I do not remember you,
if I do not set Jerusalem above my highest joy.
                (vv. 1–6; NRSV)

Background

In ancient Israel, the book of Psalms constituted a major part of the liturgy of Temple worship, as well as a resource for daily prayer within the family. These poems covered the wide range of human emotions and experience from praise and thanks to grief and lament. Because the sacred poems fully embrace common human experience and enable us to initiate a conversation with God, they have remained an important prayer resource for Judaism as well as for Christianity.

In a situation such as the closing of a long-established parish church, praying psalms of lament enables the grieving members to name their troubles, fears, anxiety, pain and sense of loss. Before any of us can experience healing, we must honestly and prayerfully name and confront our pain. Through psalms of lament, we bring our problems out into the open, placing them before God with faith and trust. God hears and answers with steadfast love, faithfulness, and mercy—the hallmarks of His covenant with Israel (see Exod 34:6-7, NRSV).

Theologian Walter Brueggemann has noted the diminishment of the sense of honest lament in contemporary U.S. society.[1] He believes that in order to embrace authentic praise and thanksgiving, as well as healing, we must first confront and name our sinfulness, guilt, anger, loss, and pain. This produces a catharsis that enables us to move forward in faith.

Healing—and the movement from grief to a "new orientation" in the faith life of those experiencing the painful loss of a church closing—can be enhanced through a meditation on Psalm 137. After the destruction of the Jerusalem Temple and the deportation to Babylon in 587 B.C.E., the people of Israel sang a song of lament. Their song was not only to lament the loss of their homeland and place of worship, however. It was also a sincere plea to keep open the conversation with the God whom they trust will eventually reestablish them in a new Temple.

We mourn the closing of parish buildings. But we, like our Israelite forebears, must express our lament in a context of openness to God in our hopes for a renewed parish. Central to the theology of Psalm 137 is remembering that the exiles find comfort, hope, and new strength through their memory of the Holy City of Jerusalem and the Temple in which they worshiped. Despite the mockery of their captors (v. 3), they will not give in to sacrilege and mockery. Their faith in God's covenant love en-

---

[1] Walter Brueggemann, "The Formlessness of Grief," *Interpretation: A Journal of Bible and Theology* 31, no. 3 (July 1977) 267–75.

ables them to pray with an implicit hope that one day a new Temple will be built in which they will again worship together.

Remembering is central to our eucharistic worship. We remember God's love manifested in Christ as together we partake in the spiritual sharing of food and drink as a faith community. So too, remembering the richness of our former parish life gives us hope that our communal life will be renewed in our new or restructured parish.

Verse 1

By the rivers of Babylon

Between the Tigris and Euphrates rivers in Babylon (modern day Iraq) there existed an elaborate system of canals, the "rivers" of Babylon. This land was very different and unlike the familiar confines of Jerusalem, which made the exiles' sense of loss even more painful. They found comfort by remembering Jerusalem, Temple worship, and communal life.

Having to leave one's home parish to worship in a new or restructured community will be unfamiliar and somewhat uncomfortable at first. It is only natural and healthy to remember our past, as the Israelites do in verse one. Naming our loss, and remembering the good things we had, becomes the first step before we can look with hope to a new experience of parish life.

- What losses are you experiencing?

- What memories will continue to be a part of your faith foundation?

Verse 2

On the willows

The exiles will hang their harps—instruments used in Temple worship—on the trees, since they are grieved by the loss of their land and Temple.

The anger and alienation that may result from a parish closing will cause some members to be disappointed. We need to name these feelings honestly.

- Describe your feelings at a time of loss.

- How do you pray at such a time? Alone? With others?

Verse 3a

Our captors asked us for songs

Here and in verse four the word "songs" refers to the Temple liturgy, where music and song were essential aspects to the joyful and reverent worship of God. Now that the Temple has been destroyed and the Israelites exiled, the Babylon captors taunt them by asking them to sing songs in praise of the God who seems not to exist. This presents a major theme found in the lament psalms, the taunting by oppressors who question the existence of the God of Israel: "Where is your God?" (42:3, 10; 14:1).

Verse 3b-4

Sing us one of the songs of Zion

Despite the taunts, the psalmist, speaking for the exiles, cannot even think of singing under false pretenses. Again this shows the implicit faith and trust of the exiles who will not make their worship a mockery. They will save their music for the future worship in the restored Temple.

As a people united through our common baptism in Christ, we are challenged to maintain faith and trust in God as we look to the future in our new or restructured faith community. During the painful and uncertain times of transition, this faith sustains us. Although it will be difficult to sing joyfully during our period of mourning, our underlying faith should enable us to realize that the Church transcends a particular building. We are the People of God, made one in baptism and called to community.

- What opportunities and possibilities do you see in the losses and changes we are experiencing?

Verse 5

If I forget you let my right hand wither

Implicit in this verse is the psalmist's hope of restoration. If he/she forgets Jerusalem and loses faith, he will never again be able to play and sing songs of the Lord in Jerusalem. The image of a withered hand, the hand he/she would use to play the harp, conveys the importance of his/her remembrance.

Likewise, we must not forget our faith community and give up hope for the future—the time when we also will be restored and restructured and will once again sing and play before the Lord.

Verse 6

Let my tongue cling to the roof of my mouth

Should the psalmist (representing the community of faith) forget Jerusalem, he/she will lose the ability to sing again in the restored Temple, as depicted in the image of the tongue clinging to the roof of the mouth.

Failure to remember our identity as a community of faith weakens our faith and lessens our hope for a restoration of community life. Like the singers of Psalm 137, we must honestly name and embrace our loss, also remembering that our identity as a Christian community has its foundation in our baptism, not in bricks and mortar. The closing of a church or the merging of parishes can cause much pain and a sense of loss. However, remembering that our life as a Christian community lies deeply rooted in God's steadfast love, we will maintain faith and hope as we embrace changes in our parish life.

- What treasures, memories, sacred objects, or pictures, etc., do you bring with you from your former parish?

- As members of this church community, to what are we called?

Additional Psalms for the "Ascent" to a New Community

"Songs of Zion," Psalms 120–34, are called the "songs of Zion," "psalms of ascent," or "songs of ascent" (NAB and NRSV) because the Israelites sang them on their annual pilgrimages to Jerusalem. We pray these psalms in preparation for our "pilgrimage" to our new and restructured faith communities.

A few "psalms of ascent" include:

Psalm 121—God's sure protection

Psalm 122—Prayer and praise on entrance to the Holy Place

Psalm 125—Trust in God's protection from evil and abundance of peace

Psalm 133—Prayer for unity within the community of faith

Selected Bibliography

American Catholic Culture and the Immigrant Church

Dolan, Jay P. *The American Catholic Experience: A History from Colonial Times to the Present*. Garden City, N.Y.: Doubleday, 1985.

———. Jeffrey M. Burns, Carol L. Jensen and Steven Shaw eds. *The American Catholic Parish: A History from 1850 to the Present*, vol. 2. New York: Paulist Press, 1987.

———. R. Scott Appleby, Patricia Byrne and Debra Campbell, eds. *Transforming Parish Ministry: The Changing Roles of Catholic Clergy, Laity and Women Religious*. New York: Crossroad, 1989.

Ellis, John Tracy, ed. *The Catholic Priest in the United States*. Collegeville, Minn.: Saint John's University Press, 1971.

Figueroa Deck, Allan, S.J. *The Second Wave: Hispanic Ministry and the Evangelization of Cultures*. New York: Paulist Press, 1989.

Greeley, Andrew. *The Catholic Imagination*. Berkeley: University of California Press, 2000.

———. *The Catholic Myth: The Behavior and Beliefs of American Catholics*. New York: Collier Books, 1991.

Hoge, Dean R. *Converts, Dropouts, Returnees: A Study of Religious Change Among Catholics*. Washington, D.C.: The United States Catholic Conference; New York: Pilgrim Press, 1981.

McGreevy, John T. *Parish Boundaries: The Catholic Encounter with Race in the Twentieth-Century Urban North*. Chicago: University of Chicago Press, 1996.

Mitchell, Nathan D. "What's Next in Catholic Liturgical Movement," part 3, "The Loss of Catholic Culture." *Rite* (May–June 2001) 5.

Schoenherr, Richard A. and Laurence Young. *Full Pews, Empty Altars: Demographics of the Priest Shortage in the United States Catholic Dioceses*. Madison: University of Wisconsin Press, 1993.

———. *Goodbye Father: The Celibate Male Priesthood and the Future of the Catholic Church*. Oxford: Oxford University Press, 2002.

Steinfels, Peter. *A People Adrift: The Crisis of the Roman Catholic Church in America*. New York: Simon & Schuster, 2003.

Chicago Resources

Archdiocese of Chicago, Office of Research and Planning. *Data on the Organization, Resources and Activities of the Archdiocese of Chicago*. Chicago, 1998.

Baldwin, David. "There Is a Sweet, Sweet Spirit in This Place." *Environment and Art* 3 no. 8 (October, 1990) 58–61.

Behr, Michael J. "Superparish Envisioned." *The Chicago Catholic*, July 15, 1988.

Bernardin, Joseph. "Chicago Parish and School Closings-Consolidations Announced." *Origins* 19, no. 35 (February 1, 1990) 565–71.

"Englewood Pastoral Planning Report." Submitted to Joseph Bernardin by the Englewood Planning Committee, December 19, 1983.

Forster, Patricia, O.S.F., "The Chicago Story and Boundaries to Parish Restructuring," in *Diocesan Efforts in Parish Reorganization: A Report*. Clearwater, Fla.: Conference of Pastoral Planning and Council Development, 1995.

Koenig, Harry C., ed. *A History of the Parishes in the Archdiocese of Chicago*, 2 vols. Chicago: Archdiocese of Chicago, 1980.

Pick, Grant "Resurrection." *The Reader* (Chicago), August 9, 1991.

Paprocki, Thomas J. "Parish Closings and Administrative Recourse to the Apostolic See: Recent Experiences of the Archdiocese of Chicago." *The Jurist* 55 (1995) 875–96.

Skerrett, Ellen, Edward R. Kantowicz and Steven Avella. *Catholicism, Chicago Style*. Chicago: Loyola University Press, 1993.

Forgiveness and Reconciliation

Alken, Martha, O.P. *The Healing Power of Forgiving*. New York: Crossroad, 1997.

Accattoli, Luigi. *When a Pope Asks Forgiveness: The* Mea Culpas *of John Paul II*. Trans. Jordan Aumann, O.P. Boston: Pauline Books and Media, 1998.

Appleby, Scott R. *The Ambivalence of the Sacred: Religion, Violence and Reconciliation*. Lanham, Md.: Rowan & Littlefield, 2000.

Baum, Gregory and Harold Wells, eds. *Reconciliation of Peoples: Challenge to the Churches*. Maryknoll, N.Y.: Orbis Books, 1997.

Brennan, Patrick J. *The Reconciling Parish: A Process for Returning of Alienated Catholics*. Allen, Tex.: Tabor, 1990.

Cummings, Owen F. "Reconciliation and Penance: Some Needed Distinctions." *Chicago Studies* 34, no. 2 (August 1995) 145–57.

Dallen, James. "Reconciliation in the Sacrament of Penance." *Worship* 64, no. 5 (September, 1990) 386–405.

———. *The Reconciling Community: The Rite of* Penance. New York: Pueblo, 1986.

Dallen, James and Joseph Favazza. *Removing the Barriers: The Practice of Reconciliation.* Chicago: Liturgy Training Publications, 1991.

Donnelly, Doris. "The Human Side of Forgiveness." *New Catholic World* 22, no. 7 (January–February 1984) 28–30.

———. *Learning to Forgive.* New York: MacMillan, 1979.

———. "Binding Up Wounds in a Healing Community." In *Repentance and Reconciliation in the Church*, ed., Michael J. Henchal, 11–31. Collegeville, Minn.: Liturgical Press, 1987.

———. "Reconciliation and Community." In *Reconciliation: The Continuing Agenda*, ed., Robert J. Kennedy, 34–42. Collegeville, Minn.: Liturgical Press, 1987.

Enright, Robert and Joanna North, eds. *Exploring Forgiveness.* Madison: University of Wisconsin Press, 1998.

Eugene, Toinette. "Reconciliation in the Pastoral Context of Today's Church and World." In *Reconciling Embrace*, ed. Robert F. Kennedy, 1–16. Chicago: Liturgy Training Publications, 1998.

Favazza, Joseph A. "The Eucharistic Table, A Reconciling Table?: Our Belief, Our Experience, Our Dilemma." In *The Many Presences of Christ*, ed. Timothy Fitzgerald and David A. Lysik, 87–104. Chicago: Liturgy Training Publications, 1999.

———. "Reconciliation: A Journey, A Process, A Little Hang Time." In *Removing the Barriers: The Practice of Reconciliation*, ed. James Dallen and Joseph Favazza, 36–37. Chicago: Liturgy Training Publications, 1991.

Green, Robin. *A Step Too Far: Explorations into Reconciliation.* London: Darton, Longman and Todd, 1990.

Hay, Mark, O.M.I. *Ukubuyisana: Reconciliation in South Africa.* Doctoral thesis, Catholic Theological Union, 1997.

Hughes, Kathleen, R.S.C.J. "Reconciliation: Cultural and Christian Perspectives." In *Reconciliation: The Continuing Agenda*, ed. Robert Kennedy, 114–30. Collegeville, Minn.: Liturgical Press, 1987.

———. "Reconciliation: Disquieting Pastoral Reflections." In *Repentance and Reconciliation in the Church*, ed. M. Henchal, 57–77. Collegeville, Minn.: Liturgical Press, 1987.

Hyde, C. *To Declare God's Forgiveness: Toward a Pastoral Theology of Reconciliation.* Wilton, Conn.: Morehouse Barlow, 1984.

John Paul II. *Reconciliation and Penance.* Washington, D.C.: United States Catholic Conference, 1984.

————. "First Sunday of Lent: Service Requesting Pardon." *Origins* 29, no. 40 (March 23, 2000) 646–48.

————. "Jubilee Characteristic: The Purification of Memory." *Origins* 29, no. 40 (March 23, 2000) 648–50.

Kennedy, Robert J., ed. *Reconciliation: The Continuing Agenda.* Collegeville, Minn.: Liturgical Press, 1987.

Lapsley, Michael. "My Journey of Reconciliation in South Africa: From Freedom Fighter to Healer." *New Theology Review* 10, no. 2 (May 1997) 21–23.

Lederach, John Paul. *Building Peace: Sustaining Reconciliation in Divided Socie-ties.* Washington, D.C.: Endowment of the United States Institute of Peace, 1997.

————. *The Journey Toward Reconciliation.* Scottsdale, Pa.: Herald Press, 1999.

————. *Preparing for Peace: Conflict Transformation across Cultures.* Syracuse, N.Y.: Syracuse University Press, 1995.

Nassal, Joseph. *Premeditated Mercy: A Spirituality of Reconciliation.* Leaven-worth, Kans.: Forest of Peace Publishing, 2000.

Patton John. *Is Human Forgiveness Possible?* Nashville: Abingdon Press, 1985.

Peck, M. Scott. *People of the Lie: The Hope for Healing Human Evil.* New York: Simon & Schuster, 1983.

Peters, J. "The Function of Forgiveness in Social Relationships." In *Forgiveness*, ed. C. Floristan and C. Duquoc, 3–11. Edinburgh: T. & T. Clark, 1986.

Schreiter, Robert, C.PP.S. "Creating Circles of Listening in a Parish." *Initiative Report* 3 (March 2001) 3–6.

————. *The Ministry of Reconciliation: Spirituality and Strategies.* Maryknoll, N.Y.: Orbis Books, 1998.

————. *Reconciliation: Mission and Ministry in a Changing Social Order.* Boston Theological Institute Series, vol. 3. Maryknoll, N.Y.: Orbis Books, 1992.

————. "Reconciliation as a Model of Mission." *New Theology Review* 10, no. 2 (May 1997) 6–15.

————. "Entering the Healing Circle: The Practice of Reconciliation." In *The Healing Circle: Essays in Cross Cultural Mission*, ed. Steven Bevans, S.V.D., Eleanor Doidge, L.o.B., and Robert Schreiter, C.PP.S., 176–87. Chicago: CCGM Publications, 2000.

Signe, Howell and Roy Willis, eds. *Societies at Peace: Anthropological Perspectives.* London: Routledge, 1989.

Steenkamp, William. "Michael Lapsley." *Cape Times*, July 17, 1997.

Studzinski, R. "Remember and Forgive: Psychological Dimensions of Forgiveness." In *Forgiveness*, eds. C. Floristan and C. Duquoc, 12–21. Edinburgh: T. & T. Clark, 1986.

Ting-Toomey, Stella. "International Conflict Styles: A Face Negotiation Theory." *International & Intercultural Communication Annual* 12 (1988) 213–35.

Tutu, Desmond. *No Future without Forgiveness*. New York: Doubleday, 1999.

Udal, Joanna. "Reconciling among Nations: The Role of the Church." *Ecumenical Review* 49, no. 1 (January 1997) 61–77.

Upton, Julia, R.S.M. *A Time for Embracing*. Collegeville, Minn.: Liturgical Press, 1999.

Volf, Miroslav. *Exclusion and Embrace*. Nashville: Abingdon, 1996.

———. "The Social Meaning of Reconciliation." *Interpretation: A Journal of Bible and Theology* 54, no. 2 (April 2000) 158–72.

Williams, Rowan. *Resurrection*. London: Darton, Longman and Todd, 1982.

Working For Reconciliation: A Caritas Handbook. Vatican City; Caritas Internationalis, 2003.

Worthington, Everett L., Jr. *Dimensions of Forgiveness: Psychological Research and Theological Perspectives*. Philadelphia: Templeton Foundation Press, 1998.

Institutional and Parochial Restructuring

Alternative Staffing of Parishes. New York: National Pastoral Life Center, 1987.

Arbuckle, Gerald A., S.M. "Merging Provinces." *Review for Religious* 53, no. 3 (May–June 1994) 352–63.

———. *Refounding the Church: Dissent for Leadership*. Maryknoll, N.Y.: Orbis Books, 1993.

Barton, Joy. "Parish Cluster Planning: Laying Deep Foundations." *Church* 10, no. 1 (Spring 1994) 35–37.

Birket, Dwight. "Parish Consolidation: A Rural Diocese's Model." *Church* 10, no. 2 (Spring 1994) 36–39.

Caron, David G. "Information Packet on Parish Closing." Miami, Fla.: privately published, 1999.

Clark, Suzanne and Robert Duggan. "Strategic Planning: What It Did for One Parish." *Church* 12, no. 2 (Summer 1996) 26–31.

Cobble, James F., Jr., and Charles M Elliot, eds. *The Hidden Spirit: Discovering the Spirituality of Institutions*. Matthews, N.C.: Christian Ministry Resources, 1999.

Coriden, James. "Parish Closings: Getting Down to Cases." *New Theology Review* 9, no. 3 (August 1996) 103–6.

Cosgrove, Charles H. and Dennis D. Hatfield. *Church Conflict: The Hidden Systems behind the Fights*. Nashville: Abingdon Press, 1994.

Couturier, David B., O.F.M. Cap. "A Spirituality of Refounding." In *Religious Life: Rebirth through Conversion*, ed. Gerald A. Arbuckle, S.M., and David L. Fleming, S.J., 85–87. New York: Alba House, 1990.

———. "At Odds with Ourselves: Polarization and the Learning Cultures of Priesthood." *Seminary Journal* 9, no. 3 (Winter 2004) 64–71.

———. "The Learning Cultures of Religious Life." *InFormation* 6, no. 5 (November–December 1998) 1–10.

Dallen, James. *The Dilemma of Priestless Sundays*. Chicago: Liturgy Training Publications, 1992.

Dorsch, Larry W. "The Rituals of Parish Consolidation." *Church* 17, no. 1 (Spring 2001) 30–35.

Duggan, Thomas J. "Massive Church Closings and Changing Urban Religion: The Current Detroit Experience." An abstract prepared for the annual meeting of the Society for the Scientific Study of Religion. Virginia Beach, Va. (November 1990).

Federation of Diocesan Liturgical Commissions, "Rituals for the Closing of a Parish Church," *FDLC Newsletter* 24, no. 5 (January 1998) 49–53.

Fisher, Rita, I.H.M. "The Grace of This Place; Closing a Church." *Liturgy 90* 27, no. 2 (February–March 1996) 9–11.

Gallagher, Maureen, ed. *Continuing the Journey: Parishes in Transition*. Kansas City, Mo.: Sheed and Ward, 1988.

Handy, Charles. *Understanding Voluntary Organizations*. London: Penguin, 1988.

Harris, Joseph Claude. "The Shrinking Church in Big Cities." *Church* 10, no. 3 (Fall 1994) 28–30.

———. "The Shrinking Supply of Priests." *America* 183, no. 14 (November 4, 2000) 16–17.

Law, Eric F. *Inclusion: Making Room for Grace*. St. Louis: Chalice Press, 2000.

———. *The Lion Shall Dwell with the Lamb*. St. Louis: Chalice Press, 1993.

Lippard, Lucy R. *The Lure of the Local: Senses of Place in a Multicentered Society*. New York: New Press, 1997.

Mahony, Roger. "As I Have Done For You," *Origins* 29, no. 46 (May 4, 2000) 746–55.

McConinaha, Scott A. "Parish Merger Event Features Comedy, Fried Fish." *Catholic Herald* (Milwaukee), June 7, 2001.

McManus, William. "A Funeral for a Parish." *Liturgy 90* 22, no. 2 (February–March 1991) 6–7.

Pilla, Anthony. "Steps Toward Collaboration among Parishes." *Origins* 30, no. 39 (March 15, 2001) 622–28.

Power, David, O.M.I. "Worship in the Absence of a Priest." *New Theological Review* 15, no. 4 (November 2002) 29–40.

Rexhausen, Jeff, Michael Cieslak, Mary L. Gautier and Robert J. Miller. *A National Study of Recent Diocesan Efforts at Parish Reorganization in the United States: Pathways for the Church of the 21st Century.* Dubuque, Iowa: Loras College Press, Archdiocese of Dubuque, and the Conference for Pastoral Planning and Council Development, 2004.

Roland, Chris. "Buildings, Cathedrals and the Gospel." In *The Hidden Spirit: Discovering the Spirituality of Institutions,* ed. James F. Cobble, Jr. and Charles M. Elliot, 52–62. Matthews, N.C.: Christian Ministry Resources, 1999.

Schnier, David James. "A Process Model for Top Management to Evaluate and Define a Mission Statement for Consolidated Roman Catholic Parishes." Masters thesis, Webster University, 1997.

Schweickert, Jeanne S.S.S.F. *Standing at the Crossroads: Religious Orders and Reconfiguration.* Chicago: Convergence, 2002.

Simons, Thomas G. "Requiem for a Church: Closing St. Francis de Sales Cathedral." *Environment and Art Newsletter* 70, no. 2 (April 1994) 16–19.

Slatter, Stuart. *Corporate Recovery.* London: Penguin, 1987.

Wilson, George, S.J. "Why Close St. Ben's?" *America* 184, no. 5 (May 17, 2001) 20–22.

Wink, Walter. *Engaging the Powers: Discernment and Resistance in a World of Domination.* Minneapolis: Augsburg Fortress, 1992.

———. *The Powers That Be: Theology for a New Millennium.* New York: Doubleday, 1998.

———. *When the Powers Fall: Reconciliation in the Healing of Nations.* Minneapolis: Fortress Press, 1997.

Ritual Theory and Pastoral Care

Anderson, Herbert and Edward Foley, Capuchin. *Mighty Stories, Dangerous Rituals.* San Francisco: Jossey-Bass, 1998.

———. "Ritual Moment and Pastoral Process: Rethinking Pastoral Theology." In *Finding Voice to Give God Praise,* ed. Kathleen Hughes, R.S.C.J., 151–62. Collegeville, Minn.: Liturgical Press, 1998.

Bell, Catherine. *Ritual: Perspectives and Dimensions.* New York: Oxford University Press, 1997.

———. *Ritual Theory, Ritual Practice.* New York: Oxford University Press, 1992.

Driver, Tom F. *The Magic of Ritual: Our Need for Liberating Rites that Transform Our Lives and Our Communities.* San Francisco: HarperSanFrancisco, 1991.

Foley, Edward, Capuchin. "Pastoral Care as Liturgical Common Ground." *New Theology Review* 13, no. 3 (August 2000) 26–33.

Francis, Mark R., C.S.V. *Liturgy in a Multicultural Community*. Collegeville, Minn.: Liturgical Press, 1991.

———. *Shape a Circle Ever Wider: Liturgical Inculturation in the United States*. Chicago: Liturgy Training Publications, 2000.

Friedman, Edwin H. *Generation to Generation*. New York: Gilford Press, 1985.

Goizueta, Roberto S. *Caminemos con Jesus: Toward a Hispanic-Latino Theology of Accompaniment*. Maryknoll, N.Y.: Orbis Books, 1995.

Goffman, E. *Interaction Ritual: Essays on Face-to-Face Behavior*. Garden City, N.Y.: Doubleday, 1967.

Granfield, Patrick, O.S.B. "The Concept of Church as Communion." *Origins* 28, no. 44 (April 22, 1999) 753–58.

Greeley, Andrew. "Authority as Charm." *America* 18, no. 1 (November 20, 1999) 10–14.

Grigassy, Daniel P. "Nonsacramental Rites of Reconciliation: Forsaken or Disguised?" *Liturgical Ministry* 4 (Winter 1995) 11–21.

Kübler-Ross, Elizabeth. *On Death and Dying: What the Dying Have to Teach Doctors, Nurses, Clergy, and Their Families*. Simon & Schuster, Touchstone, 1997.

Lane, Belden C. *Landscapes of the Sacred: Geography and Narrative in American Spirituality*. New York: Paulist Press, 1988.

Lathrop, Gordon W. *Holy Things*. Minneapolis: Augsburg Fortress, 1993.

Minuchin, Salvador and H. Charles Fishman. *Family Therapy Techniques*. Cambridge, Mass.: Harvard University Press, 1981.

Mitchell, Nathan D. *Liturgy and the Social Sciences*. Collegeville, Minn.: Liturgical Press, 1999.

Moore, Thomas. *Care of the Soul*. New York: HarperCollins, 1992.

Power, David, O.M.I. "Sinful Church, Divine Pardon." *New Theology Review* 17, no. 1 (February 2004) 57–69.

———. "Worship in the Absence of a Priest," *New Theology Review* 15, no. 4 (November 2002) 29–40.

Ramshaw, Elaine. *Ritual and Pastoral Care*. Theology and Pastoral Care, ed. Don S. Browning. Philadelphia: Fortress Press, 1987.

Searle, Mark. "The Journey of Conversion." *Worship* 54, no. 1 (March 1980) 35–53.

Turner, Victor. *The Anthropology of Performance*. New York: PAJ, 1988.

———. *Dramas, Fields, and Metaphors: Symbolic Action in Human Society*. New York: Cornell University Press, 1974.

———. *Ritual Process: Structure and Anti-structure*. New York: Cornell University Press, 1969.

Underwood, R. L. *Pastoral Care and the Means of Grace*. Minneapolis: Fortress, 1993.

Westerhoff, J. and W. Willimon. *Liturgy and Learning Through the Life Cycle*. New York: Seabury, 1980.

Whitehead, James D. "The Practical Play of Theology." In *Formation and Reflection: The Promise of Practical Theology*, ed. Lewis S. Mudge and James N. Poling, 36–54. Philadelphia: Fortress Press, 1987.

Whitehead, James D. and Evelyn E. Whitehead. *Method in Ministry: Theological Reflection and Christian Ministry*. Kansas City, Mo.: Sheed & Ward, 1995.

Trauma, Grief and Recovery

Arbuckle, Gerald A., S.M. *Change, Grief, and the Renewal of the Church: A Spirituality for a New Era*. Westminster, Mass.: Christian Classics, 1991.

Brueggemann, Walter. "The Formlessness of Grief." *Interpretation: A Journal of Bible and Theology* 31, no. 3 (1977) 267–75.

Buckland, Stephan. "Ritual, Bodies and 'Cultural Memory.'" In *Liturgy and the Body*, ed. Louis-Marie Chauvet and Francois Kabasele, 49–56. Maryknoll, N.Y.: Orbis Books, 1995.

Cane, Patricia Mathes. *Trauma, Healing, and Transformation: Awakening a New Heart with Body, Mind, Spirit Practices*. Watsonville, Calif.: Capacitar, 2000.

Grant, Robert. "Trauma in Missionary Life." *Missiology: An International Review* 23, no. 1 (January 1995) 61–82.

Henderson, J. Frank. *Liturgies of Lament*. Chicago: Liturgy Training Publications, 1994.

Herman, Judith. *Trauma and Recovery*. New York: Basic Books, 1992.

Janoff-Bulman, Ronnie. *Shattered Assumptions*. New York: Free Press, 1992.

Jefferson, Andrew M. "Remembering and Restoring; An Exploration of Memory and Narrative in Relation to Psychotherapy with Torture Survivors." *Torture* 10 (December, 2000) 107–11.

Kassmann, Margot. *Overcoming Violence: The Challenges of Churches in All Places*. Geneva: World Council of Churches Publications, 1998.

Kemp, Raymond B. "The Healing Parish: Admitting Addictions." *Church* (Spring 1991) 11–15.

May, Gerald. *Addiction and Grace*. San Francisco: Harper & Row, 1988.

McBride, J. LeBron. *Spiritual Crisis: Surviving Trauma to the Soul*. New York: Haworth Pastoral Press, 1998.

Means, Jeffrey J. *Trauma and Evil: Healing the Wounded Soul*. Minneapolis: Fortress Press, 2000.

Noer, David. *Healing the Wounds: Overcoming the Trauma of Layoffs*. San Francisco: Jossey-Boss, 1993.

Sellner, Edward C. "The Fifth Step and the Sacrament of Penance." *The Furrow* (April 1983) 214–39.

———. "The Event of Self-Revelation in the Reconciliation Process: A Pastoral Theological Comparison of A.A.'s Fifth Step and the Sacrament of Penance." Doctoral dissertation, University of Notre Dame, 1980.

Van der Kolk, Bessel A., ed. *Psychological Trauma*. Washington, D.C.: Psychiatric Press, 1987.

Whitfield, Charles. *Alcoholism, Attachments, and Spirituality*. New York: Perrin, 1985.

Zimmerman, Mari West. *Take and Make Holy: Honoring the Sacred in the Healing of Abuse Survivors*. Chicago: Liturgy Training Publications, 1995.

San Francisco Resources

"A Journey of Hope toward the Third Millennium: The Pastoral Plan of the Pilgrim Church of San Francisco." May 19, 1996.

Burns, Jeffrey M. *San Francisco: A History of the Archdiocese of San Francisco*. Strasbourg, France: Éditions du Signe, 2000.

Cinel, Dino. *From Italy to San Francisco: The Immigrant Experience*. Stanford, Calif.: University of Stanford Press, 1982.

Corona, Al. "Immaculate Conception Priest Cuts Large Figure." *San Francisco Examiner.* September 29, 2000.

Martin, Glen, "Bernal Heights United in Grief and New Fear," *San Francisco Chronicle.* June 25, 1996.

Montesano, Phillip. "St. Anthony's Parish, 1893–1993: A Short Sketch." A privately published history of Saint Anthony of Padua Parish on its Centenary, July 23, 1993.

Quinn, John R. "Decree of Merger of the Personal Parish of Immaculate Conception to the Territorial Parish of St. Anthony." San Francisco, December 1993.

Quinn, John R. "A Shepherd's Call." A homily on the occasion of the initiation of the archdiocesan planning process, December 15, 1995, as quoted in "A Journey of Hope Toward the Third Millennium: The Pastoral Plan of the Pilgrim Church of San Francisco," 52–60.

Victoria, Vicki. "Immaculate Conception Church Defeats Closure." *The New Bernal Journal* (San Francisco), December 1993–January 1994) 1–3.

Roman Catholic Liturgical Resources

Calabuig, Ignacio, O.S.M. *The Dedication of a Church and an Altar: A Theological Commentary*. Washington, D.C.: United States Catholic Conference, 1980.

———. *Liturgical Time and Space: The Rite of Dedication of a Church*. Collegeville, Minn.: Liturgical Press, 2000.

Collins, Harold. *The Church Edifice and Its Appointments*. Westminster, England: The Newman Bookshop, 1946.

Crichton, J. D. *The Dedication of a Church: A Commentary*. Dublin: Veritas Publications, 1980.

Favazza, Joseph A. *The Order of Penitents, Historical Roots and Pastoral Future*. Collegeville, Minn.: Liturgical Press, 1988.

Fink, Peter E., S.J., ed. *Reconciliation*. Collegeville, Minn.: Liturgical Press, 1987.

Fitzgerald, Timothy and David A. Lysik, eds. *The Many Presences of Christ*. Chicago: Liturgy Training Publications, 1999.

Mannion, M. Francis. "Penance and Reconciliation." In *The New Dictionary of Sacramental Worship*, ed. Peter Fink, 98–118. Collegeville, Minn.: Liturgical Press, 1990.

Morlino, Robert. "Service for the Healing of Memories." *Origins* 31, no. 23 (November 15, 2001) 382–85.

Osborne, Kenan B., O.F.M. *Reconciliation and Justification: The Sacrament and Its Theology*. New York: Paulist Press, 1990.

Simons, Thomas G. *Holy People, Holy Place*. Chicago: Liturgy Training Publications, 1998.

Wuest, Joseph, C.S.S.R., *Matters Liturgical: The Collectio Rerum Liturgicarum*. New York: Frederick Pustet, 1959.

Selected Index of Persons and Subjects

249